Kicking Off Around the World

Kicking Off Around the World

55 Stories From When Soccer Met Politics

Ramon Usall

Translated from the Catalan
by Luke Stobart

PLUTO PRESS

Kicking Off Around the World was first published in Catalan as *Futbolítica* by Ara Llibres in 2017 and translated and updated into Spanish by Altamarea Ediciones in 2021.

English language edition first published 2024 by Pluto Press
New Wing, Somerset House, Strand, London WC2R 1LA
and Pluto Press, Inc.
1930 Village Center Circle, 3-834, Las Vegas, NV 89134

www.plutobooks.com

This English edition of *Futbolítica* is arranged via Red Rock Literary Agency Ltd. and Oh! Books Literary Agency

The translation of this work has been supported by the Institut Ramon Llull

LLLL institut ramon llull
Catalan Language and Culture

British Library Cataloguing in Publication Data
A catalogue record for this book is available from the British Library

ISBN 978 0 7453 5042 4   Paperback
ISBN 978 0 7453 5044 8   PDF
ISBN 978 0 7453 5043 1   ePub

Publisher's Note: Although the subtitle of this book in North America is *55 Stories From When Soccer Met Politics*, the game is referred to as 'football' throughout, reflecting the predominant international usage.

This book is printed on paper suitable for recycling and made from fully managed and sustained forest sources. Logging, pulping and manufacturing processes are expected to conform to the environmental standards of the country of origin.

Typeset by Stanford DTP Services, Northampton, England

Simultaneously printed in the United Kingdom and United States of America

Contents

Preface to the English language edition   viii

Introduction   1

1. Britain and Ireland   7
Manchester City FC   8
Tottenham Hotspur FC   12
Liverpool FC   16
Forest Green Rovers FC   20
British Ladies FC   24
Celtic FC   28
Star of the Sea Youth Club   35

2. France and Italy   39
Red Star FC   40
SC Bastia   45
Juventus FC   51
Torino FC   56
AS Roma   60
Inter Milan   65

3. Iberian Peninsula   70
Associação Académica de Coimbra   71
Atlético de Madrid   78
Madrid FC (Real Madrid)   85
Rayo Vallecano   95

FC Barcelona   101
CE Júpiter   110
Spanish Girl's Club   117

4. Central Europe and Scandinavia   122
Berliner FC Dynamo   123
FC Union Berlin   128
SC Tasmania von 1900 Berlin eV   134
FC St Pauli   139
Polonia Warszawa   144
Ajax Amsterdam   149
Hakoah Vienna   154
Christiania SC   159

5. The Balkans   164
GNK Dinamo Zagreb   165
HNK Hajduk Split   170
FK Sloboda Tuzla   176
FK Velež Mostar   182
Olympiacós Piraeus   188

6. Eastern Europe and the Caucasus   192
FC Olt Scorniceşti   193
FC Dynamo Kyiv   198
FC Shakhtar Donetsk   203
FC Karpaty Lviv   208
FC Stroitel Pripyat   213
Klub Oktyabrskoi Revolutsii (Lokomotiv Moscow)   217
FC Akhmat Grozny   221
Qarabağ FK   227

7. The Middle East and Central Asia   234

   Erbil SC   235

   Al-Wehdat SC   240

   Shaheen Asmayee FC   246

8. Africa   251

   Racing Universitaire d'Alger   252

   Club Atlético de Tetuán   257

   JS Massira   262

   Hafia FC   267

   The Passive Resisters SC   272

9. The Americas   277

   New York Ramblers   278

   SC Corinthians Paulista   282

   CD Cobresal   288

   Colo-Colo   294

   Mushuc Runa SC   299

   CD Euzkadi   304

Bibliography   309

Crests   313

Preface to the English language edition

Ramon Usall

The book you have in your hands is the reviewed, expanded, and updated version of a work that was published in Catalan in 2017 and in Spanish in 2021. In Iberia it quickly became a yardstick for historical writing on the footballing world analysed from a social and political perspective. The original edition of *Kicking Off Around the World* was called *Futbolitica* – an invented word created from blending the Catalan words for 'football' ('*futbol*') and 'politics' ('*política*') to represent the close relationship between the two phenomena, which I explore through the rest of this book.

I was inspired to write this book to prove that football is a sport with clear political implications and interpretations, despite some people insisting on denying this. To some extent the work could be seen as inspired by the tradition arguing that in the twentieth century soccer developed to become a 'total social fact' – as sociologist Norbert Elias and journalist Ignacio Ramonet described it – and which as such has often been a mirror reflecting the human condition. The story is told by bringing together 55 histories of clubs from around the world: ranging from Britain – the cradle of the sport – to the Americas, the Middle East, and Africa. *Kicking Off Around the World* is written against the commonly voiced view that 'politics should be kept out of football'. Indeed this book has been written with mistrust towards those who voice this kind of idea. What such people tend to mean by this is that football should not mix with political stances that question the status quo and existing power relations. The idea guiding this book is that football *is always* a political phenomenon whether we like it or not; the main question is what politics are at work. The politics in football are shown by championships being organised in accordance with state borders, the World Cup making the states compete for sporting dominance, and clubs often being flagships for groups in society with religious, cultural, language or national particularities, amongst many other things.

The presence of politics in football has been made very clear by recent world events. A major example is the rise of the women's game, which has not stopped growing in public visibility (and acclaim) since 2017. This was shown in the media attention given to the recent Women's Champions League and World Cup tournaments, which saw women's growing empowerment and fight for full equality played out. Particularly important in this regard were the events that took place around the Spanish team's victory in the Women's World Cup in the summer of 2023. This saw a clash between the players and the Spanish footballing authorities sparked by the women footballers being treated in a way that fell far short of respecting the equal treatment that is preached by our societies. The sexism prevalent in both the world of soccer as well as in society as a whole was clearly on display in the non-consensual kiss that the President of the Spanish Football Federation Luis Rubiales gave to one of Spain's star players, Jennifer Hermoso. This unleashed what became a true feminist social revolt that ended Rubiales' presidency, and which forced the federation to commit to measures aimed at achieving real equality between the women's and men's national teams.

Politics in football could also be seen at the men's 2022 World Cup in Qatar – a country with an absolute monarchy that systematically violates human rights and condemns women to subordination. The competition was a telling example of 'sportswashing' – using sport as a device to clean up one's global image; and this will be repeated in Saudi Arabia in 2034 – showing once again that FIFA is much more concerned about making money and promoting business than guaranteeing respect for civil rights.

The outbreak of war in both Ukraine and Gaza has also shown how the game reflects the politics of our times. In these very pages you will be able to discover the story of how, in the dying years of the Soviet Union, Dynamo Kiev (Kyiv) became a true Ukrainian national team – even wearing its country's colours. And you can find out how Shakhtar Donetsk – a club currently exiled far from its Donbas birthplace – has become a perfect metaphor for the war that has devastated the Donetsk and Lugansk regions at the heart of the current Russia–Ukraine conflict. Regarding the Palestinian case, you will be able to read how a club created in a Jordanian refugee camp – *Al-Wehdat* – effectively became Palestine's national team before FIFA recognised the Palestinian national squad – as happened in 1998.

Besides these stories, the fact that football is testimony to the conflicts of our age can be confirmed by developments such as the Israeli national team competing in Europe despite being geographically situated on a different continent. This was clearly for geopolitical reasons and rooted in the Israeli federation's expulsion in 1974 from the Asian Confederation of Football that the Israeli federation had helped set up. With this book I hereby invite readers from the English-speaking world to discover more than 50 stories that show that football and politics indeed go hand-in-hand a lot more frequently than we might think.

Introduction

From the birth of modern football in industrial England in the second half of the 19th century, clubs in which football was played became more than just sports outfits. The collective nature of playing the sport helped strengthen clubs' community identity, leading them to take on the role of representing a town or city, neighbourhood, educational institution, parish, or even a specific political ideology.

Over the years, playing and watching football has become a truly global phenomenon, helping reaffirm the representational side of many clubs and seeing them frequently acting as mouthpieces for their communities. This is well-known in Iberia. For decades, we have been hearing that *Barça* (Barcelona) – one of the biggest sporting entities in this part of the world – is 'more than just a club'. It is demonstrated by its intense history, one closely linked to Catalonia's. This has often made the Barcelona team a major political player expressing the aspirations of the Catalan community; from the club supporting Catalonia's first taste of modern self-government (the *Mancomunitat* of Catalan provincial representatives, 1913–1925) to *Barça*'s iconic appeal for opponents to the Franco dictatorship (1939–1975) and its fans whistling over the Spanish national anthem to protest the Primo de Rivera dictatorship (1925–1930).

Indeed, some pinpoint the start of the transition to democracy in Spain to 17 February 1974 (while Franco was dying but still alive) when Barça stormed Real Madrid's Bernabéu Stadium, beating the home side by a historic 0–5, as signifying a reversal of fortunes in Spanish football. Such a claim is a simplification, but *Barça* has clearly played a historic role at certain points in recent Spanish history. In a different way, this is also true of Real Madrid, whose history is a faithful reflection of Spain over the last century. Examples include when under the Second Republic (1931–1939) the club stopped being '*Real*' – meaning 'Royal' or royalist – and how as European champions under the Franco regime, the club projected to the world a positive image of Spain and greatly aided the dictatorship in ending its international isolation.

Practically all the regions of the planet in which there are national conflicts have their *Barça* or Madrid. In fact, in almost every stateless nation some entities have adopted the role of representing their community in sport. This is the case of the Basque Country's Athletic Bilbao, with its unique policy of only signing footballers born in the Basque territories to reaffirm its Basque identity; Corsica's SC Bastia, whose greatest successes coincided with the rise of its nationalist movement; the two Celtics – both Glasgow and Belfast – representing the Irish republican community; Al-Wehdat, created in Jordan's refugee camps, which became Palestine's footballing voice; Dinamo Zagreb and Hajduk Split in Federal Yugoslavia's Croatia; and Arafat Yerevan in Soviet Armenia. The list is long. The clubs which, in varied places and historical contexts, have ended up embodying the aspirations of the national communities to which they belong are truly legion.

But football clubs that are political players are not limited to those who are a banner for nationalist ambitions. As an example, we have FC Sochaux – the first professional club in France. This was created under the auspices of the district's main factory, run by the Peugeot car company, which sought to encourage its workers to identify with its public image. Sochaux's team wore the corporate logo and colours.

Yet just as clubs have been set up to defuse class tensions, others have made social alliances a cornerstone of their identity. More specifically many clubs in history have been associated with the working class: Racing Club de Lens in the mining region of northern France; Rayo in Madrid's working-class Vallecas neighbourhood; Sloboda from industrial Tuzla in Tito's Yugoslavia; Torino, which captured blue-collar workers' desire to beat a Juventus aligned with the FIAT employers; or, closer to my home, the modest Atlético Baleares, formed in early 20th-century Mallorca as a club identifying with the island's working people.

A football club's symbolism is often so pronounced that looking at its history allows us to revisit most of the events that have shaped the contemporary era. No dictator worth their salt has failed to use a club for propaganda purposes. As Franco did with Real Madrid, the Portuguese dictator Salazar tried to overcome his international isolation through the European performances of Lisbon's Benfica. With Eusébio in its squad, the club became the chief representative of the Portuguese imperialist notions championed by the local autocrat. The same approach had previously been taken by Benito Mussolini, the Italian fascist leader. He understood that the sport could be a vehicle for spreading his ideology by instrumentalising the successes of the national *squadra azzurra* (blue team) to justify his idea of a triumphant Italy. Later, other dictators did the same. These included Romania's Nicolae Ceaușescu, who placed his son Valentin at the helm of Steaua Bucharest, which became the first club from Eastern Europe to lift the coveted European Cup. Ceaușescu also gave crucial aid to the forming of a top-flight team from his home village of Scornicești. Likewise, Augusto Pinochet in Chile took advantage not just of Colo-Colo – the country's biggest club – but also of several teams created under his rule in militant mining settlements. These aimed to avoid social conflict by applying the classic tactic of giving people 'bread and circuses' – one as ancient as Rome itself.

The other side to the attempts to place football at the service of the powers-that-be is that throughout its history the beautiful game has also been used to question dictatorial rule. For example, the right-wing Portuguese Estado Novo regime faced some of its strongest opposition in a football ground; Académica de Coimbra, a club set up by the university students' association in the central Portuguese city of Coimbra, staged a vibrant protest during the 1969 Portuguese Cup final. Also, some of the football clubs that became the playthings of tyrants had a rebellious past which refused to be erased from popular memory. For instance, the Colo-Colo lionised by Pinochet had previously enjoyed one of its moments of greatest glory under Salvador Allende's left-wing Popular Unity government, when the club ended runner-up in the *Copa Libertadores* (Liberators' Cup), the South American club competition whose very name recalls the continent's liberation from European colonial subjugation. The same Colo-Colo that the dictator would later instrumentalise proudly posed at the La Moneda palace next to a smiling President Allende, who saw the squad as excellent ambassadors for the Chile of that time.

Real Madrid has tended to be identified with the dictatorship and conservative Spanish nationalism, and its most renowned historical figure Santiago Bernabéu was a known Franco supporter. Yet the club has a republican past which those running the club today seem little interested in reclaiming. This is the Madrid of the Second Republic, which scrapped the royalist name given to it by King Alfonso XIII. It even had a President, Antonio Ortega, who was executed at the end of the Spanish Civil War for being a republican army colonel and Communist Party member.

4

As can be seen, there is no event in contemporary history that it would be impossible to explain through the trajectory of a football club. Nazism's vile obsession with persecuting Jews destroyed Hakoah Wien, one of the many openly Jewish clubs in Europe in the first third of the 20th century. The deadly Balkan conflicts at the end of that century had as a prelude a match that pitted together the two teams representing Croat or Serbian nationalism, which would later collide in an all-out war. This was the game played on 13 May 1990 between Dinamo Zagreb and Red Star Belgrade, which ended in a pitched battle. It signalled the start of the gradual break-up of Yugoslavia, an ethnically diverse country which under President Tito's rule had dreamed of fellowship between nationalities – as was perfectly embodied in the Velež Mostar team, until the subsequent and tragic Bosnian War shattered that dream of unity and fraternity. Another football match – not on this occasion between clubs but national squads – was even the spark for a lightning war between Honduras and El Salvador in 1969. Tensions between both countries developed around a qualifying play-off for the 1970 World Cup in Mexico. After both teams had won at home, the decider held on neutral ground fuelled enough animosity between the two states that it triggered the 'soccer war' – as dubbed by Polish journalist Ryszard Kapuściński.

The politics of colonialism have also been played out through football; colonial powers forced the inhabitants of annexed territories to play the European game, only for the occupied peoples to use the sport as a device to challenge colonial power. History is full of anecdotes on colonial clubs, such as Atlético de Tetuán, the top club in the Spanish protectorate of Morocco, which became the first African team to play in the top tier of a European league; or Racing Universitaire d'Argel – one of the colonial clubs in French Algeria – which

5

was the first team in the world to be able to boast having a future Nobel Prize winner in goal. These clubs that served the needs of colonisers were very soon being challenged by teams formed out of the native population. Among many such cases was Espérance de Tunis, which would represent Muslim Tunisians' struggle for liberation from occupation.

We can therefore see that there are a multitude of historic episodes that can be read and interpreted through football clubs. The partition of Germany after the Second World War, the building and later fall of the Berlin Wall, and the strategic importance of this city during the Cold War, are good further examples. Albert Camus, the goalkeeper for colonial Algiers' university team, once claimed that he owed everything he had learned about morals, life, and people's obligations to football. Loosely paraphrasing him, we can say that our recent world history, which is the ultimate word on humanity's morals, can be understood by examining the role of football and its clubs over the last 150 years. Welcome, then, to this modest lesson in late-modern history through the stories of 55 politically extraordinary clubs: a short world tour of these unusual political agents that have often had historic impacts, and ones that are often much bigger than they might at first seem.

1
Britain and Ireland

Celtic FC fans with a large Irish tricolour flag outside their stadium while awaiting the arrival of the 1967 European champions

Manchester City FC
The humanitarian origins
of the petrodollar club

The year 2008 marked a turning point in Manchester City's history. That year, the club's precarious financial situation meant its ownership was transferred away from Thaksin Shinawatra – former Thai Prime Minister and businessman accused of corruption. Taking up the helm was now the Abu Dhabi United Group, a United Arab Emirates (UAE) company headed by Sheikh Mansour bin Zaled Al Nanyan, minister and member of the UAE royal family. This greatly enlarged City's spending power, making it one of the archetypal 'football-business' clubs.

Its team had until then been in the shadow – particularly regarding international limelight – of its local rival Manchester United. Yet now City's bottomless funding capacity triggered growing hatred towards the outfit chaired by Khaldoon Al-Mubarak – the man the Abu Dhabi firm placed to run the club. Although there were already several British clubs which had been bought by unconventional foreign billionaires, City became the main target for opponents of a modern football characterised by a loss of community identity of clubs seemingly awash with money.

Reproaches against City's owner company being linked to UAE's governing monarchy were joined by the common criticism that the petrodollar club lacks a past. Nothing could be further from the truth. Manchester City is a club brimming with history, even if it is now in the hands of those who may be unaware of it. Although City was officially founded in 1894, its life spans back to 1880. Then, several members of the Anglican St Mark's Church in Gorton – in the city's east – decided to set up a team out of solidarity.

Football, then, was far from being the popular sport it is today in Manchester. The people of the UK's industrial capital preferred rugby and cricket and only had one organised football club. These were the circumstances in which the parish clergy, who had helped create a cricket team in 1875, set up the St Mark's (West Gorton) football team, so it would allow for sport in the winter months as well.

The club's aims were very clear: to avoid young people's increasing estrangement from the church and to give them the opportunity to do physical activity to stay clear of alcoholism and growing gang violence. These were chronic problems in an east Manchester that was hard hit by unemployment, precariousness, and poverty. This was even more the case as the area, which previously had been an idyllic pastoral one, had developed within decades into a focal point for the steelmaking and railway manufacturing industries. Despite St Mark's being a Church of England club that aimed to halt the growing divorce between youth and church, its humanitarian nature meant that its ranks were open to all players – regardless of religious beliefs. The team's debut game – now part of City's ancient history – was held on 13 November 1880. This was against another religious team from Macclesfield, exemplifying the fact that a significant number of clubs from that era originated from the church's attempt to direct young people towards its beliefs. Despite the West Gorton club's noble goal of putting an end to the violence plaguing Manchester's working-class districts, it not only failed to stop this scourge, but its pitch was the setting for several violent incidents.

The changes that football was undergoing at that time meant that soon after being created, St. Mark's changed its name a few times. After a short-lived merger with Belle Vue, a team for which St Mark's' captain also played at that time, the club became Gorton Association FC, a name seeking to affirm that the club belonged to the working-class Gorton neighbourhood. When it moved stadiums in 1887 to one located in the Ardwick suburb – another Manchester industrial district in that era – the club chose to call itself Ardwick Association FC.

The links clubs had with working-class communities in that era were clear from many matches such as the one in 1889 in which City's predecessor took on Newton Heath – Manchester United's forerunner. This match was played to raise money for the families of 23 workers who had died in an explosion at the Hyde Road colliery, next to the club's Ardwick home.

The club had several notable successes, such as its victory over Newton Heath in the 1891 Manchester Cup, and its involvement in setting up the League's Second Division the following year. Yet Ardwick's financial difficulties led it to decide to reorganise itself in 1894, becoming the Manchester City we know today.

The new City became the most popular club in Manchester, so much so that until the last decade it held the record attendance for an English league game (apart from matches played at Wembley). In a March 1934 cup tie, its Maine Road stadium hosted no fewer than 84,569 spectators.

Before the sheikhs arrived, the Sky Blues could boast of having won two league titles, four national cups, and a European Cup Winner's Trophy. Their popularity led them to claim to be the Manchester team with most supporters from within the city, ahead of United which had a legion of supporters from elsewhere in Britain. Hence, the rivalry between the two sides has often led 'the Citizens' to see 'the Red Devils' as unrelated to Manchester. For that reason, when City signed the Argentinean striker Carlos Tévez from United, he was welcomed with a provocative 'Welcome to Manchester' poster campaign.

So, despite the club being bought up by the sheikhs prompting greater dislike of the 'Sky Blues' and a negation of its history, the truth is that the petrodollar City of today is the grandchild of the Anglican parish club that was created out of solidarity and charity. Just one of many contradictions highlighting the nature of the present football-business model. A world where practically everything can be bought; apart from history, that is.

Tottenham Hotspur FC
Spurs' Jewish imprint

The image English football has had of Tottenham Hotspur – popularly known as Spurs – is that it is a Jewish team. Little does it matter that the most generous estimations are that only 5 per cent of the club's fans are of this religion. A bigger factor has been that the stands at White Hart Lane – Tottenham's old stadium that was demolished in 2017 – were abundant with the Star of David, including Israeli flags, and that the side's supporters are known as the 'Yid Army'.

Tottenham's Jewish support is much reduced today despite the last three people chairing the club since 1982 all having been of Jewish extraction. Yet, historically speaking, the Jewish community has formed a large part of the club's membership, especially in the early 20th century.

The Jewish community in London grew considerably at the end of the 19th century and the beginning of the 20th because of the many Jews fleeing from persecution in Eastern Europe and particularly Russia. Many of the new Jewish Londoners settled in the Tottenham neighbourhood, in the city's north, in an area undergoing industrial expansion that required the labour this immigration could provide.

One of the key things which enabled integration of these mainly working-class Jewish migrants was the local football club Tottenham Hotspur. This had been established in 1882 and already aroused passions among the district's inhabitants. Many of the Jews arriving from Eastern Europe became regulars at White Hart Lane, a reality that was reinforced by a second generation of Jewish supporters born in the neighbourhood and who fully identified with the club. This was important in terms of forging Spurs' identity.

Thanks to this second generation, and particularly after the First World War, the number of Jewish fans in the club's stands grew steadily until Tottenham became the most popular team among members of London's Jewish community. By 1935, White Hart Lane would have as many as 10,000 Jewish spectators – corresponding to almost a third of the stadium's total capacity.

This was crucial to Spurs gaining a Jewish identity in the English footballing mindset of that period. It was perhaps precisely because of that association that its stadium was chosen by the English Football Association to host a friendly between England and Nazi Germany in December 1935. Because of Hitler's openly anti-Semitic policies, the Jewish community saw the event as an affront.

Spurs' Jewish fans led an attempt to stop the match from taking place, arguing that it insulted not just the Jewish community but also 'all freedom-loving people' in Britain. Despite a substantial proportion of Tottenham fans opposing the match, White Hart Lane not only hosted the friendly – ending in a 3–0 win for England – but also bore witness to the German team giving the Nazi salute as the swastika flag hung shamefully over the match. However, the controversial National Socialist banner did not fly for long as, just after kick-off, a home fan climbed up to the grandstand roof and managed to pull it down.

Fascism had also been flourishing in the United Kingdom and Spurs' Jewish fans became the scapegoat for organisations like Oswald Mosley's British Union of Fascists. This party accused Tottenham's Jews of being 'unable to comprehend the decency and fair play that characterised British sportsmanship'. A truly cynical exercise, as the words were uttered by the person most responsible for countless violent incidents on the streets of London – episodes that led the fascist party to be banned in 1940.

Over the years, Tottenham has consolidated its Jewish identity. This is despite its directors' reluctance to enthusiastically embracing such an affinity. Jews continued to flock to White Hart Lane, although over the decades they have become less and less a mainstay of the club.

It was not until well into the 1960s, by which time the Jewish community far from embodied Spurs as it had done in the 1930s, that rival fans began to attack Tottenham as an all-Jewish club. Throughout the 1970s and 1980s, when violence and racism were the order of the day in most British stadiums, Spurs were met at away games with anti-Semitic behaviour. These included Nazi salutes, hissing that mimicked that of gas chambers, or chants such as 'Does your rabbi know you're here?' and 'Spurs are on their way to Auschwitz, Hitler's gonna gas them again'.

The response to insults, which were aimed at all Spurs' fans, not just its Jewish minority, was for supporters to reaffirm the Jewish identity the club had forged over the decades. As well as Star of David flags becoming commonplace in its stands, its supporters proudly embraced the pejorative term 'Yid'. This is how the 'Yid Army' came about; the name by which Tottenham fans are known.

Over time, this self-labelling as 'yids' has been repeatedly challenged due to the derogatory nature of the term. Indeed, in September 2013, the Football Association and police went as far as banning its use, even among Spurs fans. The considerable controversy this sparked went as far as 10 Downing

Street, prompting the then Prime Minister, Conservative David Cameron, to state that there was a substantial difference between 'Spurs fans self-describing themselves as "Yids" and someone calling someone a "Yid" as an insult'. Despite such words, several Tottenham fans were arrested and charged for using the controversial language. Although the charges were later dropped, the episode stands in stark contrast to the lack of determined action to prosecute the anti-Semitic slurs that Spurs' fans are often subjected to.

Ironically, the willingness to prosecute the word 'Yid' only encouraged its use among Tottenham fans after a period in which the term seemed to have fallen into disuse. The episode underlined the Jewish imprint that has shaped the London club's identity.

Liverpool FC
The fans that took on the Iron Lady

The first game Liverpool played after Margaret Thatcher died was in Reading five days later – on 13 April 2013. At the stadium, 'Reds' fans who had travelled to watch their team had no qualms about loudly celebrating the death of the former Conservative Prime Minister. The passing of the 'Iron Lady' was the subject of numerous chants and banners to remember the brutal clash between the city of Liverpool, and especially the supporters of its top team, and Thatcher during her time in 10 Downing Street.

It was not the first time that season that the Liverpool fans had remembered the ex-PM. On 15 September 2012, while the club visited the Sunderland stadium, the Merseyside fans sang the warning that 'When Maggie Thatcher dies, we're all havin' a party'. It was their way of celebrating the conclusions of an independent report, published days before, on the Hillsborough tragedy in which 96 Reds supporters were killed in April 1989. The report blamed those terrible events on the incompetent actions of the police authorities whose actions were whitewashed at the time by Thatcher, while Liverpool fans themselves were blamed for the catastrophe.

The Hillsborough events formed the peak of a tense relationship between Reds fans and an Iron Lady who had been championing a crusade against working-class football fans.

She particularly did so against Liverpool supporters, who had sometimes been at the centre of serious incidents. These included those during the 1985 European Cup final at Heysel stadium in Brussels, which sadly resulted in 39 deaths, for which Liverpool hooligans were the main offenders.

The animosity towards the PM by the Reds faithful was not only football-related but revolved greatly around a political matter: Merseyside's impoverishment because of the Iron Lady's austerity programme. Her policies, which started being applied in 1979, led to the rapid decline of a city once hailed as 'the New York of Europe' with steadily increasing unemployment and poverty. This also led to a heroin epidemic along with local strikes and mass riots; the average Briton viewed Liverpool as the country's 'lavatory', and one bereft of any single cleaning product.

The first big revolt in Liverpool under Thatcher began in 1981 in Toxteth, one of the city's most impoverished districts, and pitted the local black population against law enforcement officers. Altercations and riots led to a person being killed – run over by the police – and 500 arrests. Thatcher's unwavering support for the officers' actions – thereby endorsing a culture of police impunity – only added to the hatred towards her that was already stirring in the proletarian city.

At Anfield Road, Liverpool's footballing temple, it became commonplace to hear anti-Thatcher chants. These especially came from Anfield's legendary Kop stand, whose supporters would chant 'Maggie, Maggie, Maggie. Die, die, die!'.

Liverpool's grassroots were made up of the same working class that was hit hard by Thatcher's policies. This meant that during her time in office, opposition to the Conservative government became a cornerstone of Reds fans' identity. Chants against her, and in solidarity with the many social struggles that were then taking place in Liverpool, became frequent among fans; and the rift between the fans and government deepened and ossified after Hillsborough.

Before that tragedy, the city of Liverpool had shown its dislike of the Iron Lady in other ways. As a case in point, in 1983 the city voted to run its Town Hall one of the most left-wing tendencies in the Labour Party: Militant. This Trotskyist faction became one of the biggest headaches for the Prime Minister by breaking budget caps and refusing to implement the millions of pounds of cuts that the Conservative government had planned for the city.

In 1984, the Irish Republican Army (IRA) tried to kill Margaret Thatcher during the Conservative Party Conference held in Brighton. Such was the contempt that the hard-suffering working class of the northern industrial city felt towards the Iron Lady that many Liverpool fans bemoaned that she had not joined the five members of the party – including one Westminster MP – who had lost their lives.

Paradoxically, it was in this decade of increased deprivation in Liverpool that the city became the true capital of English football. During the Thatcher years – from 1979 to 1990 – Liverpool FC won eight league titles, and Everton – its city rival – two. In other words, the title went to the Merseyside capital in ten out of the twelve championships played. This gave some consolation for its inhabitants who saw football – one of the main forms of community activity – as an arena where the Iron Lady could be challenged.

As if these achievements were not enough, Liverpool added two more continental trophies to its cabinet: the 1981 and 1984 European Cups. More was not possible because due to the Heysel disaster, the team was banned from European competitions for a decade – eventually reduced to six years. This was an exemplary punishment by UEFA, which Margaret Thatcher cheered on. After all, it penalised one of her main enemies: Liverpool supporters – who had dared to stand up to the Iron Lady.

Forest Green Rovers FC
When football also wants to save the planet

One fine day in 1889, the Anglican clergyman Reverend Peach set up a football team to represent the hamlet of Forest Green, near to the town of Nailsworth in Gloucestershire (England). Little would he know that over a century later the club he had organised would still exist and be a model of footballing policies to save the environment.

Although the name Forest Green Rovers might suggest that protecting the environment had always been a defining feature of the club, in truth the struggle to preserve the planet only became a priority in 2010. That was when the Rovers were bought by Dale Vince, the green-energy businessman who has been central to the profound change to the club's identity. Any appeal the sporting entity had to ecological longings was simply due to it seeking to represent the small village of Forest Green, which, as its name suggests, is in a wooded area. Therefore, for its first 120 years, Forest Green Rovers had nothing to do with the environment apart from the interest its name might arouse among environmentalists.

The sporting entity, whose players originally wore black-and-white-striped jerseys to which were added a crest that was a near carbon copy of that of FC Barcelona, competed in the regional soccer divisions. There, it scored some notable successes such as in its glorious 1982 season when it won the

Hellenic League, plus the Football Association (FA) Vase, which the Rovers lifted in no lesser a venue than Wembley Stadium. In 2010, however, it entered a deep sporting and financial crisis. That is when Dale Vince stepped in, first as a major shareholder and then as club chairperson. Life at Forest Green would be radically transformed and never be the same again.

Vince was a former hippy who left school in his teens to backpack around the world and later turned into a successful green-energy entrepreneur. He headed Ecotricity, a company that produced electricity using wind turbines, which could boast of yearly profits totalling hundreds of millions of pounds. He decided to invest in football but picked the modest Forest Green Rovers to do so.

Under Vince's watch, changes soon began to take place. Their clear purpose was to turn Forest Green into a committed environmentalist club and global example. The outfit's new manager's first change involved the food at the club. Vince banned red meat and gradually brought in an exclusively vegan diet for all those at the club – the same he followed himself. The most interesting thing, however, was that the chairman did not just limit this to the players but made the vegan regime compulsory in all the stadium's food stands. Therefore, fans' traditional hamburgers, sausages, and soft drinks – 'hideous food', in Vince's own words – made way for hummus, quinoa, and vegetables, often accompanied by a soya or oat drink. In no time, Forest Green Rovers became the first fully vegan club on the planet.

The changes to the menu were part of a set of steps to make the club an ecological benchmark. Thus, it was chosen to have a totally organic pitch where cow excrement replaced the usual fertilisers and other chemical products. The grass was to be mown by a solar-powered robot and the clippings handed out to local farmers. These developments happened alongside installing solar panels, re-using rainwater, promoting the use of electric vehicles, recycling, printing matchday programmes on eco-friendly paper, and using chemical-free paint for the maintenance of the ground.

These transformations have enabled the club to greatly reduce its carbon footprint, helping it win a United Nations award in recognition of its fight against climate change. The accolade came after another, in this case awarded by the Institute of Groundsmanship, honouring its playing field's environmental sustainability.

Such measures have contributed to forging the club's new ecological image, which has been completed by the introduction of a new crest and strip colours. The dominant shirt colour is now green – the quintessential environmentalist hue – and a new logo has replaced the one inspired by Barça's shield. Although some of the steps were not liked by the most nostalgic supporters, Vince justified them, arguing the need for Forest Green Rovers to build its own identity – one that did not crudely imitate that of FC Barcelona.

Besides the respect that the changes to the club have aroused in the environmentalist scene, the transformation has also had a very positive social and sporting impact. By becoming a vegan and environmentalist club Forest Green has internationalised its audience, and attendance at its ground has quadrupled since 2010. This growth is also to do with the club's 2017 feat of winning promotion to League Two (the fourth division) – a fully professionalised division. If that was not enough, after five seasons in that league, the team won the right to compete in League One from the 2022–2023 season where it would face such well-established teams as Bolton Wanderers, Sheffield Wednesday, and Derby County – to give just a few examples.

Thanks to these two promotions, Forest Green Rovers made Nailsworth – which has just 6,000 inhabitants – the smallest town ever to compete in professional football in England and Wales. Vince's ambition, however, is not limited to getting the club to the third flight of English football. His dream is to take it to the Championship (the second), and who knows maybe one day even to the Premier League itself.

The green industrialist, who in his youth was an activist against Margaret Thatcher's policies and nowadays has views close to those of the Green Party, is already planning a new stadium for his Forest Green club. This will be a venue entirely built from wood, with seating for 5,000 spectators but expandable to hold 10,000 if the club achieves its Premier League dream. It also aims to have a complex developed around it for eco-friendly firms – called EcoPark – which itself would become a world-first model of its kind. All these good examples show us that football can also do its bit in the global struggle for the planet and to stop climate change. A struggle in which the future itself is at stake.

British Ladies FC
The feminist origins of women's football

Like its male counterpart, football played by women originated in industrial England in the latter half of the 19th century. Then, the growing popularity of the male version of the sport inspired many young women to want to take part. The first women's matches, however, were folk activities associated with the act of marriage, including tussles between married and unmarried women, which was more a showcase for young British men to find a wife than about appreciating women's competitive sport.

The first serious women's football games took place in 1881, when a Scottish team played an English one in a series of matches played in Edinburgh, Glasgow, and northern England. Yet even then, women's football was far from being normalised, as shown by the fact that the players had to use false names. It was also demonstrated by many matches ending in chaos – even with violent pitch invasions – probably as a consequence of the prevailing sexism. The young sportswomen who had played in the match were forced to flee as fast as they could.

Conservative Victorian Britain did not approve of women playing football and there were constant sexist criticisms in the press which condemned such players for their appearance, attire, and playing ability. These went as far as claiming

24

that football was a male-only sport and that it was not a desirable activity for women. Some doctors colluded with this approach, providing supposedly medical arguments which claimed that women could lose fertility by playing the game and thus compromise the role society gave women. They were quick to join the campaign to ban young British women from playing football.

Yet these sexist approaches did not stop the group of young females who, in 1894, published an advert in the *Daily Graphic* with the aim of enlisting women players to form the first women's football club in history. Despite all the pressure society put on them to desist, 30 women heeded the call. On 1 January 1895, the pioneering British Ladies Football Club was created, to be managed by Spurs player Bill Julian – one of the few male footballers who dared to publicly back the women's sport.

Among the clubs' promoters were two key figures in the inseparable struggle of women to play football and fight for self-emancipation. The first was Florence Dixie who, despite being an aristocrat – the Marquess of Queensbury – was also an active sportswoman, traveller, writer, war correspondent, and one of the very first feminists. The second was the young middle-class player Nettie Honeyball – a name that was in fact an alias – who had penned the *Daily Graphic* advert together with Dixie. Both women were committed feminists who advocated not just the right for women to play football but also for them to vote, go to mixed schools, have equal access to all professions, and even the right for the crown to be passed on to the monarch's first-born daughter.

Honeyball took up being the club secretary while the Marquess of Queensbury became the chairperson of the new British Ladies. The fact that the club's top post went to an aristocrat did not stop most of the footballers coming from more humble backgrounds.

Despite class differences, Dixie shared feminist convictions with the team members. One of these was Helen Matthews: a prominent Suffragette who had already participated in the 1881 women's matches – in the Scotland jersey.

The British Ladies made their public debut in London on 23 March 1895. The match attracted 10,000 spectators and pitted two teams from the club: one made up of its players from northern Britain and the other with those from the south.

The game was clearly a step forward in the fight for women's football to be recognised. For the first time, women players were able to play without wearing a corset or high-heeled shoes. All the same, the reaction to the match in the major newspapers ranged from censorship to mockery. This did not put off the fervent players who, within the space of a year, played nearly a hundred exhibition games across Britain. These were not just women's sporting events but also battles for women's rights.

Indeed, the British Ladies' activities helped draw attention to some of the issues raised by the feminist movement. They questioned the expectations of Victorian society, such as over the attire women should wear, the feminine 'ideal', and women's identity.

Nettie Honeyball herself stated that she had helped set up the club with the aim of 'proving to the world that women are not the ornamental and useless creatures that men have pictured', adding that playing football was an act 'of emancipation' that dared suggest that one day 'ladies may sit in parliament and have a voice in the direction of affairs ... which concern them'.

The club secretary's feminism was complemented by that of its chair. Florence Dixie was a Suffragette who defended full equality between the sexes (and not just the right to vote), including the right for women to wear the same clothing as men – as the women players had done in their matches. Dixie also authored a feminist science-fiction novel titled *Gloriana: The Revolution of 1900*. The book depicted a United Kingdom that had recognised women's right to vote – making the novel ahead of its time – and reaching the end of the 20th century with a female government delivering peace and prosperity.

Despite the zeal of those driving it, British Ladies had a regrettably brief existence. It disappeared in September 1896, just over a year after its first match, as it lacked the funds needed to keep its activities going.

Women's football slipped back into obscurity and witnessed the Football Association (FA) Council banning male teams from playing women's teams (even in charity fixtures). The dream of those pioneers who made football a tool to demand women's emancipation was left behind.

Celtic FC
An Irish republican symbol in the heart of Scotland

Few clubs in the world have as much political symbolism as Glasgow Celtic. The act of wearing the club's shirt on the streets of Belfast reveals its wearer to be a republican nationalist sympathiser. Wearing it on some New York Avenue indicates one belongs to the large Irish diaspora in the United States.

Despite the club's home being Glasgow, the key to understanding and explaining Celtic is its Irish identity. The unique sporting entity was officially created in 1888 at the behest of Marist Brother Walfrid (the Roman-Catholic Community name for Andrew Kerins). Its first major goal was to raise money for the inhabitants of Glasgow's East End – an area mostly comprising of Irish immigrants who in many cases lived in extreme poverty. Its second was to create links between the Irish-Catholic community and the traditionally Protestant native Glaswegians.

Despite Celtic's clear resolve to build bridges between the two communities, the club proudly displayed its Irish roots. From the shamrock in its crest to the club's name and its green-and-white-striped jersey, everything making up the club reflected that it was created out of Irish immigration and was seen as such outside Celtic.

Soon after being founded in 1895, Celtic's directors went as far as proposing limiting the number of protestants among its players. This was rejected and the club remained open to people from all religious beliefs, even though a large majority of both its players and fans were Catholic.

Glasgow Celtic had a strong symbolic foundation. It was a humble working-person's club and was the team for Irish immigrants but also the rest of the East End. It was a non-sectarian club that welcomed both Catholics and Protestants – a mixture that its bitter enemy Rangers was not able to claim.

Celtic's uniqueness helped give it a political identity originally associated with early Irish nationalism represented by the movement for Home Rule. This was the attempt at constitutional reform during the late 19th and early 20th centuries, which would grant autonomy to an Ireland that for centuries had been subjected to London's colonial diktats. In Celtic's early years, many of its players and staff voiced support for freeing Irish-nationalist political prisoners or opposed Britain's colonial war against the Boers in South Africa.

The Irish nationalism Celtic became identified with linked with a left-leaning politics encouraged by the surroundings in which most of its supporters lived: a very deprived working-class neighbourhood. The rise of the labour movement in the first third of the 20th century was especially strong in Glasgow – one of the most highly industrialised cities in Britain. This meant that much of Celtic's grassroots did not just identify with Irish nationalism (which, thanks to a war waged by the old IRA, managed to win the Irish Free State in 1921) but also with the labour movement (which was less tied to the British state and related symbols than the conservatism it rivalled).

Because of its growing social and sporting importance, Celtic came to play a key role in the Irish-Catholic community's identity. This was no longer defined exclusively in religious and political terms but also began to use soccer for its cultural identification.

The community alignment with the club deepened with the emergence of the conflict in the six Irish counties still under British rule. The pre-eminence of Irish republican ideas among Celtic supporters turned Parkhead – the district which is home to 'Paradise' (the nickname fans gave their stadium) – into a platform for pro-Irish ideas in each of the Glasgow club's home matches.

Since 'the Troubles' broke out in the north of Ireland in the late 1960s, Celtic fans have increased their political identification with a united Ireland. In fact, Celtic became an accidental participant in the Northern Irish conflict as the sympathy shown towards it, because of the conflict taking place at that time, was a clear declaration of support for Irish republicanism. As a result, the green and white shirts and the murals with the Celtic crest or images of the club became very popular on the streets of Derry and Belfast – cities from where thousands of Celtic supporters would regularly travel to Parkhead to follow their beloved team's endeavours.

Pro-republican literature – comprising dozens of different newspapers – was sold *en masse* at the gates of Celtic Park (Parkhead). The stadium itself was filled with thousands of Irish tricolour flags and rebel songs inspired both by the early 20th-century war for independence and the new IRA's resistance in the six counties still under British control.

Of all the Irish flags displayed at Paradise, one had a particular significance: that ever-flying over one of the sporting venue's stands as a reminder of the club's Irish roots. Practically from its beginnings, when the whole of Ireland was under British domination, Celtic had an Irish flag aloft at its ground. And this was above a turf which, incidentally, had been brought over from Ireland's county Donegal in 1892, thanks to the patronage of Michael Davitt – founder of the Irish National Land League and nationalist activist. Davitt claimed, 'the green sod brought from dear old Donegal will prove so slippery that any Saxon rival who ran over it will fall a cropper!'.

The first Irish flag that flew at Celtic Park was not yet the tricolour by which the Republic of Ireland is today identified but a green flag featuring a harp – the symbol used by Irish nationalists in the 18th and 19th centuries. The Irish tricolour (a flag symbolising peace – symbolised by white – between the Catholic religion – green – and the Protestant faith – orange) was first raised at the stadium in 1922. This was one year after the war for independence, after which the Irish Free State was recognised, and the island partitioned.

That flag itself was laden with symbolism as it was a gift to Celtic from the new free state government on behalf of the Irish people. From then on, it stayed above Paradise for three decades: being exposed to the harsh Glaswegian weather throughout. In 1951, the club's manager, Jimmy McGrory, asked for the tattered flag to be lowered (taking the opportunity of Celtic being away on tour in Ireland) for cleaning and repair.

It turned out that no Glasgow flag maker would accept the order to repair or make a new Irish flag, which exposed the sectarianism prevailing in the 1950s. In response to this, Celtic's manager wrote to Éamon de Valera – the historic pro-independence leader and then Prime Minister of the recently proclaimed Republic of Ireland – to explain the conundrum. The *Taoiseach* immediately responded by sending in the name of the Irish people a new tricolour flag that was soon raised at Celtic Park.

Despite its peaceful symbolism, the Irish banner met with quite a backlash, especially from within the Protestant community, which regarded the flag's permanent flying in Glasgow as a provocation. Sectarianism against the Irish-Catholic community, which was a daily occurrence among pro-British Protestants, extended to the institutions. In 1952, after some serious clashes during a derby match with Rangers, the courts made the Scottish Football Association ban any display of flags that might be deemed offensive to supporters from other clubs. The ban was particularly aimed at forcing Celtic to remove the tricolour flag from its ground, which the club refused to comply with on the grounds of its Irish roots. Eventually, the federation was forced to back off under pressure from the other league clubs who all feared suffering a sharp fall in revenue if Celtic were expelled from the competition.

The controversy over the Celtic Park tricolour did not end there. In 1972, a magistrate once again ordered the flag to be taken down. They claimed that some people found it offensive at a time of rising sectarian violence in Scottish football and greater tensions in the north of Ireland – when the IRA resurfaced. Celtic's response to the legal instruction was to, once again, refuse to remove its banner, proudly reiterating the club's Irish roots.

Along with the tricolour, republican songs also became an essential element in shaping the club's pro-Irish identity. Whether in Glasgow or on away trips, Celtic fans would frequently sing such songs. These include: 'The Boys of the Old Brigade' – a song about the war for independence and the first IRA; 'The Fields of Athenry' – a ballad about colonial Ireland's Great Famine explicitly calling for resisting the British Crown (and which can be heard at Paradise before each game); and 'Celtic Symphony' – an anthem written by the Wolfe Tones to celebrate Celtic's centenary and which contains explicit support for the IRA and the withdrawal of British troops from Ireland.

Celtic's Catholic, nationalist, and republican identity has hardened the judgements of others towards its supporters. During games in Scottish stadiums with mainly Protestant fans, Celtic followers have been subjected to sectarian jibes. This has only strengthened fans' identification with Catholicism and the republican movement. That said, the club's management has not always approved of the strong association with Irish republicanism and has tried several times to deter its fans from overtly expressing their political convictions.

For instance, this was done by Jock Stein, the legendary Protestant manager who helped Glasgow Celtic win the 1967 European Cup. When addressing his team's supporters at half-time during a 1972 match against Stirling Albion, he asked them to spare the IRA-supporting chants for the pubs and streets and stick to slogans to spur on Celtic's players. Supporters respected Stein's wishes during the second half of the game, but soon the republican chants returned to the Celtic Park stadium, where they still ring out.

In 1996, the club's directors promoted the 'Bhoys Against Bigotry' campaign which sought to banish republican songs, which it saw as sectarian, from Celtic's collective repertoire. However, a significant section of its followers rejected this decision, seeing it as an attempt to re-write the club's history and disassociate it from republicanism.

In this regard, the UEFA fined Celtic in November 2021 for pro-IRA chants by some of its fans during a Europa League match. The fine was met by the Green Brigade – the youngest and noisiest pro-Irish fan group – unveiling a banner with the words 'Fuck UEFA', which led to the club being given an additional fine.

Despite attempts to change the essence of the team, Celtic is still a club linked to the Irish republican cause: one that is simply for freedom and justice. It is a continuation of the same fight which in 1888 led Brother Walfrid to create a club like no other. One that is an icon for Ireland and its republican cause, despite its domicile being in the heart of Scotland.

Star of the Sea Youth Club
The club of Bobby Sands and the Northern Irish tragedy

On 5 May 1981 and after 66 days of hunger strike demanding political status for republican prisoners, Bobby Sands' life faded away. The IRA leader's tragic death – the first of ten among the H-block hunger strikers – made him a universal symbol of Irish freedom. This was largely because while protesting the prison regime introduced by British PM Margaret Thatcher, Sands was elected as a member of parliament.

Over his short but intense 27 years, Bobby Sands showed many different sides to his personality. These included being an underground Irish republican fighter and leading IRA prisoners inside Long Kesh prison, but also being a father, poet, journalist, and storyteller – learning to be the latter three during his years in prison. But we must add to this list a further lesser-known side to Sands: the footballing past of the H-block martyr.

In his teenage years in the late 1960s, Sands played left-back for one of the north of Ireland's most promising teams. This was none other than the Star of the Sea Youth Club; a team from the Rathcoole neighbourhood in north Belfast. The club had clear Catholic overtones, as it adopted one of the titles – Star of the Sea – by which the Virgin Mary was traditionally known. The same applied to the school the young Bobby Sands attended: a religious school named Stella Maris.

Despite its Catholic connections, Star of the Sea was always known for being open to and accepting young players from any creed; thereby, rejecting the sectarianism and segregation that permeated very many Northern Irish communities and sporting organisations. In a way, Star of the Sea was a mirror image of its Rathcoole home, which was an estate built during the 1950s where a majority of Protestant families lived with a significant Catholic community – making up almost a third of the local people. It was indeed where the Sands family moved, in the early 1960s, to escape the sectarian siege they suffered while living in the Protestant slum area of Abbots Cross.

The relatively peaceful cohabitation between Catholics and Protestants in Rathcoole spawned the forming of a club that welcomed all those doing sport, regardless of their beliefs. Liam Conlon was a club founder and guiding hand. One of the basic rules he introduced was the banning of religious discussions and communitarian symbols in the club's public areas. His aim was strictly limited to sport: to develop the best youth football team in Ireland. This was managed in 1969, when Star of the Sea was crowned as youth football champions for the whole of the Irish isle. That young generation, with its talented left-back named Bobby Sands, won trophy after trophy over two years – in which it only was defeated a couple of times.

In a north of Ireland that began being torn apart following the Catholic community's revolt for equal rights, Star of the Sea initially resisted, remaining one of a few spaces of mixed-faith cohabitation. In its ranks were Catholic, Protestant, and even Mormon players. Yet such a club was not able to survive the mounting war between the IRA, on the one hand, and the British Army and Unionist paramilitary forces, on the other.

Indeed, the 1969 Irish champions became a real metaphor for 'the Troubles' the six counties (Northern Ireland) went through between the late 1960s and the signing of the Good

Friday (peace) agreement in 1998. Its ranks did not just include a prominent future republican activist, such as Sands, but also young men who would go on to join armed loyalist organisations. This happened with the Mormon Terry Nichol and Protestant Michael Atcheson, who were both imprisoned for their activity in the Ulster Voluntary Force (UVF).

Sands, Nichol, and Atcheson had gone from sharing the club strip and dressing room to taking up arms against each other in the conflict that shook the north of the island. As if this was not enough, there were also other tragedies. Raymond McCord was a teammate who managed to get a trial for Manchester United – even if this was unsuccessful. He saw the UVF, which two of his old teammates had joined, murder his son and try to do the same to him on three occasions. McCord was in fact Protestant but was accused by his co-religionists of colluding with the republican movement because he regularly denounced sectarian violence. Protestant paramilitary groups were also responsible for the killing of the brother of Paddy Davison, another Star of the Sea player who was Catholic.

The escalating Irish war ended, then, with the disbanding of the multi-faith outfit that had been proclaimed Irish champion. Most of the Protestants left the team because it was increasingly identified as Catholic. Only Raymond McCord tried to preserve – with little success – the club's non-sectarian stance. A tough enterprise while Rathcoole, the club's birthplace, was becoming an exclusively Protestant ghetto. In 1993, Stella Maris, the Catholic school that shared with the football club a reference to the Virgin Mary in its name, had to close.

Likewise, Bobby Sands' family was once again forced out of their home, in 1972, due to sectarian pressure. This time they moved to Twinbrook, a Catholic district in West Belfast.

The north of Ireland thus entered a turbulent period in which Star of the Sea players went from complicity in the changing room to brutal infighting. This was a struggle that led to the sacrifice of that promising left-back who died as a martyr to the Irish cause in those bitterly remembered H-blocks.

2
France and Italy

Gianni Agnelli greets Juventus FC players during training in 1972.
Source: RCS Quotidiani, unlimited use

Red Star FC

The red star lighting up the sky of a Parisian *banlieue*

Until very recently, Paris was the only major European capital without a soccer club that was a continental leader. The only Parisian team among the top French footballing clubs was Paris Saint-Germain (PSG). Yet, before its Qatari petrodollars appeared, PSG could only boast of having won two league titles in what was a rather brief history – spanning back no further than 1970. The arrival of Nasser Al-Khelaïfi, head of Qatar Sports Investments, to the lavish Parc des Princes turned the club into one of the most financially muscular teams in Europe. The world stars that the Qatari fortunes were able to sign made the Parisian club a symbol of commercial football today. Qatari oil revenue seemed able to buy absolutely anything it wanted.

Everything? '*Non!*' as the indomitable Gauls would say. If there is one thing that Al-Khelaïfi and company cannot buy, it is history. And compared to other international teams, Paris Saint-Germain's background is not so rich. Just in Paris itself, we can find clubs with a far greater tradition, but admittedly less money. The best example is Red Star; the legendary club which on more than one recent occasion reached *Ligue 2* – the French second division. It has been striving to rekindle its glory – success that the almighty Qatari-capital PSG now wants all for itself.

40

Unlike its billionaire neighbour, Red Star FC has a long history. It was founded in a bar in Paris' seventh *arrondissement* (district), backed, among others, by Jules Rimet. He was to be the chairman of the French and international football federations and would lead the creation of one of the most successful projects in the sporting world: the World Cup. Although the club's name might suggest otherwise, Red Star was originally a bourgeois club. Indeed, its name had more to do with the Anglophilia of its promoters than any pro-Bolshevik sympathies. The name Red Star seems to have been suggested by Miss Jenny, the Rimet family's English governess, and quickly accepted by the society's other founders. Jenny took such a name from the Red Star Line transatlantic steamer company. Therefore the name had nothing to do with the communist ideology that, nevertheless, would infuse much of the club's future.

Initially, the Red Star team – first wearing a navy blue and white strip – played its matches in the exclusive Champ de Mars area – very close to the Eiffel Tower. Yet it was soon pushed out of there by growing real-estate speculation. Thus began an odyssey which saw the bourgeois Red Star club play at different grounds. These included Bir-Hakeim at the site – also close to the legendary tower – that would later house the infamous Winter Velodrome used by the Nazis to hold the Jews they rounded up in 1942. In 1909, Red Star would finally settle in the brand-new *Stade de Paris* in the working-class town of Saint-Ouen – next to the famous *Marché aux Puces* (flea market).

Moving from Paris' smart seventh district to one of its working-class suburbs (*banlieues*) radically transformed Red Star's character. It quickly went from being a bourgeois club to being one for workers and the urban poor. This mirrored what was generally happening to the game, which despite being

41

promoted by the bourgeoisie, was gaining popularity among the lower classes.

That was the context in which Red Star's history of success, which was particularly notable in the 1920s, began being created. From 1921 to 1923, the Saint-Ouen club won three French Cups in a row. The first of these was in a historic final against Olympique de Paris – its main rival at the time. Ironically this club would merge with Red Star, in 1926, providing the green and white strip that Red Star still wears today.

The illustrious 1920s, in which the club added another cup to its trophy cabinet, brought professionalisation, which swept through French football over the following decade. Red Star was indeed one of the first clubs to become professional and frequently played in the top flight of French football.

The Nazi occupation of the country, from 1940, was met by another of Red Star's golden ages. The club won its first major title of the period, the *Coupe de France*, in 1942. Shortly after, it signed the player who became the club's true icon: Rino della Negra, a player who juggled his sporting pursuits with fighting in the resistance to the occupation. As a member of the immigrant Partisans – led by the Armenian Missak Manouchia – della Negra took part in several actions. This included the attack on the Italian National Fascist Party headquarters in Paris, and the killing of Nazi general Von Apt – one of the highest-ranking officials overseeing the occupation.

In the last letter Rino della Negra wrote before the Nazis executed him at Mont Valérian in February 1944, he sent a last message to his teammates and others at the club: 'I bid good morning and farewell to everyone at Red Star', the young resistance fighter signed off.

Della Negra was not the only martyr that the Saint-Ouen club had to mourn during the Second World War. Eugène Maës, a

Red Star player from 1910 to 1914, died in the Dora-Mittelbau concentration camp in Germany in March 1945.

Red Star's identity, which had been profoundly working class since the club moved to Saint-Ouen, began being associated with the Partisan resistance and communist imaginary following the Nazi occupation. Consequently, after Paris was liberated, the club was chosen to host a match, held on 3 September 1944, in which it played the Parisian club Racing to raise money for the families of the 'Free France' fighters who gave their lives to free the capital.

Strangely France's liberation marked the beginning of Red Star's decline. It lost the 1946 Cup final and went through several mergers – some bizarre, such as joining up with Toulouse; a club and city more than 600 kilometres from Saint-Ouen. After that, the club failed to live up to the glory it had enjoyed since the 1920s. It suffered many humiliations, such as in 1955, when it failed to go up to the first division despite winning this right on the pitch. It was blocked from doing so because its directors were being prosecuted for embezzlement.

Despite its decline, Red Star's political symbolism has remained intact. A good example of this is the new name which the old *Stade de Paris* took after the war ended: Bauer, taken from the street in which it was located. The road itself had been named in homage to Jean-Claude Bauer; a doctor from Saint-Ouen, who had also joined the anti-Nazi resistance and was shot at Mont Valérien in 1943.

Red Star's political allegiances were also clear when, at the height of the Algerian War in 1959, the club signed former Stade de Reims player Mohamed Maouche. This was just after the player heeded the call by the Algerian National Liberation Front (the main movement fighting French rule in the country) to join Algeria's anti-colonial national team. The criticisms levelled at Maouche by the section of French society that backed the colonial occupation did not stop Red Star from opening its doors to him and enabling him to play in the metropolis again.

The fact that the milieu around Red Star was overtly communist greatly helped construct the club's image. As an illustration, the Saint-Ouen Town Hall was run throughout the 1945–2014 period by the French Communist Party. Red Star became popularly known as 'The 93 Communists' Club'. The number corresponds to the *department* (county) of Seine-Saint-Denis – a historic stronghold in Paris' red belt.

Among the historical actions that have reinforced the described link was the club's role in the May 1968 revolt. During this dreamlike time, the club spearheaded the playing of a charity game to fund the workers' strikes shaking Saint-Ouen and almost all of France. Furthermore, two members of the Red Star team were among those who occupied the headquarters of the French Football Federation, just as the students had done at the Sorbonne, demanding 'football for footballers'.

Promotion to *Ligue 2* in both 2015 and 2018 forced the club to relocate to Beauvais and to the Jean-Bouin stadium in Paris' fashionable 16th district. Despite temporarily abandoning Bauer (because the old stadium did not meet professional-league standards), Red Star remained an icon for those with anti-fascist and left-wing inclinations. In the stands of the different grounds the club has played in, there has never been a shortage of tributes to Rino della Negra or Clément Meric – a young anti-fascist Red Star fan murdered by a group of right-wing extremists in central Paris in 2013. Over a century has passed since Red Star was founded in Saint-Ouen, and the club has more and more outrageously rich and powerful neighbours. Yet, thanks to young people preserving the club's rebellious traditions, a red star still lights up the sky of a particular Parisian *banlieue*.

SC Bastia
Corsica's rebel soul

On 13 December 2015, Corsica had a historic election day. For the first time ever, the regional elections were won by a coalition comprising pro-independence and other national- ists – including Femu a Corsica and Corsica Libera. Four days later, historic pro-independence leader Jean-Guy Talamoni was sworn in as President of the Corsican Assembly. Corsican nationalism had gained control of the country's main institu- tion. This was a milestone that the Corsican national movement had sought since it burst onto the scene in the 1970s.

Until then, and despite the important role in society that Corsican patriotism had played over recent decades, the Cor- sican Assembly had always resisted such a government being formed. And pro-Corsican sentiment had always been spread through popular institutions. Notably, these included a football club closely aligned with the pro-independence movement: Sporting Club Bastia, which has traditionally been considered one of the leading examples of Corsican national aspirations (and has Talamoni himself as a fan). Thus, as has happened in many stateless nations around the world, Corsicans have a soc- cer club with a remit beyond the strictly sporting, and which has become a platform for feelings of national belonging.

The club did not have this symbolism when it was set up in the early 20th century; it picked it up decades later, when SC

Bastia evolved into becoming Corsica's footballing champion and national symbol for the Mediterranean island's inhabitants. In fact the club was founded (in 1905) by a Swiss national, Hans Ruesch, who taught German at the town's high school and who came to Corsica via Barcelona. Once Ruesch settled on the island, he decided to promote such a venture, as his fellow countryman Hans Gamper had done in the Catalan capital.

During the first phase of its history, Bastia was no more than a sports club and was not associated with any pro-Corsican political symbolism. Indeed, in its early days, football was seen in Corsica as indicating identification with the French metropolis because the island's clubs played in the Gallic competitions. This participation reinforced the idea that football strengthened Corsica's subordination to France.

It was from the 1970s that the ties between football and nationalism became closer and Sporting Bastia emerged as the main soccer club representing the Corsican nation. The recently professionalised Sporting Club Bastia had just achieved the greatest sporting feat in its history, when it won the French second-division championship in 1968. This enabled it to reach the top flight of French football – an unprecedented achievement for a Corsican club.

Sporting became the Corsican sporting ambassador *par excellence* because its boom in the 1970s coincided with the rise of Corsican nationalism. A contemporary movement for the island's independence developed after events in Aléria in 1975, in which a revolt by small wine farmers turned into a true national revolution. Shortly after, the Corsican National Liberation Front (FLNC) was created.

After its promotion, Bastia achieved an even bigger success when it reached the 1972 French Cup final. Although it lost this to Olympique de Marseille, the Corsican fans used the occasion to demonstrate their national pride, filling much of Paris' Parc des Princes stadium with flags featuring the *testa mora* (Moor's Head) – the Corsican national emblem. This runner-up spot was followed by coming third in the 1977 league and – most impressive of all – the club's revered run in the next season's UEFA Cup, where it managed to qualify for the final.

To reach that final, Bastia successively disposed of Sporting Lisbon, Newcastle, Torino, Carl Zeiss Jena, and Zurich's Grasshoppers. Its last opponent was PSV Eindhoven, who themselves had knocked out *Barça* in the semi-final. Amid the nationalist upsurge, the Corsicans' progress in the European competition was regarded as a source of national pride, and the whole island rallied around their beloved team.

This support helped it defy the big European capitals' teams despite Bastia being a town of only 40,000 inhabitants. Yet it did not stop the club from losing against the Dutch team in a final marred by a first leg played on an unplayable pitch – owing to Corsica being hit by torrential rain a few days earlier. A goalless home draw was followed by a 3–0 defeat at Eindhoven, so the PSV players ended up lifting the cup.

It wasn't until 1981 that Bastia won its first and only major trophy. The Corsicans again reached the *Coupe de France* final, but this time triumphed against Michel Platini's then-almighty Saint-Étienne again in a Parc des Princes brimming with Corsican flags.

Bastia's golden era, when it was a key ingredient in Corsican consciousness, came to an end when the club was relegated to the dreaded second division in 1986. Paralleling difficulties affecting Corsican nationalism, which suffered serious fragmentation in the late 1980s, SC Bastia hit a low point and suffered the most dreadful event of its history. This was the Furiani stadium disaster, taking place on 5 May 1992, before a cup semi-final between Bastia (the home side) and Olympique de Marseilles. Just before kick-off, a specially installed temporary stand collapsed, tragically leaving 18 people dead and more than 2,000 injured.

Jean-Guy Talamoni was then the speaker of the Corsican Assembly for the pro-independence party A Cuncolta Nazionalista (which was seen as the political wing of the armed group *FLNC-Canal Historique*). Around the time of the disaster, figures linked to the party took over directing the soccer club. Until then, it had been directed by Jean-François Filippi – a businessman and mayor of the village of Lucciana. Although Filippi had been elected on a right-wing mandate, he had a close relationship with the pro-independence wing of the *FLNC-Canal Historique*. This was shown when the club's private security was entrusted to Bastia Securita; a company created by A Cuncolta and which employed leading activists from the aforementioned party.

Jean-François Filippi was murdered in 1994, after he had quit being club chairman in advance of the trial over the Furiani tragedy. His death, which was never fully explained, was one of the many killings that shook Corsica at the time and can largely be explained by the fratricidal war between the different nationalist factions. The practical consequence of his death was for Sporting Club Bastia to fall under the direct influence of A Cuncolta and *FLNC-Canal Historique*.

Gaining such control satisfied the strategic interest pro-independence groups had in the club. However, it was also driven by the other nationalist faction, represented by the *FLNC-Canal Habitual* and Movement for Self-Determination, having acquired the chairmanship of Athletic Club Ajacci – the other big Corsican club (although one with much less support among the island's people than Sporting).

So it was in that period that Charles Pieri, the *FLNC-Canal Historique* leader, became the effective chairman of SC Bastia, despite not holding a formal position in the Bastia hierarchy. He was regularly seen in the VIP suites watching SC Bastia matches – whether at the Furiani or when the team played away.

In 1994, Pieri managed to guide the club up to the French first division and keep it there for over a decade. However, this wasn't without controversy. It is believed that the sponsorship of the Corsicans' shirt from 1995 to 2004 by the travel company Nouvelles Frontières, had simply been a veiled way of paying the revolutionary tax that the FLNC demanded from such companies operating in Corsican territory. This was suspected because one of the central struggles by pro-Corsican fighters was against French companies doing island-related tourism – making them a target for attacks. It should be added that, in 2004, Jean-Guy Talamoni was charged with extortion of this kind against Nouvelles Frontières to benefit the pro-independence magazine *U Ribombu* – A Conculta's mouthpiece. It was alleged that the travel firm had included advertising in the magazine to pay the revolutionary tax. (Talamoni was eventually acquitted.)

In the 21st century, pro-independence politics has lost influence within Sporting Bastia's power structure. However, the club's symbolism remains intact. This has been shown by events such as its fans whistling over the *La Marseillaise* (French national anthem) in the 2002 cup final – in which Bastia was beaten by Brittany's Lorient. This so outraged President Jacques Chirac that he threatened to leave the stadium. There were also the chants in the 2015 League Cup final where the Corsican supporters reiterated 'We are not French' during a match against Paris Saint-Germain. Finally there have been continued calls to display the *testa mora* – also a club symbol

– in pre-match ceremonies despite the French Professional Football League having banned using such symbolism.

It is precisely prohibitions of this kind that have led Talamoni and many other pro-independence Corsicans to denounce what they see as 'anti-Corsican racism' by the French footballing authorities. SC Bastia's forced relegation to French football's fifth division on financial grounds can be seen as the latest instance of this. As historian Didier Rey has argued, both the powers-that-be and the media have a biased and often unfair image of Corsica and its football. This fuels victimhood among Corsicans, which has often been met radically or violently.

All the same, we are a long way off from those images of Corsica as bandit territory in which everyone went around armed – even to the stadium. The pacification of Corsican society and the disappearance of the armed struggle have helped point the footballing spotlight in the right direction: seeing SC Bastia as a unique institution which, despite having lived through tough times, is still able to draw around it almost all of Corsican society. This has made the club's Corsican-language motto '*Uniti Vinceremu!*' (United We Shall Win!) seem even more true. Maybe this is why, during the high points in Sporting Bastia's history, the club has had as many as 10,000 season ticket holders – a quarter of Bastia's population or a third of the total number of people living on the island. Such impressive figures show that the club truly is Corsica's rebel soul.

Juventus FC
A puppet of the masters of Italy

Juventus Football Club is an Italian institution. The *Vecchia Signora* (Old Lady) – an intriguing nickname for a club whose formal name means 'youth' in Latin – is the club that has acquired most silverware in Italy's history. Specifically, by the end of 2022–2023, it could proudly claim having won 36 *scudetti* (league shields; and it would have been 38 if Juventus had not been stripped of two thanks to the Calciopoli scandal). And it could boast of having picked up 14 *Coppa Italias* (Italian Cups). In other words, it has won more titles than any of its domestic rivals.

Besides being the Italian club with the most honours, it also has the biggest fan base. Yet the contradiction is that it doesn't have the most supporters in its home city Turin. There, Torino FC has more fans than its local arch-rival despite having a far more modest trophy record. Even though it has the most national trophies as well as most supporters, Juventus has a less-celebrated record: it is the most hated team in Italy. This reaction is closely related to the perception that Juventus is rich and arrogant. It is also because of its link with the owners of the Fabbrica Italiana Automobili Torino – the Turin-based car company better known by its initials (FIAT) – the firm that probably best epitomised Italian industry in the last century.

When Sport Club Juventus was created in 1897 by a group of Turin students, it could not have been predicted that their new outfit would become such a 20th-century national icon. Despite the club's association with the FIAT-owning Agnelli dynasty only developing years later, Juventus' first big sporting success came quickly: victory in the all-Italian league in 1905. After that, however, it went through two decades of stagnation, when the Italian championship was dominated by other clubs from the same Piedmont region, particularly Pro Vercelli.

The history of Juventus took a sharp turn after 24 July 1923. This was when Edoardo Agnelli was elected as club chairman. He was the son of Giovanni Agnelli: the founder of FIAT in 1899; and the person key to turning the car manufacturer into a leading Italian firm and symbol of northern Italy's industrialisation. Thus began the bond between the corporation and the soccer club.

The control that FIAT bosses acquired over the club through Edoardo Agnelli had the blessing of the fascist authorities which had just been formed (itself partly thanks to collusion by corporations such as FIAT that saw Mussolini's National Fascist Party able to guarantee economic stability).

The capital that FIAT invested in the club and the close relationship company bosses had with the country's new rulers ushered in a long period of success for the Turin team. In 1926, Juventus won its second Italian championship. This was one of the last to take place in which separate league tournaments were played in the north and south of Italy and then a match between the winner from each would determine the national champion. Fascism saw this organisational model as deviating from that of a strong and united Italy, so it decided to restructure football in 1929 to create the top-flight *Serie A* – as it is known today.

It was in the early years of the *Serie A* that Juventus gained its winning reputation: picking up five *scudetti* in a row from 1931 to 1935. This was also when it developed the image among the working class as being a club at the service of the employers and state rulers. It was no coincidence that it was during fascism that *Juve* became successful, rich, and able to attract the very best players by paying them astronomical salaries for that time. In 1932, during the club's glory days, the Agnellis funded the building of a new stadium named after Benito Mussolini. It then was made the venue for the 1934 World Cup hosted by fascist Italy. These were nods to the connection between the club's masters and the extreme-right regime.

The end of Mussolini's dictatorship did not, however, create big waves for the giant Turin-based corporation. Indeed, FIAT has always had great power and influence in Italy no matter who has governed. This is the reason why the company that is the essence of Italian capitalism in the last century is commonly known as '*Fiatalia*' (Fiat + Italy).

Edoardo Agnelli died in 1935 – during the last year of Juventus' golden five. Yet his sons Gianni and then Humberto would go on to become club chairmen in 1947 and 1955, respectively. This involvement helped preserve the company's strong relations with the authorities that had been developed under fascism. These were then extended to successive post-war governments, particularly those of the conservative Christian Democracy – a party with which the Agnelli family has always had a special relationship.

Because of its industrial success, Turin became a magnet for migrants from southern Italy during the 1950s and 1960s. Such people – derogatorily labelled '*terroni*' (peasants) – came to the Piedmont capital seeking a job at FIAT. The new Turinese population became Juventus fans – unlike their native counterparts, who followed Torino. Juventus' new supporters then acted as ambassadors for the club when going back south on their holidays, in the process helping give the *Vecchia Signora* the biggest fan base in Italian club football.

Blue-collar identification with the employers' club proved the success of FIAT's strategy towards Juventus. The Agnellis did not just financially benefit from the club but acquired popularity and helped bring about social consensus with their class enemies.

The substantial backing given to the employer-linked club by migrants at the bottom of the social ladder was a big contradiction. Yet Juventus had supporters as unlikely to be colluding with the Italian bourgeoisie as Palmiro Togliatti, who was General Secretary of the Italian Communist Party (PCI) for over three decades. It is worth recalling one of Togliatti's funnier quotes, when asking fellow communist Pietro Secchia, 'What has *Juve* done? And you want to start a revolution without knowing what *Juve* has done?'. It is surprising that the leading figure of communism in Italy shared footballing allegiances with a Juventus chair closely linked to the Christian Democracy the PCI was fighting with all its might (until the party's 'Historic Compromise' period).

Circumstances such as these allowed Agnelli to boast of the draw Juventus had among the working class in the south. Indeed, he went as far as to publicly claim that 'one of the precise reasons why migrants chose to go to Turin during the mass migration of the fifties and sixties was to see Juventus'. Yet such assertions clash with the fact that often *Juve* has not managed to fill the *Stadio Comunale* – the renamed Mussolini stadium – even if it draws thousands of supporters to watch its away games in the south. This confirms the idea that Juventus' support is widespread across Italy but in a minority in Turin. The latter was revealed when the current Juventus stadium was built to seat 40,000 spectators, which contrasted with the capacity of the club's earlier stadiums: 70,000 in the case of the *Stadio Delle Alpi* (also used by Torino FC) and 65,000 in the case of the Comunale.

Undeniably FIAT's link with Juventus has determined its history, making it mirror Italian history over the last century. A good example of this is that the several heads of the Turin firm and club were targeted in attacks by the revolutionary left during the *anni di piombo* (Years of Lead) – from the late 1960s until well into the 1980s.

It is worth sharing the anecdote that during that period of intense political tension Juventus offered a sum quite a bit lower than the modest Vicenza club to sign Paolo Rossi, the rising star in Italian football (regarding whom a co-ownership deal was eventually made). This was for a simple reason: the Agnellis did not want to give a spendthrift image to workers at a time in which FIAT was being affected by the international oil crisis and was laying off hundreds of workers.

Juventus's FIAT links still make it a sporting entity full of contradictions today. It is a club loved and hated in equal measure. It is a club with powerful connections that has received incomprehensible favours throughout its history: benefits that are frequently cited by adversaries to explain Juventus' unparalleled trophy record. A club which has been at the centre of a match- and competition-fixing scandal – *Calciopoli* – leading it to be stripped of two titles and relegated for the first time in its history to the depths of the second division. All in all, Juventus is a club that for almost the whole of the last century was a puppet in the hands of the FIAT employers, who for many have been the true masters of Italy.

Torino FC
When the workers beat the bosses

Piedmont, the Italian region with Turin as its capital, has historically been the country's industrial powerhouse – alongside Lombardy – ever since the industrialisation process began there in the 19th century. Indeed, the region has been the home, from 1899 onwards, of what have probably been the most important Italian industrial factories: those of FIAT. As discussed in the previous chapter, FIAT has had an intimate relationship with football in Turin.

As Piedmont is an industrial area, this has also made Turin a major site for class struggle – particularly between the working class and the ruling class. The city was the birthplace and first capital of the 19th-century united Italian state. Then it became the arena for the first worker organising, the first anti-fascist movement, and a key player in the strike movement that brought down *il Duce* (Mussolini). A city with such a proletarian history was not going to have a game untouched by class divisions. Consequently, football support in Turin became split between two clubs: Juventus and Torino – the latter being a club more than familiar with the social divisions of the Piedmont metropolis.

Juve was the first of today's Turin clubs to be established – taking place back in 1897 – and the *Toro* (Bull) – the Torino Football Club's nickname – was not created until 1906. It began as a merger between Football Club Torinese – formed in 1904 – and a group of Juventus dissidents led by the club's ex-chairman, Alfredo Dick, who disagreed with the professionalisation of the *Juventinos*.

In the early 20th century, the two bitter rivals began to forge their own identities: Juventus became associated with the bourgeoisie; Torino with the proletariat. This was helped greatly by the Agnelli family's acquisition of the *Vecchia Signora's* chairmanship in 1924, strengthening Juventus' bond with the big Piedmont industrialists. Conversely, rising class conflict against the employers helped strengthen the workers of Turin's sympathies towards Torino, making it the choice of the Piedmont proletariat.

The different class identifications of the two clubs was perfectly summed up by local writer Mario Soldati in his book *The Malacca Cane* (its original Italian title being *Le due città* – literally *The Two Cities*):

> The two men crossed the Piazza Vittorio, and they were already talking about football. Naturally Emilio was a Juventus fan; the team for the masters, the pioneers of industry, the Jesuits, the self-righteous, the educated; in short, the bourgeois rich. Also naturally Girauto supported the *Toro*; the team for the workers, the migrants from nearby regions or from the Cuneo and Alessandria provinces, those that had gone to the technical college; in short, the petit bourgeois and poor.

However reductionist this may seem, Soldati's 1964 work perfectly captured the social and footballing division of the time. Before the large-scale migration from southern Italy in the 1950s–1970s period, it was hard to find a single worker in Piedmont who followed Juventus. Likewise, it was almost impossible for a bourgeois member of high society to show a footballing preference for Torino.

Yet, history can play tricks and despite Juventus having several Agnellis as *presidente*, the only club that has officially incorporated the Turin company's name into its own official name is actually Torino – becoming Torino FIAT in 1944. That was the name with which the *Toro* played in the last league championship under fascism. It had already been forced to change its name to Associazione Calcio Torino, because its previous one was felt to be too foreign-sounding.

By creating Torino FIAT, the fascist regime tried to do away with the class struggle and push the club's fans to identify with FIAT and therefore their employers. In the end, those promoting the change did not get their own way as fascism's defeat meant all reference to the Piedmontese firm was removed from the club's name.

The period immediately after the Second World War saw a peak in the rivalry between Torino and Juventus. Italy had been battered during the war and the combination of the need for reconstruction and rising social tensions allowed the Italian Communist Party (PCI) to become the focus of Italian workers' desire for equality and freedom. It emerged as one of the country's biggest political forces.

This was when the '*Grande Torino*' (Great Torino) legend was forged. The team won four league contests in a row from 1946 to 1949 but then entered the eternal history books after the Superga air disaster, in which 18 Torino players were killed while flying back from a friendly match against Benfica in Lisbon.

That tragic accident, which took place only four match-days from the end of the season did not stop it from becoming champion once again. This was despite having to play its youth squad – something its opponents also did out of respect for the deceased. Celebrations over the club's fourth consecutive title were, of course, greatly tinged with grief due to the loss that had preceded it.

Grande Torino's golden years helped strengthen the pride of the Piedmont workers. They would have a feast when, twice yearly, their beloved club allowed them to play against and beat their bosses – even if only metaphorically speaking and on the football pitch – as represented by the bourgeois Juventus.

It was in that era that Turin proletarians most strongly identified with the *Toro*. Even the local edition of *L'Unità* – the PCI newspaper founded by Antonio Gramsci – described Torino's players as 'true representatives of the proletariat and progressiveness'. This was an unparalleled accolade coming from a paper that, at the time, did not even have its own sports section.

Piedmont's large-scale industrialisation in the post-war decades encouraged people to migrate from southern Italy and settle in and around Turin to work in its large factories. This led to the paradox of these new workers not having the same sporting sympathies as their Turin colleagues and swelling the ranks of the bosses' club's *tifosi* (fans).

This turn prompted a new way of seeing a person who identified with Torino. They became the '*torinesità*' (truly Turinese). The *Toro* thus presented itself as the only true Turin team, as well as the most popular one in the city and region.

Despite a weakening of ideological identification in Piedmontese society in recent decades, we can still observe how class rivalry pits the two Turin teams against each other. While Juventus is known for more than half its supporters being right-wing; the opposite is the case with Torino, whose supporters are mainly left-leaning. This reflects the fact that Torino has stayed true to its history. It is a history that explains why, despite Juventus' sporting superiority, Torino is still the best-loved team in the Piedmont capital. After all, it is the club that once allowed the workers to beat the bosses.

AS Roma

The people's heart of the Eternal City

Before the home matches of Associazione Sportiva Roma, the faithful in the *Stadio Olimpico* of the 'Eternal City' sing a heartfelt version of the southern Italian club's anthem: '*Roma Roma Roma*, heart of this City, one and only love, of so much and so many people'. This Antonio Venditti song has been a club mainstay since the mid-1970s. And the Roman singer-songwriter is not mistaken when singing of AS Roma as the true heart of the working-class neighbourhoods of the historical city.

Rome is one of the most passionate and thrilling cities there is and is beholden to football. Yet the city's club preferences are divided between AS Roma – seen as an urban team with support dispersed among the capital's working-class neighbourhoods – and SS Lazio – a more outlying club with roots in the bourgeois and particularly rural areas of the Lazio region. It is a curious split as at one point the two clubs were going to merge so that they could challenge the dominance of the northern teams – Italian football's true masters.

Indeed, after the rise to power of Benito Mussolini and his Fascist National Party (PNF) in 1922, a government obsession was to restore the glory of the Roman Empire – naturally identified with the city of Rome. Football would have a pivotal role in the attempt to do that. In the late 1920s, the fascist authorities tried to merge all the capital's clubs into a single sports entity that could challenge the footballing hegemony of the teams in the north. The latter – led by those in Genoa, Turin, and Milan – had clearly established themselves as the dominant clubs in the Italian league championship (which came before today's *Serie A*).

As a result, the chair of the Società Fascista Fortitudo Pro Roma (Rome Sports Society), the fascist leader Italo Foschi, led the project to merge the capital's three big clubs – Fortitudo, Alba Roma, and Lazio – into one team. This culminated in 1927 with the creation of the Associazione Sportiva Roma (out of Fortitudo, Alba Roma, and the small Foot Ball Club di Roma – an aristocratic outfit that wore a kit using the official city colours). Società Sportiva Lazio was not included in the merger thanks to its deputy chairman (and fascist general) Giorgio Vaccaro, who managed to keep resisting the regime's institutional pressure and safeguard the independence of a club close to the power structure.

The new Roma was created to fully identify with the Italian capital and sought to become the true footballing representative of it. This was why it took on the city's name and colours from di Roma, as well as incorporating in its crest the city's foundational symbol: the Capitoline she-wolf suckling Romulus and Remus. That way, the fans of the new club would wave banners with the symbols and traditions of the legendary Eternal City.

From the outset, the new Roma had an intense rivalry with Lazio, which went beyond the strictly sporting and had clear political and sociological meanings. Even though both clubs identified with the fascist regime, a clear social split could be seen between them. While Lazio's home base was the Parioli district, the cradle of the Roman bourgeoisie, AS Roma was based in the deprived area of Testaccio – in the heart of working-class Rome. A visible contrast created a growing image within Roman football that Lazio's main support was from the same-named region's urban and rural ruling classes, while Roma had its following in the capital's inner-city areas.

This idea was strengthened by Lazio's growing links with fascism; particularly after Mussolini became a club member in 1929. Indeed the identification between Lazio and fascism still exists today, given that a substantial section of *laziale* fans openly sympathise with the extreme right, thereby reinforcing the general view that Lazio is the right-wing club and Roma more associated with the left.

Despite Lazio's identification with fascism, it should be noted that during Mussolini's dictatorship, the *laziale* failed to win a single title. Championships continued to be won by teams from the north of the country; most notably Bologna, the biggest club in Emilia-Romagna – *il Duce*'s region – which won six league titles in the period of national fascist rule.

The first team to break the north's footballing hegemony was Roma, which won the 1942 *scudetto* played in the middle of the Second World War. The triumph was seen as a revolution in Italian football as it was the first time a 'southern' team had triumphed in a national championship.

The nature of this first Roma victory has received different and even contrasting interpretations. Mario Soldati's and the journalist Gianni Brera's thesis is that Mussolini gave a helping hand to the club that enabled them to become champions in order to replicate Roman Imperial glory. This echoed the view of Helenio Herrera, former Roma team manager for several seasons. While responding to criticisms from fans over his team's performance, the coach said,

It's impossible to win here. This club has not won the championship since 1942* and only did so then because Mussolini was the coach.

Other sources categorically deny that *il Duce* accorded any favours to Roma that would allow it to win the title. And, in fact, the only detectable aid the regime gave the club was to allow those of its players who had to do military service to do so in Rome. That way they could train with teammates and avoid having to do long weekly trips. Amadeo Amadei, who was a forward in the championship-winning Roma team, insisted that the title was won on the football field: not only had the club not been assisted by any biased refereeing but it suffered from glaring mistakes by the referee in the decisive match of the championship against Torino – thereby weakening its chances of success.

Mussolini's own footballing loyalties lay with Bologna and Lazio. This, added to the many problems the dictator faced due to the evolution of the war at the time, made it hard to believe there was any political intervention favouring AS Roma. Additionally, the regime had been in place for two decades, and been in a stronger position to interfere with Italian football, and yet the club had not been so successful.

With the fall of fascism, the cleavage in local society over football deepened. Roma's working-class character was strengthened while Lazio remained a refuge for the far right – including those nostalgic for the fascist years. Over time, this simple split has become more blurred.

Roma followers often use the derogatory label '*burini*' (roughly speaking, 'townies') against their arch-rival Lazio fans, playing on the social divisions between the two fanbases

---

* The club can now boast of having won three league titles.

(counterposing urban Roma to rural Lazio). At the same time, Lazio fans have not held back from being offensive about their rivals. Their most extreme and openly fascist supporters have devoted many banners to their footballing rivals, calling them 'Jews' in an insulting way. Two of their most outrageous and controversial have been 'Auschwitz is your homeland; ovens, your homes' or 'team of blacks supported by Jews'.

In the 1970s, clashes between both clubs' most extreme fans had a markedly ideological character. AS Roma's terraces witnessed the emergence of the *Fedayn*: a fan group from the Quadraro district which identified with the far left. This was fought by the *laziali* extremists in a period of pronounced political tensions in Italy.

Roma's footballing image is still that of a people's and left-leaning team. Yet the far right has in fact managed to carve a space in the legendary 'southern bend' of the stadium, where the most die-hard fans of the capital's club assemble. 'The Boys' – formed at the same time as the *Fedayn* in 1972 but from a different social background and with a radically contrasting ideology – have grown among the Roma hardcore. Accordingly it is sadly increasingly common to see fascist symbols and paraphernalia among such fans. This is a real paradox given the historical links between the *romanisti* and the working-class areas and left-wing politics. A contradiction which, all the same, has not stopped Roma from being the people's heart of the Eternal City; the true 'heart of this city' that Venditti sang of.

Inter Milan
When *Inter* was not Italian enough for Mussolini

After the black shirts' mass march on Rome, Benito Mussolini and fascism seized power in 1922. This ushered in one of the most terrible periods in Italian history, which was marked by intense nationalism. Among other measures imposed was a policy of *italianizzazione* (Italianisation). This sought to strengthen centralism and force the usage of Italian in the territories colonised by Rome. It also wished to eradicate foreign cultural influence and force the Italianisation of names and terms with any foreign inclination.

This will to Italianise had by no means been exclusive to fascism. In the first decade of the 20th century, the country had gone through a similar wave, which had significant effects on sport. In 1909, the Italian football federation that had been set up in 1898 with the Anglophile name of *Federazione Italiana del Football* would be renamed the *Federazione Italiana de Giuoco Calcio* (the same name fully Italianised). Two years earlier, the same federation banned foreign players from taking part in its competitions. The decision led to bitter arguments inside the main Milanese club: Milan Football & Cricket Club, which initially opposed the regulations but eventually accepted them after striking a deal with the federation.

The Milan team's approval of exclusions was to the distaste of a sizeable section of its management, who then decided to split from the club and create a new one that would specifically be characterised as accepting all nationalities within its footballing ranks. Its promoters had no difficulty in finding a name for the new club that would reflect such an identity. The words in its founding charter were, 'It will be called International, because we are brothers of the world'. Thus, Football Club Internazionale Milano was created, rejecting nationalistic Italianisation by being open to all players.

The return and strengthening of this policy under fascism put Internazionale in the crosshairs of those in charge of *italianizzazione*, despite the club's social base then mainly being the Milanese bourgeois and wealthy – the same that had welcomed Mussolini with open arms within the political context of instability and social unrest.

In a way, Internazionale started being seen as the club for the local moneyed classes thanks to its rivalry with Milan Football & Cricket Club, an antagonism which had grown since the 1910s. This was not purely a sporting rivalry but one due to the clear social gap between *Inter*'s mainly wealthy fans and the Milan FCC fans who tended to be from a working-class background. Indeed, once the rift between them developed, the Internazionale fans started to refer to the Milan fans as '*casciavit*', meaning 'screwdrivers' – a nickname pejoratively referring to the popular-class origins of most Football & Cricket Club supporters. Conversely, Milan followers labelled the *interistas* as '*bauscia*' – a strongly Milanese term for braggarts who have only gained a fortune by collaborating with the foreign rich.

Having a conservative and bourgeois background did not spare Internazionale from fascism's Italianisation policy. The National Fascist Party had a clear dislike of the club's name. This was not only because it was 'un-Italian' and therefore clashed with the regime's nationalism. It also sounded like it was linked to the Communist International founded by Lenin

66

and the Bolsheviks. This brought together communist parties from across the globe, including the Italian Communist Party, created in 1921, and which strongly opposed Mussolini's fascism.

The regime consequently took advantage of its reform of the Italian club system, which aimed to reduce the number of big teams per city where possible, to reorganise Inter and remove any allusion to internationalism from its name. For this purpose, the fascist authorities forced Football Club Internazionale to merge with Unione Sportiva Milanese – the Lombardy capital's third-most-important club. This led to the creation of the Società Sportiva Ambrosiana (SSA); a club with an unequivocally Italian name. The club also had notable Catholic connotations: first having a name referring to Saint Ambrose – Milan's patron – and secondly in its football jersey: a red cross on a white background (like the city's coat of arms). Completing the club's strip was a *fascio littoro:* an axe in a bundle of rods that had become the ultimate fascist symbol.

Although most of the new club's sporting strength had been provided by the former Internazionale, its chairmanship went to Ernesto Torrusio, formerly US Milanese chairman. This was likely due to his fascist-party membership and having been one of the founders of the first fascist paramilitary organisations (the *Fasci di combattimento* in Italian), in the Lombardy region. Despite Torrusio only remaining as head of the club for one season, he joined a hall of other prominent figures – mostly conservative political and business leaders from prosperous industrial Milan – that had run the outfit since 1909.

Torrusio's spell as SSA chairman was a complete disaster, especially in terms of the club's finances. This meant that not even his proven fascist credentials were enough to save him his job. To preserve the club, the regime's hierarchy opted to involve business interests. It did this through Oreste Simonott, who made a considerable financial investment in the club and became its chairman. Ambrosiana's name was slightly modified, from Società Sportiva to Associazione Sportiva, while Internazionale's original colours were reintroduced in its jersey.

Due to public pressure, Ambrosiana was even able to re-incorporate '*Inter*' into the club's name; to become Ambrosiana-Inter in 1932. The resulting name was a nod to *Inter*'s past at the same time as avoiding any explicit reference to its international nature, which would have allowed it to be understood to be ideologically aligned with the Communist International, which was what really bothered the regime. Besides protests from fans, the modification to the name was authorised because US Milanese had opted to recover its independent status, even if this excluded it from playing in official Italian competitions.

During the fascist years, Ambrosiana-Inter emerged as a mighty team, with Milan turning into its 'poor cousin'. This was met with animosity by the country's central and southern clubs; a reaction especially pronounced in the capital because of the traditional clash between Rome and Milan as the (respective) epicentres of political and economic power in Italy.

In the same years and despite the minor concession of allowing Inter to recover its nickname, the fascist Italianisation policy intensified. This specifically affected the sporting world, where Anglicisms were the general rule. Clubs with Anglophile names, such as Genoa or Milan, were therefore specifically renamed Genoa Circolo del Calcio and the Associazione Calcio Milano.

Italianizzazione came to an end with the regime's fall and the Partisans executing Benito Mussolini and his lover Clara Petacci in the Lombardic village of Giulino di Mezzegra in

April 1945. The anti-fascist militia took the two corpses to the birthplace of the *Internazionale*, which fascism had considered so un-Italian. In the regional capital, the two bodies were exhibited in Loreto Square; the same place in which – the year before – far-rightists had killed and publicly exhibited the bodies of 15 Partisans accused of bombing a Nazi truck parked in Milan's city centre.

A few months later, on 27 October 1945, an announcement – long-awaited by the *interista* fans – was made by Carlo Masseroni, the businessman chair of the sporting entity. He declared, 'as of today, Ambrosiana will once again be simply and exclusively named *Internazionale*'.

The period in which the club was known as Ambrosiana was rescued for *Inter*'s centenary in 2008, when the club brought back the shirt with the Saint Ambrose cross. That decision was not uncontroversial, as it prompted a legal complaint by a Turkish lawyer who saw the strip to be offensive to Muslims when worn at Fenerbahçe SK's stadium during a Champions League fixture.

Besides, having a shirt with the Saint Ambrose cross meant looking backwards to an era that would forever define *Inter*'s history. A dark period in which the team had to change its name because *Internazionale* was not seen as Italian enough by Mussolini's regime.

3
Iberian Peninsula

Madrid FC players with raised fists moments before a match in honour of the Republican Army's 21st Mixed Brigade

Associação Académica de Coimbra
The student team that defied the
Portuguese dictatorship

In Portugal in 1968, the longest-surviving dictatorship changed its public image. Antonio de Oliveira Salazar, who had ruled over the right-wing *Estado Novo* (New State) since 1932, was replaced as Prime Minister by law professor Marcelo Caetano.

Power was taken from Salazar after he suffered a clumsy fall while holidaying in Estoril, showing he was unfit to govern. Yet Salazar's inner circle hid this fact from him until his death in 1970. His successor was a long-time supporter but who had been side-lined from the circles of power during a cabinet crisis in 1958. Then, Portugal was known as the country of the three 'Fs': Fátima, fado, and football – the three pillars propping up the regime. These were specifically and respectively: Catholicism – embodied by the Sanctuary of Fátima, built in the early 1950s at the place where several shepherds said they had seen apparitions of the Virgin Mary; folk music – as symbolised by a fado that came out of society's poorest classes; and lastly football – the country's favourite sport and which, thanks to Benfica's continental triumphs, had won significant prestige for the dictatorship. The new PM was taking over an authoritarian regime that was now being assailed on several fronts.

The start of the colonial wars in Angola (1961), Guinea (1963), and Mozambique (1964) undermined the notion of

Imperial Portugal that the Estado Novo had always promoted. On top of that, different social revolts – involving workers, intellectuals, and students – took place in Portugal itself in 1962 and 1965. These were brutally repressed by the police but revealed a growing discontent in the country.

Caetano took office in such a situation and with the task of keeping happy both the dictatorship's hard core – those closest to Salazar – and the growing number of technocrats wishing for modernisation to ensure the regime survived. Among the reforms the new premiere introduced was authorising holding elections in the *Associação Académica de Coimbra*. This was the students' union in the country's oldest university – the one where Salazar himself had acquired a degree in law and a doctorate in economics and had lectured in the latter.

The lively student association had an important sports section from which the football club most stood out – having won the Portuguese Cup in 1939. As a clear nod to the Coimbra students' academic uniform, the team wore an all-black kit.

Caetano's move was aimed at curbing the rise of the students' movement, which had been particularly active in Coimbra. He feared repercussions from the May 1968 protests in France among Portuguese students. He was also very aware that university students were one of the main pillars of the opposition, as had been shown in 1962 when the banning of the first national students' meeting – to be held in Coimbra – triggered a large wave of protests.

In February 1969, a ticket named 'For the Council of the Republic', comprised of anti-dictatorship students, won 75 per cent of the vote in the Coimbra Students' Association elections. When President-elect Albert Martins was prevented from speaking at the inaugural ceremony of the university's new Faculty of Mathematics, it sparked the biggest student revolt since the beginning of the dictatorship.

The students wanted to present their demand for a democratic university to the Portuguese President – Américo Tomás – but their right to expression was denied. Vicious repression headed by the PIDE – the regime's political police force – led the rebellion to mushroom.

On 22 April, the *Associação* declared 'Academic Mourning': the remembrance traditionally observed by students after the death of an educational-community member. However, this time it was over the repression and lack of freedoms suffered. To coincide with the mourning, the union held dozens of activities – including occupations and cultural activities – in the Coimbra University grounds which allowed pupils' democratic demands to be voiced.

In the middle of this sustained mobilisation, the football section of the student organisation played in the quarter-finals of the Portuguese Cup. The team was mainly formed by Coimbra University pupils – the same who were behind the protests. It was an ideal opportunity to put football at the service of opposition to the regime. This would have the added bonus of breaking the image of the sport as a pillar for the authoritarian regime which had stemmed from Salazar's exploitation of Benfica's successes in the early 1960s.

Despite Académica de Coimbra's many hopes going into the quarter-final, it lost the first leg 2–1 away to Vitória de Guimarães. The student club's players swore they would make a comeback in the second leg and please their fans, who were mostly university students.

Just a month earlier, the Minister of Education had closed the University of Coimbra until the exam period. It was therefore unsurprising that the match played in the city, on 1 June 1969, was surrounded by apprehension. Académica went out onto the pitch in its traditional black strip. It played a magnificent match: thrashing Vitória 5–0. By doing so, the *conimbricenses* qualified for the semi-final, where they would face Sporting Lisbon. This was a golden opportunity to use football for the democratic cause that their fellow students were fighting for.

The first leg of the semi-final was played on 8 June at the Estádio José Alvalade. Académica went onto the pitch wearing an all-white kit, thereby radically modifying its traditional black one. It also wore black armbands to mark its 'academic mourning' and solidarity with the anti-regime protests then taking place on the streets of Portugal. Student mobilisation again seems to have put the wind in Coimbra's sails, which beat Sporting 1–2.

The spread of university protest to the centre of Portuguese football set off all the official alarm bells because of the sport's mass following. At the regime's behest, the footballing federation told Académica that it could no longer change its strip colours or wear an armband. In the second leg of the semi-final, played in Coimbra, Académica had to be at its most inventive to do a visible protest. The student team chose to go onto the pitch in its usual black kit but with a white stripe as a symbol of mourning. In the end, the stripe was banned and the *académicos* came onto the pitch with a white sticker over their crest: that way showing they also partook in the 'academic mourning'.

On that 15 June, the club's *Estádio do Calhabé* – now *Estádio Cidade de Coimbra* – was packed to the rafters with students keen to see their team continuing to defy the authorities, now even in a cup final. The ground was full of protest banners, as most of the public had come to it after a demonstration on the streets of Coimbra. Académica beat Sporting 1–0, thus booking a place in the final in Lisbon one week later, which would see it take on the mighty Benfica.

Académica reaching the final created a real headache for the Portuguese authorities. The decisive match was to be played in the *Estádio Nacional* – a major symbol for the dictatorship – and it seemed more than likely that the students and wider opposition movement would use the event to register their disapproval of the regime.

In keeping with this idea, the authorities took the unprecedented decision of stopping the final from being broadcast on television to avoid publicising a very likely protest that would be impossible to stop. Also for the first time, neither the President nor any member of Caetano's cabinet would attend. Instead, a very large contingent of police was deployed to suppress any opposition.

Knowing that some kind of protest would be held, the authorities even went as far as considering preventing Académica from appearing in the final. Accordingly they made Sporting Lisbon aware that this might be required. In the end, the *conimbricense* team went onto the turf of the stadium, prepared to win the cup, which they felt would be the biggest act of defiance against the regime.

Led by the *Associação Académica*, the student movement made thorough preparations for the match. Days before the event, several student delegates went to Lisbon to coordinate their efforts with the capital's opposition movement. The aim was to make the cup final the biggest protest rally in the dictatorship's history. The underground printing presses worked flat out to produce 35 leaflets that included the student movement's demands, which were thrown into the crowd during the final.

On 22 June – the big day – the Coimbra University world descended on Lisbon laden with banners and flags to cheer on its players and make its demands known. After the club received new warnings over its kit from the football federation, it decided to wear its traditional black strip accompanied by a typical university cape – to show its solidarity with the student movement.

The *Estádio Nacional* stands were bursting at the seams and dozens of Coimbra students' banners turned the venue into a huge tribune for opposition to the regime. Indeed, some see the 1969 cup final as the biggest political rally in Portuguese history.

The many slogans visible in the stands called for university freedom and condemned police repression, as well as demanding the release of those imprisoned during the student revolt. To avoid arrests by the political police during the match, the banners were raised and then quickly hidden again so officers did not have time to identify their bearers.

The stadium seemed to collapse when in the 81st minute of the match, the Académica forward Manuel Antonio put his team in the lead. Regrettably, however, the students' euphoria was short-lived. Just four minutes later, Simões equalised, taking the match to extra time.

It was during these added minutes that Eusébio scored Benfica's second to dash Coimbra's hopes of becoming champions. The cup title had slipped from Académica's grasp at the last moment. This was despite many Benfica fans wanting their opponent to win, as they sympathised with its political stand against the authorities.

Despite the defeat, the Académica contingent was received with great fanfare in Coimbra by the student-revolt leaders. The protest movement had planned in case of victory for the *Associação* President Martins to accompany the players during their victory parade. Alas, it was not to be.

All the same, Académica's rebellious run had been a real challenge to the Portuguese dictatorship and a huge platform for the student movement's ideas to be heard beyond the campuses.

Football had so often been used by the dictatorship to give it legitimacy, but this time had been put to use for democracy and freedom. History – so often unfair – did see a now-professional Académica de Coimbra overcome that defeat and lift the cup – over 40 years later in 2012. This brought some justice to the student team that had dared defy the Portuguese dictatorship.

Atlético de Madrid
The club with a thousand faces

In May 2014, Atlético de Madrid clinched the league title in Barcelona's *Camp Nou*, led by Argentinean coach Diego Simeone. Everything suggested that it had forever left behind 'the jinxed ones' image it had shouldered for four decades.

The tragic climaxes of the Champions League finals in Lisbon in 2014 and Milan in 2016, when the 'the Red and Whites' (*rojiblancos*) were thwarted at the very end by their local rival Real Madrid, were outcomes all too reminiscent of their defeat in the 1974 European Cup final at Heysel. That was when Atlético first became nicknamed 'the jinxed ones' ('*El Pupas*'). It still seems that the club will find it hard to shed that label.

If we go back further than the recent experience of a club also dubbed 'the Mattress Makers', we find a club with a thousand faces, whose trajectory closely reflects the contemporary Spanish history it is part of. Today's Atlético Madrid was created back in April 1903 in Madrid's *Casa Vasca* (Basque House). This was the social centre where students at the School of Mining Engineers who were from the Basque province of Biscay would meet, alongside others also from the large diaspora in the city. It was precisely this group that founded the club, as the Madrid branch of Athletic Bilbao. Bilbao – also from the Biscay province – had just won the first *Copa de España* (Spanish Cup) against Madrid Football Club – the team that would eventually become no less than Real Madrid (and Atlético de Madrid's most bitter rival).

Initially the club – then named Athletic Club (Sucursal de Madrid) – was no more than a subsidiary of the mentioned Basque team, which it was not able to play against and to whom it lent its up-and-coming players when requested by the Biscayan team. It also adopted the same strip: initially including a blue and white shirt and from 1910 the club's famous red and white stripes.

The growing number of Madrid-born members within the club, as opposed to being residents of Bilbao, led the Madrid branch of Athletic Club to relinquish its subsidiary status and become a fully independent sports club. Even so, the club decided to preserve its original name of Athletic Club.

Freed from Basque patronage, in 1923, today's '*Atleti*' moved to its legendary stadium the *Metropolitano*. It was there that the 'Mattress Makers' played during the tumultuous years leading up to the Civil War.

Precisely one of *Atleti*'s worst footballing memories dates from that historical period. In 1936, just before General Francisco Franco's coup d'état, Athletic Club was relegated to the second division after a disastrous season in which the league-championship trophy went to the club's former Biscayan patrons.

And that was not the end of the club's misfortunes. The far-right uprising and the war front subsequently arriving in Madrid led to almost a complete halt to the club's activity. Worse still, they led to the destruction of its stadium, located close to the university area – a site of intense fighting.

While sporting activity was suspended, the club played few matches besides the occasional one to raise money for republican organisations such as people's militias, blood-transfusion hospitals, and the Anti-Fascist Association's children's hospitals. The charity matches played by the Mattress Makers players who had not been sent to the front produced some memorable moments. One was of the Athletic Madrid squad raising clenched fists – clearly symbolising their support for the republican cause.

After the conflict began, many clubs in the Spanish championship strongly sided with the republican side. The fascist generals were aware of football's political importance, so they started creating new teams. The most important of these was the Club Aviación Nacional (National Air-Force Club), which would later become one of the forefathers of today's Atlético de Madrid.

Aviación was formed in 1937 in Salamanca – specifically at the Matacán air base. At first, it was completely made up of soldiers and its main purpose was to raise money for the fascist forces. When the crucial Battle of the Ebro began in the summer of 1938, the pro-Franco army's headquarters were moved to Saragossa (Aragon), and much of the air force went with it. This meant Aviación Nacional also moved to the Aragonese region, where it began to play official matches, going as far as becoming regional champion. Through this the outfit qualified to play in the first Supreme General's Cup – the fascist version of the *Copa del Rey* – in which it reached the quarter-final (only to be eliminated by the eventual champion Sevilla FC).

After Franco's military victory, Aviación Nacional not only refused to fold but moved its headquarters to Madrid. There, it did everything possible to earn a place in the first or second division of the 'national' league championship that would begin in 1939, after the stoppage due to the fighting.

It is little known that Aviación Nacional's initial aim was to merge with Madrid Football Club (Real Madrid) – the only footballing entity in the city that was then sure of a place in the top flight. Nonetheless, an association agreement between the two did not come to fruition: not because of ideological differences but because Madrid was unwilling to hand over any boardroom power to the military authorities running the air force club.

This first attempt failed. Afterwards, Aviación turned its gaze to the other two clubs in the Spanish capital: Club Deportivo Nacional – a team from the Chamberi neighbourhood that played in the second division before the war – and Athletic Club, which had been relegated to the same flight in the last championship held.

Athletic Madrid's seriously weak position – also due to its stadium being destroyed – forced it into an agreement with Aviación Nacional. Thus was created Athletic Aviación Club. The new outfit kept Athletic Club's strip. Yet the break with Atlético's past was shown by Aviación's first chairman being Francisco Vives, one of Franco's air force commanders, and he was joined on the board by several other officers. The aviation's imprint was also visible from the club's modified crest which now incorporated its official insignia.

The club's complicity with the Franco regime was laid bare when it was asked to take Oviedo's place in the first top-flight championship of the post-war era. The Asturian club had also had its ground destroyed but on top of that it was in a deep financial crisis. In an attempt to conceal the arbitrariness of the top-flight invitation, the footballing federation organised a play-off for the place between the two teams that went down in 1932: Athletic Club (Athletic Aviación) and Pamplona's Osasuna.

The Madrid team did not waste the opportunity and comfortably defeated the Navarrese team in a match held at the Mestalla stadium in Valencia. It was a turning point for Athletic Aviación, as the renamed club went on to win the first two league tournaments under Franco. This, alongside its part-military background, helped the club become identified with the regime in the post-war years. The idea was bolstered by the extreme-right dictatorship's use of the club for propaganda events such as the matches between Athletic Aviación and the teams from fascist Italy's air force or the German Luftwaffe that were held during the Second World War. These were indeed quite a statement when the dictatorship was claiming neutrality in the conflict.

The league triumphs in the first two seasons coincided with the club further changing its name: to Club Atlético Aviación in 1940. This allowed it to comply with the law for the 'Hispanicisation' of all institutions which banned any 'use of foreign generic terms'. Drafted by Falange leader Ramón Serrano Suñer, the law forced a change to the names of almost all the football clubs, which had been culturally dominated by the English-speaking world.

Curiously, when these regulations were later modified, Atlético opted to ignore its past and keep the Hispanicised name given to it by fascism, which it has kept to this day. This contrasted with clubs such as the Athletic Bilbao and Barcelona, who chose to revert to their original denominations.

All the same, Atlético had its name modified one more time. In 1947, the Ministry of the Air decided that the club should drop the term 'Aviación', arguing there should be no armed-forces-related team in the Spanish league championship. It was similarly decided that military officers should leave Atlético's governing board – making the club fully civilian again.

What did not end was Atlético's identification with 'Francoism', as its heads – led by Vicente Calderon – were closely linked to the regime. Rumour has it that it was Calderon's contacts with the regime's upper echelons that allowed its Manzanares stadium to be built above a major highway, which later evolved into the M-30 motorway. Madrid's mayor Carlos Arias

Navarro – later Spanish Prime Minister – initially opposed this location. He denounced it for not having a municipal building permit, sent the police to halt the works, and threatened to demolish the stand. Yet he backed down after a call from Franco's residential palace. The Manzanares stadium – now called Vicente Calderon – was officially opened in 1966.

It was in the following decade that Atlético picked up the label 'el Pupas' – a name commonly used to describe a clumsy person who has constant mishaps. This originated from the club's above-mentioned disappointment in the 1974 European Cup final at the hands of an up-and-coming Bayern Munich (who would also go on to win the next European Champions League Cups).

The Mattress Makers lost that contest in a cruel fashion. They sensed victory in the first of two finals played in Brussels, after Luis Aragonés scored with only six minutes of extra time left, breaking a nil–nil deadlock. Yet moments before the final whistle, Bayern centre-back Schwarzenbeck equalised, undoing the Atlético team's victory. In the cup final replay, the Bavarians gave the Madrid team no chance, hammering them 4–0.

On the positive side, the 'jinxed' legend helped Atlético acquire the image of being a people's club, in contrast to its eternal rival Real Madrid, which was closely associated with the power hierarchy and footballing success. Indeed, the very same Diego Simeone, who came so close to breaking with the 'el Pupas' tradition claimed 'people's team' status for the Mattress Makers.

He was half right, but the portrait of the Red and Whites is only complete when incorporating its other features: being a Basque subsidiary, military club, regime team, and (more recently) entity associated with the sinister figure of Jesús Gil y Gil. This club chairman (and construction magnate) was pardoned by Franco for manslaughter and went on to become an icon of the corruption and excesses of 1990s Spain. Atléti-co's identity – shaped over more than a century – is that of a club with a thousand faces.

Madrid FC (Real Madrid)
When Madrid stopped being royal ('Real') and had a communist chairman

The one thing that Real Madrid likes to boast about, on top of its glistening cabinet of trophies, is its history. The 100-year story of the club includes, however, an inexplicable gap when dealing with the Second Republic (1931–1939) and particularly the Civil War years (1936–1939). This is clear from the blind spot the club has regarding the figure of Antonio Ortega Gutiérrez. Gutiérrez was the communist army officer who was chair of the club during its toughest years and who was executed under Franco.

Real Madrid's official history has it that Colonel Ortega never ran the sports entity based in the district of Chamartín. This can be confirmed by the photo gallery of the club's different chairpersons on its website, the dozens of publications Madrid has authorised, and particularly the section of the club's museum on the club's history. There is not one mention of the person who led the club during those tough years.

Madrid's odd interpretation of its own history leaves not a shred of doubt over the club's will to wipe away the memory of Antonio Ortega. Yet it is a part of the white shirts' inescapable past that between 1937 and Madrid falling to the fascists in 1939, the republican colonel and Communist Party (PCE) member headed a club that epitomised republican values at the time. This begs the question of who was republican Madrid's communist chairman? And why have all those presiding over the Santiago Bernabéu stadium's box of honour – a symbolic place of power in Spain – allowed his memory to disappear?

To answer these questions, we must go back to the spring of 1939 and the city of Alicante – one of the last bastions of the Second Republic. At that time, the city was bustling with tens of thousands of republicans desperately looking to flee Franco and his now-inevitable victory. Many of those not able to catch a boat to exile in Oran (Algeria), were interned in the Los Almendros concentration camp. This had been set up by Franco's nationalists on 30 March 1939 – two days before they issued the war communique announcing their victory. The camp held near to 20,000 republican prisoners – both military and civilian – who lived in appalling conditions.

Among the uniformed prisoners was Colonel Antonio Ortega. After the makeshift detention centre was dismantled, Ortega was taken to another concentration camp (Albatera) and then to Santa Bárbara Castle, where professional military personnel were held. Ortega's time in the castle on Mount Benacantil in central Alicante, which had previously been used by the republicans to hold nationalist prisoners, was longer than that he spent in Los Almendros but only lasted a few months. After a fast-track military trial, the 50-year-old republican colonel was executed on 15 July 1939. Santa Bárbara silently witnessed Antonio Ortega's killing by garrotte – a cruel medieval device used to strangle a person. The haste with which Ortega was condemned and put to death was an indication of the importance he had acquired during the war, when the victim rose to the highest ranks of command in the republican army while becoming known for his communist sympathies.

Oddly enough, before the war, Ortega had not stood out due to his political allegiances but for his military career. This began in 1906 and developed under the Second Republic, when he received several promotions. Franco's uprising in July 1936 caught him working as a lieutenant paramilitary policeman in the Basque town of Irun, where he actively participated in stopping the putschists. This earned him enough merit to be made Civil Governor of the Guipuzkoa province on 6 August. Shortly after, he led the Republican forces in the same area. Yet this put him in the sights of the nationalist press, which accused him of having been a 'smuggler' and of being 'illiterate and uneducated'.

After the fascists took Guipuzkoa in September 1936, Ortega was posted to Madrid, where he made a decisive contribution to the city's defence against Franco's oncoming armies. Soon after reaching the Spanish capital, the Burgos-born Ortega was put in charge of a company of 300 soldiers from the Basque country. The battalion played an important role in the Battle for Madrid and held fierce battles against the nationalist forces on the Casa de Campo and Ciudad Universitaria fronts. These stopped the fascists in their tracks.

Such exploits greatly boosted Antonio Ortega's career, leading him to be appointed as a republican army colonel. This was helped by his proximity to the man overseeing Madrid's defence, José Miaja, and Ortega's membership of the PCE – the party controlling much of the republican power structure during wartime.

Of the different posts that the colonel held during the war, two were particularly relevant. First, Ortega was Security Secretary for the Negrin government. This meant, as historian Hugh Thomas pointed out, he was responsible for the arrest of the leaders of the Workers' Party of Marxist Unification (POUM), including the dissident Marxist Andreu Nin – the POUM leader who disappeared after his arrest in an operation designed by Alexander Orlov. The latter was Ortega's close

confidante and man in Spain for the NKVD – the Soviet political police and forerunner to the KGB.

Second, the communist colonel was made chairman of
Madrid Football Club; the republican name for Real Madrid
after the club came under the wing of the Workers' Cultural
and Sports Foundation (FCDA) – a socialist-inspired institution. With this background, it is unsurprising that fascist
repression targeted Ortega, a top-ranking republican officer
and steadfast communist, as well as a prominent public
figure during the war period – helped by being at the helm
of Madrid's biggest football club. What is somewhat harder to
understand, especially considering how Real Madrid is seen
today, is how someone with Ortega's background could be put
in charge of a club which, thanks to its excellent relationship
with the monarchy, had been given the name '*Real*' (meaning
'Royal'). This distinction had allowed the club to add the
Bourbon crown to its crest, which, as a token of gratitude, then
awarded an honorary club chairmanship to Alfonso, Prince of
Asturias – King Alfonso XIII's first-born son.

Madrid's royal status was rescinded after the proclamation of the Second Republic on 14 April 1931 – resulting in
the suppression of all monarchic emblems from public life.
Accordingly, Real Madrid also reverted to being called Madrid
Football Club and removed the crown from its crest, adding
instead a purple stripe. This was the colour of the Castille
region but also that which the Republic had added to the
Spanish flag.

Besides changing its insignia, Madrid substantially transformed its identity in this period away from its association
with the Madrid elites of the early 20th century. Several
staunch republicans were incorporated into the club as leading
members. One was Rafael Sánchez Guerra (who was in fact the
son of a monarchist politician). He was swept into becoming

chairman in the 1935 elections (recovering from his defeat in 1933).

The 1935 result sparked an all-out struggle for control of Madrid FC. This was eventually resolved in favour of Sánchez Guerra, thanks to the many new republican members that joined the club and now frustrated the efforts of Santiago Bernabéu and others. The latter were adamantly against a sporting entity like Madrid being in republican hands. The Madrid club traditionally had a social base that was conservative and pro-monarchy and had leaders linked to the parties allied in the Spanish Confederation of Autonomous Rights (CEDA) or to the fascist Falange.

Sánchez Guerra's chairmanship – the last in the republican period to be recognised in Real Madrid's official history – only lasted from 31 May 1935 to 4 August 1936, when the club came under the control of the FCDA. Despite this term being so short, Sánchez Guerra was able to add to republican Madrid's trophies thanks to one of the club's most memorable triumphs. This was winning the renamed President of the Republic Cup (previously the King's Cup – *Copa del Rey*). The cup final, played in Valencia on 21 June 1936, was the last official football match to be played in Spain before the war. It ended with a narrow 2–1 'meringue'* victory. This was after a sterling performance by legendary goalkeeper Ricardo Zamora who, in the dying moments of the match, made an incredible stop against a shot from Barcelona's Escolà.

The outbreak of the Civil War once again led to a shift in control of republican Madrid. The FCDO put Juan José Vallejo in charge of the club, which then had 6,000 members, a stadium for 22,000 spectators, a large swimming pool, and

---

* Translator's note: The Madrid team is known as the 'meringues' on account of the white colour of its jersey.

several tennis courts. In short, it was a sports complex that was very appealing to control during the war.

Colonel Ortega replaced Vallejo as chairman in 1937. The change caused few ripples as the club kept Pablo Hernández Coronado – its veritable strongman since the summer of 1936 – as club secretary. The appointment of a communist republican showed that the PCE wanted to have all spheres of power under its authority – naturally including the sporting arena, which was of great political importance in 1930s Spain.

Despite the lack of competition during the war years, Madrid did not remain idle. The Chamartín Stadium hosted many parades and sporting and military exhibitions. An example was the military parade, sports competition, and republican infantry display organised by the United Socialist Youth (JSU) on 26 September 1937. This involved the pitch being used by soldiers doing drills rather than footballers running around. It took place under the watchful eye of Ortega, as official host, and other distinguished political and military republicans. These included General Miaja, Colonel Valentín González – better known as 'the Peasant Farmer' – and Santiago Carrillo – the JSU leader who later headed the PCE.

Events such as this were commonplace at the Madrid ground under Antonio Ortega at a time when Chamartín also was home to the Republican Sports Battalion. This had been set up by Popular Front members at the start of the conflict and aimed to encourage those who played sport to join the fight against fascism. The battalion had been using Madrid's facilities since 18 August 1936 and had organised several activities aimed both at improving fighters' physical shape and boosting their morale.

Political and sporting events of this kind were not just held in the football ground but also in the club's other infrastructures. This was particularly so with the pool, which was very popular and used for many swimming classes.

All these activities were shaped by the war the city was living through and tended to steer clear of being too competitive. This was so with the Central Army Trophy played at Chamartín. For this, the participating teams from different military units were supplemented by professional footballers. However, the latter were limited to being no more than five per team. A unique feature of the tournament was that the winning team was not awarded a cup. This was in keeping with the principles espoused by Colonel Ortega, who sought to free the footballing world from increased competition and commodification.

There are few media records of Ortega's views as Madrid chairman. In one such piece – an interview by 'Derby' published in *Blanco y Negro* magazine in November 1938 – the communist officer defended the sport being played at the Chamartín ground during wartime as such:

> The new sport, as applied to war, has avoided … preciousness and showmanship, and is ensuring that soldiers … build their muscles, get oxygen into their lungs, and have the stamina required for any fighting today.

Furthermore, Ortega pointed to the need for football to steer away from commercial interests:

> The football [of the future] will be not at all like that played before 18 July. I mean, of course, how it will be organised. There will be no buying and selling of gambling slips or star players or of youth.

This notion of sport was complemented by the kind of matches played at Chamartín during wartime. These always had political undertones and were often charitable: raising money for a variety of organisations – from the republican army to PCE-linked anti-fascist women's organisations. At the same time, because of the lack of regular contests, Madrid requested to participate in the 1937 Mediterranean League organised by the Catalan and Valencian clubs. However, Barcelona opposed this, arguing that Madrid's physical proximity to the war was too great a threat.

With this anecdote to one side, it must be highlighted that chairman Ortega's dream of a business-free football was cut short by republican defeat in the Civil War. The Chamartín ground – the scene for very many republican military and sporting demonstrations – was left practically in ruins and pro-coup forces turned it into a prison camp. This was a real metaphor for the Spanish disaster.

With Franco winning a definitive victory, Madrid's turbulent republican period came to an end. The club's 'Royal' status and name were reintroduced, and control of Madrid was put back in conservative hands. Its heads had close relations with the new authorities, particularly from 1943, when its chairmanship was given to Santiago Bernabéu, who had been a war volunteer on the fascist side.

This is key to why, since the end of the conflict, Real Madrid has never accepted Antonio Ortega as former club chairman. The club's official historiography skips over the 1936–1939 period, as if Juan José Vallejo and Antonio Ortega had never presided over Chamartín.

Unquestionably, Madrid's self-history has been one written by the war's victors, deliberately hiding figures such as Colonel Ortega. This is because his republican and communist ideology not only clashed in general with the traditional values of the upper classes associated with the club, but also on specific issues such as bullfighting. Interestingly Antonio Ortega led a movement to abolish this activity, managing to prevent any fights from taking place in the republican zone from 1938 to 1939.

The colonel was less successful in his efforts to stamp out sports gambling, such as that taking place around Basque *pelota* courts or dog-racing tracks. Here, his approach threatened the significant earnings that the republican government received from such activity at a time when financial revenue was more necessary than ever.

To complete the portrait of this unique figure we must add that, besides his roles as chair and campaigner, he also wrote for the prestigious magazine *Cuadernos de Madrid* – edited by the Alliance of Anti-Fascist Intellectuals. A fact that refutes the criticism that some fascist publications made about him that he was illiterate and uneducated.

Antonio Ortega is the unsung figure in the Madrid club's history. A chairman who was executed by garrotte and who today's Real Madrid does not devote even the briefest mention to in its museum – contrasting with its pompous worship of Santiago Bernabéu. It was as if the club all but started with the pro-Franco supporter who served as a corporal in the occupation of Catalonia. This is despite one big overlap between Ortega and Bernabéu: their shared desire to build a large stadium for Madrid. The republican colonel expressed this will in the mentioned *Blanco y Negro* interview:

Madrid ... and I will try and make it so, should have the best pitch in Spain, the more important stadium. Madrid, which has won its right to be capital, should have everything that has been acquired by other cities that have been more cavalier with regard to the war. All of us must therefore help the great club.

Paradoxically, such a dream was fulfilled by his pro-Franco successor.

This is an example of Real Madrid's unwillingness to acknowledge its republican past and most notably chronicle its Civil War years. A memory gap led it to forget its executed chairman: the communist republican from when Madrid was not 'Real'.

Rayo Vallecano
Neighbourhood pride and class consciousness

On 21 November 2014, the working-class Madrid neighbour-hood of Vallecas was the site of the umpteenth social tragedy produced by the 2008 world financial crisis that especially hit poorer areas. Carmen Martínez-Ayuso, an 85-year-old widow living on a paltry pension, was evicted from the flat she had lived in for half a century in the street of Sierra de Palomeras in the historic centre of Vallecas. Her son was not able to pay back a personal loan that had been guaranteed by his mother and which tripled in size after being taken out.

Shocking images of Carmen being evicted – captured by photographer Andrés Kudacki – starkly portrayed the suffer-ing of an old woman driven out of her lifelong home. Most likely, without his camera being there, the eviction would not have caused any stir in the media and the event would have become just another daily eviction statistic. In Spain hundreds of thousands had been evicted since the beginning of the crisis.

But the eviction of the Vallecas resident only turned into a big media story after the Rayo Vallecano squad and their manager Paco Jémez saw the images of Carmen in the press and decided to show her their solidarity. They met the cost of renting decent housing for Carmen.

This support gained global news coverage due to its uniqueness: a club taking responsibility for an elderly woman being punished due to bank debt. It was a step which, in a league officially named after a bank ('*la Liga Santander*') and in which millionaire salaries are paid, put humanity squarely back into football. It was an example of the kindness that seemed to have been lost forever due to the sport having turned into a profit-making business.

In fact, there was nothing strange about an act of solidarity of this kind coming from Rayo Vallecano. Indeed it came shortly after a financial crisis for the Rumasa business conglomerate the club belonged to, which led to Rayo's players not being paid for more than a year.

It is also the case that modesty, neighbourhood pride, and class consciousness have been elements that symbolise Rayo: a club of the most rooted kind in a district with a long tradition of social commitment, solidarity, and workers' struggle. Possibly that is why Rayo was the only squad that joined – as requested by its fans – the general strike on 29 September 2010 against the (socialist) Zapatero government's labour-market 'reforms'. This protest was rounded off by the club closing its offices in a clear show of solidarity with the workers' struggle.

The decision was repeated on 29 March 2012 when players and staff – this time without any prior prompting by Rayo supporters – agreed to join the national stoppage called by all the unions against a new assault on working conditions – this time by Mariano Rajoy's right-wing administration.

Solidarity was again shown with the simultaneous strike held on 14 November that same year in many European countries against EU-driven austerity policies. That time club employees did not officially join the strike, in which only the Galician Celta de Vigo joined out of the top-flight Spanish clubs. Yet Rayo did limit itself to exercising in the gym, and publicly expressed its concerns over the issues behind the industrial action.

There was participation in the mobilisations that were part of the general strike by Rayo fans, led by the '*Bukaneros*' (Buccaneers spelt with a 'k'*) – the football club's staunchest supporters. This group has also been characterised by its involvement in Madrid social movements and pro-republican and left-wing politics, which has led to many of its members embracing communist and anarchist ideas. The *Bukaneros* were so involved in the strike activity that one of its members, Alfonso Fernández – known by the nickname Alfon – was arrested on his way to a picket, accused of carrying fireworks and fire-lighting material in his backpack.

Alfon's arrest and subsequent imprisonment was seized on by the Spanish government's regional delegate – the conservative Cristina Cifuentes – to criminalise Rayo followers – presenting them as akin to a 'criminal gang'. The attack unleashed a wave of solidarity and sympathy towards this particular crew who believe that loyalty to the neighbourhood's working-class identity is as important as supporting their soccer team.

Since then, banners in support of Alfon have been very visible in the stands of the Vallecas stadium – alongside the Spanish republican flags that were already a regular fixture. Accompanying them were messages remembering Carlos Palomino, a young anti-fascist who was killed in Madrid in 2007 by a far-right soldier, and who was a regular in the *Bukanero* stand. That killing underlined another component in Rayo followers' identity: their anti-fascism.

The key to Rayo Vallecano fans' leftist traditions is not so much the *Bukaneros* but the working-class character of the district. This also inspired the *Peña Los Petas* supporters' group

---

* Translator's note: in the alternative scene in Spain the letter 'c' in words is often replaced by a 'k' to give the word a radical, even-punk sound. For instance, '*ocupa*' (squatter) becomes '*okupa*'.

– one of the club's noisiest and most fun. That group would carry a Che Guevara flag and claim 'independent-nation' status for Vallecas (or '*Vallekas*' – as most of its alternative neighbours would write its name*).

The call for local sovereignty is not as unreal as it might seem – at least if we go back to the past. It is no coincidence that in 1924, when Rayo was created (with this very name), Vallecas was a separate town from Madrid. It was only annexed by the Spanish capital in 1950.

Three years before this, and precisely to claim its belonging to the town, Rayo incorporated Vallecas' municipal coat of arms in its crest. As a gesture made in the middle of discussions over annexation, it was a true statement regarding the club's identity.

This peculiarity, and Rayo's lack of any self-reference to Madrid, stood firm until 1995, four years after the club was bought by the notorious José-María Ruiz-Mateos. This conservative businessman controversially chose to ditch the traditional name of Asociación Deportiva Rayo Vallecano (ADRV) in favour of the name Rayo Vallecano de Madrid. This is a name that the more conscious sections of fans have always rejected, seeing it as the main symbol of the club's 'Madridisation'.

Being proud of a Vallecas neighbourhood that has always stood up to Madrid's incursions has been one of the Rayo's hallmarks. Yet Rayo is the only neighbourhood club in Spain that has managed to both gain mass support and firmly establish itself among the elite clubs – particularly since winning promotion to top-flight football for the first time in 1977.

Rayo's other distinguishing feature is its working-class nature which has not wavered since its beginnings. Indeed, the

---

* Translator's note: See previous footnote.

first official competition it played in was organised in 1931 by the Workers' Sport Federation (FDO), the body that was encouraging working-class people to do sport even ahead of the Second Republic being declared (on 14 April of that year). It also promoted socialist and communist ideals within such activity. It was precisely from this federation that the Workers' Cultural and Sport Federation (FCDO) sprang. This was the worker-oriented organisation that coordinated holding the International Workers' Olympiads (sporting competitions held parallel to the official Olympics and which excluded the Nazis).

Due to its nature, the federation that first incorporated Rayo into competitions was unsurprisingly disbanded after Franco's victory in the 1936–1939 War. From then on, the Vallecas outfit joined the Castilian Football Federation to play in the matches organised by the new Spanish federation.

Despite its working class and locally rooted nature, Rayo has also had important links with the Madrid oligarchy that has sought to control it. This was shown by one of its closest collaborators during the period of far-right rule being Santiago Bernabéu; a known fascist and chairman of Real Madrid. In the 1960s, Rayo made him an Honorary Member and gave him a gold and diamond insignia. This was for his services to the club, which was then still in the lower flights of Spanish football at the time.

The controversial businessman Ruiz-Mateos was another figure who tried to pervert Rayo's historic identity. He managed to become the club's biggest shareholder in 1991 when it was turned into a public limited company. In 1994, he gave the chairmanship to his wife Teresa Rivero, who became the first woman to head a top-division Spanish club.

That unique turn led to Rayo's stadium being named after her in 2004. The change was endorsed by referendum but was

later revoked in another referendum in 2011. The whole experience was a good democratic exercise and ended up with the
venue being called the name it has to this day: none other than
Vallecas Football Ground.

Supporters initially showed enthusiasm towards Ruiz-
Mateos' running of the club but this waned; ending disastrously
when the club entered bankruptcy proceedings in 2011. Then,
the squad, with fans' support, campaigned hard to save it using
the slogan 'Rayo, yes; Rumasa, no!'.

Despite attempts at 'depersonalising' the club, new episodes
of this kind have occurred since Raúl Martín-Presa took over
as chairperson. But Rayo fans have remained faithful to the
club's working-class history. The club's chronicles include
chapters such as the support given to their evicted neighbour,
Carmen Martínez. It was symbolic of the impoverished and
troubled Vallecas neighbourhood – the same that keeps Rayo's
heart beating. A modest club but one with a dignity that many
of its rivals have lost. In short, a working-class club proud of
where it comes from.

FC Barcelona
Army of unarmed people

Catalonia has had a turbulent history, fraught with violent episodes. Yet since the arrival of Franco's fascism, and helped by the spread of historian Jaume Vicens i Vives's view of Catalans as having historically been a 'people of peaceful spirit', a pacifist culture has imbued Catalan society.

Catalan nationalism, unlike the Basque variant, has rarely expressed itself in violent terms and the movements for conscientious objection and refusal to do compulsory military service, were widely followed in the Catalan lands. This is one reason why the Spanish army was an institution with thin roots in Catalonia. Another was that it was seen as a foreign force.

In Catalonia the mission of defending the territory – in theory carried out by the state army – has been taken up by organisations that have little relationship with the military tradition. Among these is a sporting entity that has taken on a very notable role in promoting and defending Catalan sentiment: Futbol Club Barcelona – better known locally by its nickname '*Barça*'.

Manuel Vázquez-Montalbán was one of Barcelona's foremost intellectuals, labelling himself as a 'journalist, novelist, poet, essayist, anthologist, prologue writer, humourist, critic, gastronome, *Barça* fan, and generally prolific person'. He stood out most for his involvement in communist and anti-fascist politics, as well as for his love of FC Barcelona. He defined the club as 'the unarmed army of a country whose identity was crushed'.

The metaphor is somewhat over-egged, yet it does identify one of the most important roles that the club – founded by Hans Gamper in 1899 – has had ever since. This is none other than defending Catalonia and its national identity.

Vázquez-Montalbán's definition, quoted in *Catalònia* magazine – a publication that promoted Catalan culture internationally and was produced in many languages – was echoed years later by Bobby Robson. As manager of the '*blaugrana*' (Blue-and-Burgundy) team in the 1996–1997 season, Robson perfectly understood the club's social, political, and cultural significance, stating that 'Catalonia is a country and *Barça*, its army'. To explain his similar use of a military allegory as the author of the Pep Carvalho detective novels, Robson said 'every time we played in Spain it was a battle as we were representing Catalonia'.

The army metaphor is by no means the only one used to define *Barça*'s symbolism. Vázquez-Montalbán himself, in the many articles he wrote on the club in his prolific career, saw this to be 'a means of being in contact with the Catalan people's own history', 'an instrument of emotional attachment with the country', 'a badge of identity', 'Catalonia's liver: a delicate collective organ through which passes almost everything that happens in the country', 'Catalonia's eternal spiritual reservoir', 'its epic recourse', and 'a declaration of principles on being Catalan'. Not much really.

Whether it is an army, liver, means of contact, or spiritual reserve, FC Barcelona has certainly stayed closely associated with Catalonia, to the point that it became one of the nation's most archetypal banners. Despite what is usually thought, the historic relationship between *Barça* and Catalonia is not just rooted in the Franco period but goes back to the club's very foundation.

The first significant chapter that turned *Barça* into a club identified with the Catalan cause was in 1908. An assembly that year added a second objective to its statutes, on top of promoting doing sport. The added aim was 'the promotion of and participation in the social, cultural, artistic, scientific and recreational activities that are necessary to maintain the representativeness and public image enjoyed by the club, the result of a permanent tradition of loyalty and service to members, citizens, and Catalonia'.

This mission statement would gradually be implemented through concrete measures. A Catalan flag ('*Senyera*') started to be flown at the club headquarters – next to the Spanish and *blaugrana*-club flags – in 1916. The same year, Catalan was introduced as the club's day-to-day language – after the overtly pro-Catalan Gaspar Rosés became chairman. *Barça* participated in the acts celebrating Catalonia's National Day (*la Diada*) from 1919. Lastly, in 1922, it had its statutes written wholly in Catalan.

Amidst such decisions, Barcelona performed its first clear political act when it chose to join the campaign in favour of a Catalan statute of autonomy led by an assembly of councillors from the Catalan provinces (*Mancomunitat*). This support was praised by the newspaper *La Veu de Catalunya* – linked to the bourgeois pro-Catalan party la Lliga Regionalista. The paper wrote, 'FC Barcelona has gone from being a club from Catalonia to being the club of Catalonia'.

Since then, *Barça* has become progressively incorporated into the pro-Catalan imaginary, as confirmed by the club's 1920 annual report. This declared, 'We are FC Barcelona because we are from Catalonia. We do sport because we are building a homeland'.

The start of that decade saw the creation of the first Catalan parties that decidedly favoured independence. It was also a period of symbolic acts that bound *Barça* to the nationalist tradition. The club started calling its fourth team 'Separatists' in 1920. Additionally one of the designs for the future stadium in Les Corts included the pro-independence Catalan flag ('*estelada*') atop the main stand in 1922. This is not to speak of the two days of mourning that the club held in 1920 after the death of the Sinn Féin Mayor of Cork – while a political prisoner and hunger striker – during the war for Irish independence.

Not surprisingly, the dictatorship of Miguel Primo de Rivera reacted to these developments, clamping down on the club's conduct. It banned both the use of the Catalan language and the club's participation in the *Diada* ceremonies.

Yet the dictatorship's main act of repression against *Barça* took place in 1925 after a friendly between the sporting entity and Club Esportiu Júpiter. The match was a tribute to the *Orfeó Català* Choral Society – another big pro-Catalan organisation threatened by Primo de Rivera.

Before kick-off, the public packing the stadium loudly whistled over the Spanish national anthem (the *Marcha Real*). This peaceful protest against the dictatorship and its crackdown on pro-Catalans was heavily punished: *Barça*'s stadium was ordered to close for six months – a ban later reduced to three – and its chairman was forced into exile. Instead of such repression achieving its goal, it reinforced the symbolic nature of a club that, once the dictatorship fell and the Second Republic was proclaimed, reinstated many of the activities that Primo de Rivera had prohibited.

Barça reintroduced Catalan as its working language. It did so to such a degree that it organised Catalan grammar courses in the 1930s, which had as one of its teachers the outstanding linguist Pompeu Fabra – creator of the rules of modern Catalan. The club also participated again in the *Diada* activities, paying the traditional homage to the martyrs during Barcelona's fall to the Bourbons in 1714. At the same time, *Barça* was the target of a relentless fight for control between the supporters of the different political wings of Catalan nationalism: the Lliga Regionalista and the republican left of Catalonia (ERC).

The club's political side was once again shown when Josep Suñol was chosen as club chairman in 1935. Suñol was an ERC MP in Madrid and editor of the *La Rambla* newspaper: a publication that advocated linking sport with being a republican citizen.

Suñol's tenure was short-lived. Soon after the fascist uprising on 18 July 1936, he made a trip to the republican front accompanied by a fellow journalist at *La Rambla*. The MP was arrested in the Guadarrama Mountains by nationalist troops and executed on the spot, with no right to trial. It was a clear example of the extreme violence that Francoism would inflict on the club, seeing it to be an entity 'hostile to the regime'. This ruthlessness was further exemplified when the deceased Suñol was prosecuted under the dictatorship's 1939 Law of Political Responsibilities with the aim of 'settling the guilt of those who contributed to forging red subversion'.

After the war, the Franco regime severely punished *Barça's* stance in the preceding decades – including its wartime defence of the republican cause. The dictatorship wished to humiliate the club and put regime supporters at its helm, at the same time as it filled Barcelona's stadium with fascist flags and forced its players to do the fascist salute before the monument commemorating club members who had 'fallen for God and Spain' (fighting on Franco's side).

The 1940 Hispanicisation decree passed by the fascist state, forced *Barça* to Hispanicise its name – as happened with Athletic Madrid and other clubs – to become Club de Fútbol Barcelona. It was also forced to change the *Senyera* on its crest for something resembling a Spanish flag.

Just before then, the sporting newspaper *Marca* – created in 1938 in the Spanish zone under Franco's control – had proposed that *Barça* be punished for its Catalan nationalism by being renamed '*España*' (Spain). This was never actually implemented but it illustrated the aversion that the club's Catalanness aroused among the sectors backing the new regime.

Despite the repressive measures and having directors forced upon *Barça* who were complicit with the dictatorship, most of the club's fan base remained loyal to their principles and fought impositions through small peaceful actions. An example worth highlighting is when the *blaugrana* fans refused to travel home by tram (despite the rain) after playing against Racing de Santander at the Les Corts stadium in 1951. By walking *en masse* they thereby joined strikes opposing a hike in tram fares – one of the first major social revolts under Franco.

Barça also suffered affronts such as the government interference behind the controversial signing of star player Alfredo Di Stefano by Real Madrid (instead of Barcelona). All these events led many citizens across Spain to support the Catalan club. They saw the *blaugranas* as an anti-authoritarian vehicle through which to peacefully protest against the regime.

In the post-war period, being a *Barça* member became a way of asserting feeling Catalan (as Vázquez-Montalbán noted). It was a form of protest tolerated by the regime. Despite abhorring everything the club stood for, the far-right rulers preferred the masses to chant in the stadiums early on a

Sunday evening rather than do so on the streets on workdays or engage in underground political activity.

It was during the dark period of the Franco regime that a phrase was coined that has best summarised the club's history. This is none other than *Barça* being 'more than just a club' ('*més que un club*'). It was first used by Narcís de Carreras during his acceptance speech as the new club chairman in 1968. (De Carreras, nonetheless, was a former member of the conservative Lliga Regionalista and representative of a bourgeoisie still wedded to the regime's principles.)

The expression was later popularised by another chairman Agustí Montal during his 1973 campaign for re-election to the post. A representative of Barcelona's textile employers who had rediscovered the Catalan cause, Montal played a key role in the club's history during his years as chair: 1969–1977, which coincided with Franco's final years and with the 'transition' to democracy.

During his tenure, *Barça* reintroduced using Catalan again, in its newsletter, and through its PA system. Most importantly it defied the ruling elites with an epic 5–0 win over Real Madrid at the Bernabéu on 17 February 1974. Some have come to consider that date – not without some exaggeration – as the beginning of the Spanish transition to democracy. It seemed to show that the tables were turning between dictatorial might – represented by Real Madrid – and the emerging democratic force – symbolised by *Barça*. For instance, *Diario de Barcelona* journalist Àlex J. Botines wrote of the match as a 'lesson in contemporary history', noting its clear historical implications and how it prefigured the regime change that came soon after (although with Franco dying peacefully in bed in the autumn of 1975).

With the end of the far-right dictatorship, *Barça* made a series of gestures that once again demonstrated its status as being 'more than just a club'. A month after the dictator's death, but with his regime still intact and the Catalan flag still banned, *culés* (Barcelona supporters) waved hundreds of Catalan flags during the match their team played against Real Madrid. Shortly after, club director Jaume Rosell had a bust of Franco removed from display at the club's offices; while *Camp Nou* was set to warmly receive Josep Tarradellas, the exiled President of Catalonia, on his return home.

Since then, the club has for a long time been run by an administration far removed from the grassroots *catalanisme* that has historically permeated the club's mass base. Despite this, however, the political gestures that stressed *Barça's* affinity with Catalan nationalism have only multiplied. These have ranged from the whistling over the *Marcha Real* during *Copa del Rey* finals (which were reminiscent of that performed in 1925) to the club joining the National Pact for Self Determination. They include lending out the use of *Camp Nou* for huge events in favour of Catalonia's right to self-determination, such as the recent non-binding referendums, the human chain across Catalonia, and the Concert for Freedom.

Nor should we forget the decision to play the match against Unión Deportiva Las Palmas on 1 October 2017 behind closed doors. This was in response to the Spanish police harshly repressing the referendum on independence held that same day. It was the club's response to pressure from fans to pull out of the match in solidarity with the hundreds of people across Catalonia who were injured by police. It must be added, nevertheless, that it was a protest that the same fans saw as half-hearted.

The chant for independence that *blaugrana* supporters make 17 minutes and 14 seconds into every Barcelona home match is highly symbolic. The exact time of the chant is to pay homage to the martyrs of the 1714 siege and occupation of

Barcelona (which led Bourbon Spain to ban the Catalan institutions and language. The club has also paid varied tributes to
the victims of that historic defeat since first joining the *Diada*
events in 1919). The chant was first made on 19 September
2012 – a week after the first of several gigantic pro-independence demonstrations to flood the streets of Barcelona
– during a Champions League match between the Catalan
club and Spartak Moscow.

Although *catalanisme* had historically shaped the club,
this was the first time ever that a large majority of supporters at *Camp Nou* openly expressed backing for independence.
Dr Josep Trueta, a staunch pro-Catalan and member of the
Catalan National Council in exile until his death in 1977, once
said that Catalonia would become a fully sovereign nation 'the
day *Camp Nou* cried out for independence'.

The match in which pro-independence sentiment poured
around the stadium took place the day after the death of
Santiago Carrillo – the former General Secretary of the
Communist Party of Spain. He had predicted that Catalonia
would eventually become an independent state but that he
would not live to see it. If we heed Trueta and Carrillo's pre-
dictions, Catalan statehood will sooner or later come true. It
will probably only be then that *Barça* stops being the army of
an unarmed people – as it was described by the much-missed
Vázquez-Montalbán.

CE Júpiter
With the star as its banner

Like many clubs formed in early 20th-century Europe, Club Esportiu Júpiter started life in a beer house. Specifically this was the Cebrián, at the heart of the working-class Barcelona district of Poblenou on 12 May 1909. Júpiter's main promoter was David Mauchan, one of many Scottish workers that the Fabra i Coats textile factory brought in due to the merger between the firm from the Sant Andreu neighbourhood and a textile manufacturer from the outskirts of Glasgow.

Mauchan set up a new sports society that brought together the small clubs in the neighbourhood. He was helped to do this by his brothers Jean and William, who, like himself, played for a team known as '*Escocés*' (The Scot), as well as by local footballers playing for Stadium Nacional and Anglo-Espanyol – two small amateur outfits in the district.

On that May night, Júpiter was created. Its name did not refer to the supreme Roman God, as one might initially imagine, but to the hot-air balloon that had just won a contest on the nearby Mar Bella beach. Its promoters were little aware that the club whose name had popped up over beers would end up reflecting Catalan political history in the early 20th century.

From the outset, Júpiter stood out as a club very closely identified with the Poblenou neighbourhood and its working-class inhabitants at a time of social conflict in the area's factories. The football team quickly drew in workers linked to anarchist trade unionism – the dominant wing of the union movement in the early century.

These workers would spend part of their free time playing football on the Camp de la Bota wasteland. The site would play a significant role in Barcelona's history, and this was not just because of Júpiter's first matches. Camp de la Bota later housed a shanty town for those who came seeking work related to the Universal Exhibition held in Barcelona in 1929. It was also the site of hundreds of shootings of republican prisoners after the fascist victory in 1939. It again became a slum area during the wave of migration into Catalonia in the 1950s and 1960s. Finally, it was part of the space used for the Universal Forum of Cultures promoted by Barcelona Town Hall in 2004.

When the club joined the Catalan footballing federation in 1912, it left the Camp de la Bota esplanade to move to the Carrer Taulat ground – in Poblenou. It laid down deep roots in the neighbourhood while playing there and later – in 1921 – in nearby Carrer Llull, where it spent its golden age.

By then, Júpiter had introduced a crest that was highly symbolic as it featured the *Senyera* (red and yellow Catalan flag) crowned with a blue star. The star therefore made the image a forerunner to the pro-independence Catalan flag (the *Estelada*, which also includes the colour blue and a star). The latter first appeared in a document by the Pro-Catalonia Committee – the organisation set up to win national recognition from the League of Nations – on 11 September 1918. This strengthened Júpiter's pro-worker and pro-Catalan identity at a time of frequent episodes of violence between employers and workers. The identity was such that a legend was created that the club's players used its facilities to store weapons and away matches to transport them – inside leather footballs – to reach armed anarchist groups such as *Los Solidarios*. Many of the players themselves were linked to anarcho-syndicalism.

The club paid a price for its association with the workers' movement and Catalan nationalism when a 1923 coup d'état, led by General Miguel Primo de Rivera, brought in a military dictatorship that cracked down on the two movements. In April 1924, a judge named Cristóbal Fernández made a formal complaint against Júpiter to Barcelona's Civil Governor due to the club's pro-Catalan insignia. He argued that this 'clearly dissimulated the Catalan separatist flag' popularised at the time by *Estat Català* – the pro-independence party created by Francesc Macià in 1922. The Civil Governor ended up banning the crest, which had to be swapped for another in which a Barcelona city crown and the teams' colours replaced the *Senyera* and the star.

Ironically, notwithstanding the repression suffered under the dictatorship, the 1920s was the period when Júpiter reaped some of its biggest sporting successes: most commendably becoming the Spanish second-division champion in 1925 (and having won the Catalan second-flight championship that same year).

These victories by Júpiter were accompanied by *Barça*'s triumph that year in the cup. This tournament was for the champions of the different regional competitions in the Spanish state and was in that era treated as the Spanish championship. This coincidence led the two Barcelona teams to be given a triumphant welcome in the Catalan capital in which supporters celebrate both their achievements.

As Júpiter had won the Spanish second division, *Barça* invited it to play a friendly on 14 June 1925. This was to pay homage to the *Orfeó Català* – a choral society with great nationalistic symbolism which had been clamped down on by the military dictatorship.

The match was played in a very tense atmosphere. It included a pre-match performance by the British Royal

Marines Band, who played '*God Save the King*' (the British national anthem), which was met by a respectful silence. Then it played the *Marcha Real* (the Spanish equivalent), which was loudly whistled over by the 14,000 spectators filling the *blaugrana* Camp de Les Corts stadium.

According to the authorities, the whistling added to the fact that when the match's authorisation was requested, it was not specified that it would be in homage to the *Orfeó Català*, which ended up being banned by the dictatorship for some months. These two things led Barcelona to suffer harsh reprisals: its stadium shut, and its chairman was forced into exile.

The end of that dictatorship and the subsequent proclamation of Spain's Second Republic once again changed Júpiter's history and allowed it to reinstate its original crest. This was performed in a highly symbolic ceremony, held on 25 September 1931, before a match pitting Júpiter against Palafrugell. Then, the club's captain handed Francesc Macià, now President of the restored *Generalitat* (Catalan government), an insignia featuring the club's old symbols: the *Senyera* and star.

During the early 1930s, Júpiter went through a second golden period. Its crowning glory came in 1934, when the club managed to reach the second division of the Spanish League, where it managed to stay for two seasons.

Júpiter again showed its political commitment during the stormy year of 1936 – when the Civil War started. It joined then the Catalan Committee for People's Sports – the body that was to organise the 1936 People's Olympiad and which defended promoting and rooting sport among the popular classes.

Before the eventually thwarted July 1936 Olympiad, the committee organised a tournament in which worker teams from different territories in the Spanish state played each other in solidarity with Ernst Thälmanm, the German Communist Party leader who had been imprisoned by the Nazis. In the final, played at Júpiter's ground, the team representing Asturias won, triggering the jubilation of a public showing its solidarity with the 1934 miners' insurrection in this region.

Júpiter's legendary association with the workers' movement was strengthened because of the fascist uprising on 18 July 1936 (which also scuppered the Barcelona People's Olympiad that was to begin the following day). Rapidly after the coup began, Júpiter's ground became a meeting point for worker-party supporters, many of whom lived in the vicinity of the stadium, who sought to organise the popular insurrection against the far-right revolt. There, worker militants had collected a significant stockpile of weapons that they would use to stop the attempt at taking control of Barcelona.

During the war that followed the locally unsuccessful coup d'état, Júpiter did not stop playing and still found the time to win the Catalan second-flight championship. All the same, the most significant matches played at Carrer Llull at the time were benefit matches for the different republican institutions, such as *Socorro Rojo* (Red Aid), the blood bank, and the people's militias. These once again showed the club's commitment to the anti-fascist cause.

Yet this political commitment led once again to Júpiter paying a high price. Indeed, several of its players were called up to fight at the front where some even lost their lives; and at the end of the war, another club footballer, Carlos Ibáñez, was shot dead at Camp de la Bota – the same place where the Poblenou club began playing.

With the history it had behind it, Júpiter was seen by the Franco regime as a club 'opposed to the regime' and inflicted on it the same repression it had suffered under Primo de Rivera. Consequently, the Poblenou brigade once again had to ditch its starred crest and bring back the one it used during the previous dictatorship. Yet this time the attempts to stamp out its working-class, pro-Catalan, and revolutionary character went a bit further. Franco's authorities were not content with changing the club's imagery but also changed its name, forcing it to adopt that of Club Deportivo Hércules. Changing its name from a Roman God to that of a Greek hero had no other purpose than attempting to obliterate any symbolism the club had garnered over its three decades of existence.

The complete suppression of Júpiter's identity was to be completed by merging Hércules with *Real Club Deportivo Español* (Barcelona's Espanyol) and making the new club a subsidiary of the latter one. The big ideological differences between the two clubs' fans and the rejection of the idea by the Español supporters meant the plan did not end up coming to fruition.

The CD Hércules name lasted no more than a season, as the club regained its original name in 1940. This decision amounted to no more than a pretence of a claimed relaxation in treatment towards the club, as Franco's state apparatus continued targeting a club that stood for everything the regime detested.

Júpiter subsequently entered a period of decline, taking it far from its 30 glorious years in which it reached 2,000 members and would compete for the Barcelona footballing throne with the two giants of the city (*Barça* and Espanyol).

The club's woes continued. In 1948, it was forced into exile from its original Poblenou neighbourhood. After having become familiar with its Carrer Llull stadium, the club now had to leave Poblenou and settle at the Verneda ground in the Sant Martí district. Banishment from Poblenou was a big blow for a club closely linked to its neighbourhood and it correspondingly lost much of its identity. This took it to the verge of disappearing.

The first decision made during the dictatorship to revive at least the memory of the original Júpiter came in 1959 when the club brought back the grey and maroon kit it is identified with today and that its team had worn in the 1920s. This meant dropping the green and white shirts worn during the Second Republic and the early years under Franco (but not returning to the white and sky-blue strip that Júpiter first wore either).

Yet the big step the club made to restore its past did not come until years after the end of the far-right dictatorship when, in a meeting held in 1989, club members agreed to reintroduce the original crest. As a result, on 2 September 1990 – the first day of the new season – Júpiter wore the four stripes and star on the breast of its jerseys. It was an act of justice which gave back the club the pro-independence star that had always been its banner, and which had triggered vicious repression from the Primo de Rivera and Franco dictatorships. An act to remind us that this modest but inspiring club has closely reflected Catalonia's traumatic history over the 20th century.

Spanish Girl's Club
A dream frustrated by the First World War

Like almost everything to do with the beautiful game, women's football first came into being in Britain at the end of the 19th century. Specifically, the first club exclusively made up of women – British Ladies – was set up in 1895 – championed by the feminist aristocrat Florence Dixie.

The club only lasted for approximately a year. Yet despite this brief existence, British Ladies acted as a spur for new initiatives beyond Britain's borders that wanted to promote football played by women. The best example was that of the Spanish Girl's Club,* the first women's football club in the Iberian Peninsula, which was created in Catalonia in April 1914.

Spanish Girl's, whose name was clearly inspired by British Ladies, was the initiative of Paco Bru, an Espanyol player at the time (although both before and after then he played for *Barça*). Bru was a Madrid-born footballer but who had spent his whole sporting career in Catalonia, even becoming one of the most important figures in Catalan football before the Civil

---

* Translator's note: The Anglicised name was chosen at a time when few would have spoken or written the English language in Spain, and I suspect that the club should have been called 'the Spanish Young Women's Club' as the name is likely a translation from 'Club de chicas españolas'. 'Chicas' can be translated as both 'girls' and 'young women'.

War. He was a jack-of-all-trades, having at different times acted as a player, manager, referee, club director, and even journalist.

Convinced of the female sex's sporting potential, Bru introduced in Catalonia the idea that the British Ladies had briefly put into practice in the UK despite being hampered by the English Football Association (FA). The 'Parakeets' (Espanyol) player assembled 50 aspiring female footballers and their families and started up the Spanish Girl's Club – the pioneering team of its kind in Iberia. Bru had to overcome a lot of misgivings, particularly over young women wearing short trousers or showering together after a match. The prevailing sexism in Catalan society in that era meant that most people did not approve of young women having these freedoms or even playing a sport which, until then, had been restricted to men. This led to the Spanish Girl's often being contemptuously labelled 'tomboys' or 'butch' – insults that Paco Bru always responded to with an alternative description for those daring female pioneers: 'sportswoman',* a term imported from Britain, just like the idea for the team.

After outlining his intentions for the club and picking the team, Bru got started on the initial training, which lasted a month and a half. In that time, Spanish Girl's consolidated itself as a perfectly organised club, even having its own premises – in Consell de Cent in Barcelona. This acted as a meeting point, and it hosted the *Amistat* Leisure Society.

The first-ever women's football game played in the Iberian Peninsula happened on 9 June 1914 at the Espanyol ground in the Barcelona street of Indústria. It seems that despite being a charity match, Spanish Girl's could not find any men's team

---

* Translator's note: See previous note. Bru used the English word exactly as it is written here. 'Sportswomen' (with an 'e') would obviously be preferable.

willing to play against them. This was likely due to general disregard towards women's football but was probably also encouraged by the (English) FA's 1902 ban of male and female clubs playing each other – even in charity games.

This setback did not put off Paco Bru and his young women players, who chose to go onwards with their initiative, which was specifically aimed at raising money to fight tuberculosis. Spanish Girl's chose to split into two teams, which were given the names 'Montserrat' and 'Giralda' in honour of the Catalan monastery and iconic Sevillian monument of the same name. The two sides from the Spanish Girl's Club went onto the turf of the Espanyol stadium on 9 June 1914 to play the first women's football match in Iberian history.

The match was quite an event and attracted a large crowd to the Parakeet ground under the watchful eye of none other than the Captain-General of Catalonia – former Minister of War César Víctor Augusto del Villar. He bore witness to the Giralda women beating Montserrat 2–1.

Yet, as had occurred with the British Ladies, and as would happen almost everywhere where women began playing soccer at that time, Spanish Girl's was on the receiving end of considerable rejection in a society tainted by sexism and traditionalism. A good example was a report on the event in the *El Mundo Deportivo* sports paper. This said,

We were not happy about women's first appearance in the virile game of football. This was not just because of its poor sporting side. The descendants of our mother Eve had to get into such unbecoming and unsightly postures, they killed female beauty.

Regardless of the fierce disapproval they faced, Spanish Girl's played each other again two days later – again at Espanyol's

Indústria venue. The match ended in a 1–1 draw, leading Montserrat and Giralda to play each other once more, this time in Sabadell on 14 June. This was the first game Spanish Girl's played outside Barcelona ended in a resounding 1–4 victory by the team named after the Catalan monastery.

The Sabadell game was followed by matches in Barcelona and nearby Mataró, also in June 1914. Finally Spanish Girl's travelled to play outside the Greater Barcelona area, in Reus.

Paradoxically, records suggest that the Reus game was the last featuring the pioneering women's football team in Catalonia. The club had agreed to away fixtures in Tarragona, Valencia, Palma, and Pamplona, and even had planned a tour for that August in the south of France. Yet, the events Europe went through in that summer of 1914, when the First World War broke out, led all the Spanish Girl's matches to be cancelled.

The pioneering women's football team was therefore one of the first casualties of the war that would devastate the world from July 1914 to November 1918. Oddly, the disappearance of the women's game in Spain contrasted with the revival of the women's game in several of the countries at war. This was because a large proportion of men of fighting age were sent to the battlefields, and due to the need to maintain the rear guard's spirits by holding leisure and sporting activities.

After the Spanish Girl's short-lived experience, Iberian women's football hibernated for a long time, only reappearing (in Catalonia) in the late 1960s. The high point after its return was Christmas Day 1970. Then, 60,000 people filled the *Camp Nou* stands to see the young women from the *Selecció de la Ciutat de Barcelona* (Barcelona City Team) – the embryo of today's *Barça* Women – take on those of Unió Esportiva Centcelles.

Both Spanish Girl's and the initiatives that picked up the baton more than five decades later, were the cornerstone for the present-day success of women's football in Catalonia, which has Barcelona Women's recent triumphs as its prime example. These players are worthy heirs of those pioneers who, in the spring of 1914, dared to challenge the sexism that dominated society and whose dream was only dashed by the outbreak of war.

4
Central Europe and Scandinavia

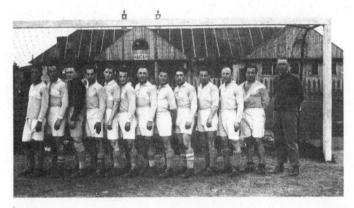

Hakoah Vienna players at the Viennese Prater stadium, where the Jewish club played at home

Berliner FC Dynamo
The *Stasi*'s club

'Footballing success will highlight even more clearly the superiority of our socialist order in the area of sport'. This bombastic sentence was uttered by Erich Mielke, one of the most feared – if not *the* most feared – men in the former German Democratic Republic (GDR). Mielke was speaking as Minister for State Security and chief of the ever-present and ever-powerful political police: the *Stasi*. However, before then he had been a first-wave communist activist and had fought in the International Brigades during the Spanish Civil War. Another passion as absorbing for him as politics was none other than football.

It was precisely this second passion that led him to be (honorary) chair of Berliner Fußball Club Dynamo from 1957 to 1989. The club began as part of a sporting institution – Sportgemeinde Deutsche Volkspolizei Berlin. This had been set up in 1949, amid the building of the new socialist Germany. It was tied to what formally emerged a year later as the *Stasi* – the state service that aimed to be 'the shield and sword of the party'. In other words, it was an instrument for fighting those who disagreed with the dominant communist ideology. In 1954, the club became Sports Club Dynamo Berlin, an entity under the Ministry for State Security – the portfolio for which was given to Mielke shortly afterwards.

The Berlin club's early years were characterised by its rather inconspicuous existence, which saw it wandering the lower flights of GDR football. But the political interest in giving Berlin a club to compete on a national and European level led the *Stasi* chiefs to decree – also in 1954 – that the best players from Dynamo Dresden – the most successful team in those years – join the Berlin team.

At the stroke of a ministerial decree, the *Stasi* thus enabled Dynamo Berlin to reach East Germany's first division and even win its first trophy: the 1959 Cup. All the same, the idea of creating a team that would reign undisputed in the GDR and show Europe 'the superiority of socialist sport' did not come to fruition. Instead, the political manoeuvre set in motion an intense club rivalry with Dresden – which later spread to the other clubs in the country's south. In sporting terms, this led Berliner Dynamo to be relegated to the second division – helped by the relatively old age of its footballers.

Aware of the need to rejuvenate the team, Mielke had big changes made at the club. Dynamo's football section was formally separated from the multi-sports entity and renamed Berliner FC Dynamo. Contrary to the *Stasi's* will, success was slow for the Berliner club. Mielke grew extremely impatient, watching frustratedly how in the early 1970s the 'capitalist' team Bayern Munich (from the Federal Republic of Germany, FRG) achieved European success; and Dynamo Dresden, its old sister club, re-established itself as the dominant club in the GDR. A turning point was only reached in the 1970s – after a long wait – when the *Stasi's* team gained dominance in East Germany.

A few years before, Mielke had become fully aware of football's political importance. This was after the GDR's victory over its Western arch-enemy, the FRG, in the 1974 World Cup played on 'enemy' territory. Communist Germany had beaten its capitalist sister on the pitch – even though the latter went on to win the World Cup.

In June 1978, after seeing Berlin's main domestic rival win its fifth first-division title in the 1970s, Mielke lost his patience. He stormed into the Dynamo Dresden changing room, bellowing that the following year, his Dynamo – the Berlin one – would become the *Oberliga* champion once and for all.

His words were prophetic in that during the following ten seasons – between 1979 and 1988 – Dynamo Berlin won the East German league championship back-to-back. It must be said that its victories were not based on sporting merits alone but on an insulting collusion between the club and the refereeing authorities and other bodies.

Mielke's ever-present *Stasi* had built up an extensive network of collaborators in German football. Players, managers, federation representatives ... No sector escaped the clutches of the political police. It aimed to keep a tight rein on a sporting arena deemed strategic for demonstrating 'socialist superiority' but also especially dangerous to the regime because of the frequent contact players had with capitalist states that were seen as the GDR's enemies.

The policing that Mielke did over his players was clearly illustrated in the case of Lutz Eigendorf, a rising star for Berliner Dynamo. On 20 March 1979, Eigendorf defied his highly powerful boss by escaping to West Germany after a friendly against Kaiserslautern. The fact that one of the flagship players for a Dynamo that was on its way to being champion for the first time would risk defecting from the 'socialist paradise' unleashed fury in Mielke, who ordered the covert assassination of his former great hope. Four years after fleeing, Eigendorf died in a suspicious car accident. After the *Stasi* files were later opened, it was confirmed that the political police had orchestrated this killing as punishment for his defection.

Dynamo's dominance in East German football did not mean it was successful on a continental level. In European contests, the *Stasi* chief could not lean on referees or federation reps, so the Berliner club did not enjoy the same glory in the European Cup that it was used to in domestic competition. Quite the opposite happened: Dynamo suffered some humiliating defeats, such as in its last European match when the 'capitalist' Werder Bremen thrashed it 5–0.

Clearly, Berliner FC Dynamo's domestic victories had more to do with its corrupt ties with the powers-that-be than the superiority of its football. The most transparent instance of political manipulation in the East German league came in 1986. That season, Lokomotiv was seeking to end Dynamo's hegemony of the game. On the 18th match day of the season, the Leipzig club hosted the Berliner team in a match that could settle the championship. After taking the lead, the home side saw an incorrect penalty decision, given in the 95th minute, allow the Berliners to equalise and stay at the top of the table. Anger over this daylight robbery spilt beyond the sporting arena and sparked a nationwide outcry. Aware that people were demanding the issue be resolved, Mielke scapegoated the match referee, Bernd Stumpf, and severely punished him.

Despite Mielke's enormous might, there was one thing he could never buy for his Dynamo, and that was being liked. His team met hostility in almost all GDR stadiums, where it was berated for being the 'champion at cheating'. In the midweek game Dynamo Berlin played in November 1989 and coinciding almost exactly with the fall of the wall dividing its city, there were only 2,000 fans in its stadium – compared to the 30,000 fans that would watch its Dresden competitor. This was a good snapshot of the support for each of the two clubs with the most titles in the GDR competitions.

This was the reason why, once the wall came down, Germany was reunified, and Erich Mielke was disgraced. BFC Dynamo became a club virtually lacking any direction, identity or future.

In 1990, the club dropped its traditional Dynamo name to be called FC Berlin to leave behind its controversial past and association with the *Stasi* – the central agent of political repression against dissidence.

A new name was not of course enough to steer the club towards success. In its home city, it was competing against Herta, the main club in Berlin's west; and Union, the most popular team in the east; and its past weighed heavily on it.

Having no clear orientation and with serious financial problems, FC Berlin chose to go backwards and again use the name Berlin FC Dynamo; aiming to revive its former golden era – if only out of nostalgia. This proved impossible, as today the club plays in Germany's fourth division. Such a reality has not stopped the club from sporting three gold stars above its crest, for being ten-times league champion in the former GDR.

Regardless of this nod to its past, today's Dynamo is quite different from the club that was the preferred plaything of the dreaded Erich Mielke. If he were around today, the former International Brigadier turned *Stasi* head would be astonished to see that now the main group of fans of 'his' Dynamo openly sympathise with the far right and unashamedly display the fascist symbols that Mielke spent his life opposing. A bizarre paradox that attests to the uniqueness of a club that was a product of its time. An era in which Berlin was the faultline in the Cold War between the two main world blocs. An age in which football was part and parcel of that conflict.

FC Union Berlin
The team that has defied the *Stasi* and capital

On 13 September 1986, East Berlin was buzzing with excitement about a derby match. This pitched Dynamo, which – as described previously – was the *Stasi*'s team and presided over by the feared Erich Mielke, against 1. Fußball Club Union. The latter was the other Berlin team, sponsored – in accordance with the GDR footballing system – by the German Federation of Free Trade Unions (FDGB) – the single union movement under East German Communism.

The derbies between the two East Berlin teams always had a meaning beyond the strictly sporting and exposed political rivalries. While Dynamo was the team of the powerful – and that autumn had won the league for the eighth time in a row – Union was seen as the people's team and drew in its stands the regime's dissidents; whether critical intellectuals, the long-and-straggly-haired, or the first East German punks.

That September 1986, Dynamo beat Union for the umpteenth time, giving it a humiliating 8–1 pounding. This was far from being the first drubbing that the trade-union team had suffered at the hands of the regime's pet favourite. Consequently, the defeat was not unduly painful for the 10,000 Union fans that had descended on their arch-rival's stadium – a similar number to the home-team fans present. They were used to losing to an opponent with the upper hand.

Indeed, the fans bearing direct witness to their team's defeat left the ground loudly chanting, in an act that was interpreted as a challenge to the authorities supporting Dynamo. This spontaneous demonstration was a political act that showed Union's supporters to be a mainstay of the opposition to the regime.

Actions such as this came as no surprise to the *Stasi*, which already knew that the terraces of the *Stadion An der Alten Försterei* – Union's home ground, located in the working-class Köpenick neighbourhood – were full of dissidents and subversives.

As an example, when the club played at home and was to take a free kick near its rival's penalty area, leading to a wall being formed, a favourite chant of Union Berlin fans was '*Die Mauer muss weg!*' (The Wall must fall!). This had an obvious double meaning that greatly annoyed the authorities who could do nothing to stop the situation as it was impossible to arrest half a stadium. For that reason, the *Stasi* set about identifying the most fervent club fans to keep tabs and files on them. After the Berlin Wall came down and Germany was reunified, the *Stasi* and other archives were opened. Some fans then discovered that the organisation's long arm was behind some rejected job applications – a Union supporter was suspected of being a dissident and therefore not the most suitable person for that job.

Union's working-class character endeared it to most East Berliners, but it did not receive any institutional backing. Even though Union was linked to the official union, it was not loved by the regime or its media – indeed the opposite was the case. Since the late 1970s, the East German media only had eyes for Mielke's club, which had won dominance by buying the best players from the other GDR clubs – frequently by forcing a sale to happen.

Union itself was repeatedly a victim of this theft – performed to bolster its city rival. This distorted competition and made it impossible for the Köpenick workers' team to match the almighty *Stasi* club at sport.

But before Dynamo became such a winning machine in 1979, Union managed to overcome its limitations and win its first major title (even if this was not to be repeated). In 1968, it picked up the East German Cup, which coincidentally shared the name of the Workers' Federation Union it was associated with (being called the *FDGB Pokal* – the cup of the German Federation of Free Trade Unions).

The historic events in Berlin in 1989 and subsequent reunification led to the disappearance of the GDR competitions and many outfits that had dominated East German football. It also saw Union having to reinvent itself, now competing in the lower tiers of Federal German football. This was not the first time the club had done so. Indeed, it had happened on many occasions since its founding in 1906 as Olympia 06 Ober-schöneweide – named after the neighbourhood that would eventually be incorporated into the Köpenick district and that permanently shaped the club's working-class identity.

It was in this initial era, and because of its original all-blue kit – like the work clothes used in the district's factories – that club supporters started being nicknamed '*schlosserjung*' – translatable as 'Metalworker Boys'. It was also in that period that a rallying cry was created that still often rings out today in the *Stadion An der Alten Försterei*: '*Eisern Union!*' (Iron Union!).

These beginnings with close ties to the neighbourhood's popular classes clearly conditioned the club's evolution. The club developed a sharp working-class identity in contrast to the other Berlin teams which had more affluent origins.

After becoming runner-up in the German championship in 1923 – one of its greatest sporting successes – the reorganisation of football by the Nazi Third Reich in 1933 meant that

Union had to struggle through different German divisions until 1945. But the biggest obstacle along its long road came at the end of the Second World War when the Allied authorities occupying Germany decreed the break-up of all the country's sporting entities. In 1945, Olympia 06 was re-created as SG Oberschöneweide and participated in the first post-war Berlin leagues until the growing Cold War tensions eventually led the new club to be split into two. The players living in West Berlin made up one club; while the others formed the club in the East, using Union for its official name for the first time, to become Union Oberschöneweide.

The restructuring of football in East Germany, after the GDR's creation in 1949, and the state control of the sport by the new communist authorities led the Berlin club to go by several different names. This was until 1966, when it took the name 1. FC Union Berlin – a name it has kept to this very day.

As Union had gone through so many changes in its history, German reunification did not involve too much turmoil for a club that then became the leading East Berlin team – thanks to Dynamo's near disappearance.

Although it maintained a high sporting level, Union's big problem in adapting to the new all-German football was financial. The former communist-country neighbourhood club was not used to being managed following capitalist logics. Despite being promoted on sporting merit to the German second division in 1994, it was denied its place there due to its economic difficulties, which were edging it towards bankruptcy in 1997.

Union's demise was only avoided thanks to its fans getting involved. They championed rescuing a club with an important history in the community and that had become a true symbol of freedom for East Berliners. During those difficult times, punk singer Nina Hagen wrote the club anthem '*Eisern Union!*'

– following the team chant. Another significant chant, '*Und niemals vergessen!*' (And never forget!) also became popular at that time. This referred to working-class memory, the difficult times, and preserving East Germany's sporting legacy.

The club timidly recovered but only to again be blocked from joining 2. *Bundesliga* (second-flight German football) for financial reasons. Promotion to the second division did come in the end after the club's glorious 2001 season in which the club not only went up but reached the German cup final (losing 4–0 to Schalke).

Nonetheless, the club's economic woes continued, and it was on the verge of liquidation in 2004. To avoid collapse, Union Berlin supporters launched the campaign '*Bluten für Union*' (Bleed for Union) in which fans gave blood in city hospitals and then put the payment received for this towards preventing the club's bankruptcy. This campaign was a real success, saving the club, and became an example for the other German clubs fighting a game dominated by financial speculation.

A similar situation arose in 2008, when Union wanted to modernise its stadium but could not pay for the refurbishment. After an appeal to fans, Union mustered 2,400 volunteers who renovated the venue in less than a year. Altogether they devoted 140,000 hours of their time – out of love for their club. Yet they insisted that three out of the four stands were standing-room-only, which led the club to have a long but eventually successful tussle with the German Football Association.

On top of this, supporters forced club directors to break an agreement a year later with the firm International Sports Promotion, a sponsor that gave the club 10 million euros, as one of its heads had worked for the *Stasi*. This was a further sign of the fans' respect for the club's anti-authoritarian history.

While having a working-class identity, Union's terraces have rejected the racism and fascism that have pervaded many of the formerly East German clubs, and the club has had impressive policies, such as not paying anything for player transfers – a policy that lasted up until recently. Developments such as these have shown Union to be as opposed to the 'business' model of football as the club was to the *Stasi* and the GDR regime in their time.

After a tough spell in the early part of the new century, Union achieved the biggest feat of its history in 2019. After reaching third place in the 2. *Bundesliga* and winning an agonising play-off against VfB Stuttgart, it managed to go up to the all-German first division.

If this were not enough, Union fans have celebrated Christmas together since 2003. They fill the stadium despite no match being played, sing carols, set off flares, and drink mulled wine – a popular German speciality. This recent tradition, which initially involved only 89 supporters but now draws around 30,000, is just another demonstration of the footballing entity's community feel, which wishes to stay faithful to a romantic notion of football. Another example of a club that has dared defy both the *Stasi* and becoming finance-driven. A club that is a true family. A true union.

SC Tasmania von 1900 Berlin eV
Cold War promotion

A quick glance at the German *Bundsliga*'s historical statistics reveals that the competition has had what has probably been the worst team ever to compete in a major European league: Sport Club Tasmania 1900 Berlin. This is a club that holds the sorry record for the fewest ever points obtained in a season (eight, to be precise), a tally complemented by the worst-ever goal difference (15 for and 108 against). This was achieved in the 1965–1966 season – the only one in which Tasmania has played in the German top flight.

Obviously, the cause of these bad stats could be traced back to the limited abilities of the Tasmania Berlin players. Yet their causes go way beyond that. It would be fair to say that the ultimate responsibility for the disastrous season lies in geopolitics; more precisely, the post-1945 Cold War, which had Berlin as a central battleground.

SC Tasmania was a club created in 1900 in today's Neukölln neighbourhood and whose name came out of a beerhall argument between sailors over the Australian island of the same denomination. Until 1965, it played in the Western Berlin regional league, which was effectively West Germany's second-tier league – as this was split into many regional contests.

When the *Bundesliga* was established in 1963, Tasmania competed with its neighbour Hertha for the honour of being picked as the Berlin team to compete in the new RFA League. But in the coming years it had to settle for playing in the regional competition which Tasmania actually won the following year.

The lowly Tasmania's history took a sharp turn in the summer of 1965. The club's West Berlin rival, Hertha, had robbed it of a place in the first *Bundesliga*, the Federal Republic of Germany (FRG)'s first division. But Hertha had violated league rules over player signings and payments, leading *Bundesliga*'s inspectors to discover a hole worth 200,000 marks in the club's accounts. It was thus blocked from promotion.

Part of the financial deficit was driven by the difficulty the club had in attracting players. This was because they would have to live in the western part of the divided Berlin: an area encircled by the wall built by communist Germany in 1961 and which isolated West Berlin from the rest of the FRG. Despite this, the *Bundesliga* did not forgive Hertha for its mismanagement and forcibly relegated the club at the end of the 1964–1965 season.

This decision had undeniable geopolitical implications as it left the top sporting competition in Federal Germany without a club in Berlin. Faced with this, the RFA authorities put pressure on the *Bundesliga* to avoid an absence of West Berliner clubs in the first division. For them, having a club from this area in the competition would help show that at least part of the Cold War-divided city remained under capitalist Germany's jurisdiction.

Thanks to such pressure, which was greatly aided by the newspapers published by the Axel Springer group – most notably *Die Welt* and the *Bild* tabloid – the German football federation chose to reverse its initial decision to hold a promotion play-off between the regional champions that had not won promotion. Instead, it simply earmarked a promotion spot for a new club from Western Berlin.

This was accompanied by the *Bundesliga* being expanded from 15 to the 18 teams it still has today. As a result, the RFA's top footballing championship had added to it the two teams promoted for their performance on the pitch – Borussia Monchengladbach and Bayern Munich – the two teams that were to be relegated at that season's end – Karlsruher SC and Schalke 04 – and the new West Berlin club.

The (latter) spot created out of Cold War needs, was initially offered to Tennis Borussia Berlin. This was the team that had won its regional league championship that same season but which was then beaten (by Bayern) during the play-off for promotion to the *Bundesliga*. But Tennis Borussia turned down the offer, as did the Berlin league's second-placed club, Spandauer SV.

Thus, the offer to take up the slot for a team representing Berlin in the *Bundesliga* fell to SC Tasmania 1900, the team that had finished the regional championship in third position. The news that Tasmania would play in the top flight reached the club only a fortnight before the competition started, giving it inadequate notice to be able to strengthen a squad that was understandably shaken by this unexpected promotion. The club even had to become fully professional, which created quite a few problems for players who in most cases had jobs outside football. Difficult conditions.

Yet the sporting entity also had a desire to represent the old German capital in the *Bundesliga*, a step of clear political meaning at a time when the ideological confrontation between the two Germanies was rife. This drove SC Tasmania – the neighbourhood club named after an Australian island created at the start of the century – to make a strong start in the league competition. Its debut on 14 August 1965 saw 81,534 people fill the Berlin Olympic Stadium, buzzing while their team beat its Karlsruher visitors 2–0. It seemed, then, that the Berlin public was beginning a courtship with the club that had taken on the mantle of representing the western part of the city. There was no sign yet of the tragedy that was about to unfold.

The love affair would soon be over. This victory was only a mirage and Tasmania would have to wait until as late as May 1966 for their second – and final – win in the league (when it defeated Borussia Neunkirchen 2–1). No less than 31 match-days had taken place in between – the longest streak any German team had had without winning a game.

This statistic is just one of many sorry records that Tasmania made during its *Bundesliga* season. Probably the most woeful is that attained when playing Borussia Monchengladbach on 15 January 1966. That game still holds the dismal record of drawing the smallest ever match attendance in the *Bundesliga*'s history: 827 spectators. It gave a barren appearance to the Olympic Stadium – a venue where five months earlier Tasmania had managed to attract 80,000 spectators.

The political gamble of giving a Berlin team promotion regardless of ability had failed. It did manage to ensure that the name Berlin was present in every weekend's football, and this helped contribute to Federal Germany's collective imagination that the city remained under its sovereignty (at least in part). Yet Tasmania's awful results week after week gave an image of the team and city that went against the aim of the politically motivated promotion.

Inevitably, Tasmania ended the 1965–1966 season in last place. Its figures were truly disastrous and included tallies that are still unsurpassed: least points in a season, least wins, most losses, the only team to not win an away match, biggest goal difference, most defeats in a row, most matches without a win …

Tasmania's figures were a real nightmare and meant that the following season, when the club was relegated to the regional league, the 1965 decision was overturned. No longer would a Berlin team be included in the *Bundesliga* for political reasons.

Consequently, in the two seasons after Tasmania's spell in the first division of Federal German soccer, there was no representative from West Berlin in the championship. This remained unchanged until the 1968–1969 season, when Hertha managed to go back up to the top.

After the nightmare of its top-tier spell, Tasmania tried to return to the top West German division, now legitimately and only based on the merit of its game. Yet this goal was never attained – despite being crowned regional champion on several occasions.

The story of the unique club ended in 1973, when financial bankruptcy brought about its demise. It left behind the memory of political promotion due to the Cold War and a season that ironically put it into the history books as the worst club to play in the *Bundesliga*.

FC St Pauli
Three times a rebel

In the traditionally sexist and homophobic footballing world, it is hard to believe that there has ever been a club headed by someone openly homosexual and an activist for LGBT rights; and who listened to club supporters and removed advertising in the stadium that its fans saw as demeaning to women.

But, yes, there has been and still is a club like that. We are talking about none other than Hamburg's Fußball-Club St Pauli, a team that has shown by example why it is a cult club for anti-fascists and others around the world.

From 2002 to 2010, Corny Littmann was chairman of St Pauli, adding to the uniqueness of the German club. As well as being the first openly gay club chairman, he is also a theatre actor: in other words, an educated and cultured man in a post normally taken by big businessmen and unscrupulous millionaires, who are sometimes sexist and homophobic to the bone.

Littmann being club head also accentuated St Pauli's anti-sexism. This was shown the year of his arrival when the magazine *Maxims* had to remove its advertising from the club's Millerntor stadium as St Pauli fans deemed it was sexist. Such a rebellion added to two unique hallmarks of the club: namely being one of the few sporting entities in the world that has incorporated both anti-fascism and anti-racism into its statutes. This went beyond the typical campaigns to eradicate racism from football, which tend to amount to no more than symbolic declarations of good intentions. Later, the club added to its statutes its opposition to sexism and homophobia.

Formally, therefore, St Pauli is a triply rebellious club: in the way conjured up by Catalan writer Maria Mercè Marçal in her poem *Divisa*:

> By chance I am grateful for three gifts: being born a woman, of low class, and of an oppressed nation: the cloudy azure of being triply rebellious.

The rebelliousness that has clustered around St Pauli is somewhat broader. Its home is the district (Sankt Pauli) from which it takes its name. This is an alternative area, including the Reeperbahn: one of the streets where prostitutes work and where there are the bars with the best atmosphere in Hamburg.

So Sankt Pauli was, then, a neighbourhood of working-class people with an intense nightlife and a substantial number of squatters who turned the area into one of the strongholds of the German squatting scene. The association between this movement and St Pauli has therefore been very close. Many squatters can be found in the Millerntor stands. Furthermore, one of the club's sporting icons was Volker Ippig, who played in goal for St Pauli from 1986 to 1992. He was much liked by fans because he lived in one of the neighbourhood's many squats. Also, Ippig had shown his political awareness by promoting solidarity events with the left-wing Sandinista National Liberation Front (FSLN) – in power in Nicaragua at the time.

Despite its remarkableness today, and its roots within the working class, St Pauli was not steeped in rebelliousness from the very beginning – being formed in 1899 and registered as a club in 1910. For instance, during Nazism, it did not stand out for taking a political stance and adapted to the Third Reich like many German workers.

Until the 1970s, St Pauli struggled through the different West German divisions. Its big sporting feat was to win promotion to the *Bundesliga* (the federal republic's top tier) in 1977 – leading to somewhat fleeting joy as the team was relegated the following season.

It must be borne in mind, however, that despite successfully gaining promotion, its stands were never very lively and only drew a few thousand fans. Indeed, it was only in the 1980s when St Pauli began its transformation into a cult local team involving alternative youth – many of communist or libertarian ideology – whose stomping ground was the Reeperbahn.

Besides the proximity of the Millerntor stadium to Hamburg's most roguish nightlife scene, another element helping its evolution was what was happening in the stands of Hamburg's other club: the almighty Hamburg SV (HSV). These were being infiltrated by the far right. Young radicals refused to share a space with neo-Nazis and racists like those at HSV so they turned to St Pauli – a club with all the ingredients to make it an example for anti-fascist football lovers.

When those young people came to the Millerntor, the stadium's atmosphere changed dramatically. Ever since, it has been usual to see alternative-styled young people; the ground became a paradise for local punks.

Instead of creating a stigma for St Pauli, the new mass of supporters helped make the club stronger and ultimately helped it achieve a legendary status. Indeed, thanks to its anti-fascist image, St Pauli soon saw the number of spectators at its stadium multiply to around 20,000.

The new supporters shaped the unique identity that defines the club today. Indeed it was they who adopted the Jolly Roger pirate flag as club symbol – one that is widely used in the club's official marketing today.

One of the first steps that the club took thanks to its new fans was to ban Nazi and far-right symbols from its ground – at a time when soccer stands in much of Europe were full of neo-Nazi activists promoting their ideology. This was the prelude to the club officially declaring itself as anti-fascist, anti-racist, and anti-sexist.

This unambiguous political stance would turn St Pauli into a unique cult club with a punk and alternative image and supporters from across the planet. This has led many music bands to mention the club in their lyrics or wear St Pauli club or supporters' T-shirts at concerts.

Such an image has also been developed through the club's use of music. When playing at home, the team goes onto the pitch to the tune of AC/DC's 'Hells Bells' and goals are celebrated with Blur's 'Song 2'.

These elements have enabled a strong bond to be created between the Hamburg club and Glasgow Celtic, which, as previously shown, is another sporting entity characterised by its political stance (in support of Irish republicanism and against sectarianism). The high point in this relationship was in November 2009 when Celtic played Hamburg SV in the Europa League group stage. Celtic supporters were then accompanied during their visit to Hamburg by a multitude of St Pauli fans who wanted to see the Glaswegians beat their arch-rival (which unfortunately did not happen).

Aware of the Celtic–St Pauli friendship, HSV fans provoked the Scottish fans by holding British flags and doing loyalist chants, a gesture that merely strengthened the bond between the two rebel clubs. For St Pauli's official centenary in 2010, it invited Celtic to play a friendly at the Millerntor.

Sankt Pauli's singularity has led to hundreds of fan clubs being set up across the world. Fan clubs which, besides supporting the Hamburg team, act as a meeting point for anti-fascists who defend St Pauli's rebel values wherever they are. An example showing the uniqueness of a club that is once, twice, three times a rebel.

Polonia Warszawa
A lesson in Polish history

On 11 November 2018, over 200,000 people joined a march in Warsaw promoted by Poland's conservative, Catholic, and nationalist government – led by the Law and Justice Party. The aim was to commemorate the centenary of Poland's declaration of independence, made on the same day in 1918. This declaration put an end to more than a century of Poland being partitioned and subjected to the empires of Russia, Prussia, and Austria.

Among the great many demonstrators in 2018 were tens of thousands of far-right Polish nationalists. These were the very ones that had been commemorating Poland's declaration of sovereignty since 2009 with a march in which ultra-nationalist, racist, and xenophobic slogans had become commonplace. The demonstrations showed how much hate had permeated Europe, which seems to have forgotten the values around which it was created.

The large extreme-right presence at the demonstration, as well as the success of previous ones, confirmed the rise of right-wing extremism in Poland, which had been plaguing the country's stadiums for decades and had turned most of its clubs' stands into platforms from which to spread divisive nationalism.

Fortunately, however, this was not the first time that Polish nationalism had used football to further its cause. In the sport's early days, it had been used by the Polish national movement but with a much nobler purpose than promoting far-right values. The aim was no less than to free the Polish nation from the grip of the empires that were ruling over it.

One of the first clubs to emerge in the part of Poland that was inside the Russian Empire was Polonia Warszawa. This was founded in 1911 out of the merger between two Warsaw student clubs: Stella and Merkury. Its key promoter was Wacław Denhoff-Czarnocki, a young nationalist activist who later pursued a military career and joined the underground Polish Military Organisation in the First World War.

It was Denhoff-Czarnocki himself who christened the new club Polonia. This was the Latin name for Poland, which gave it an unmistakably patriotic and nationalist meaning at a time when the country was occupied by the German, Russian, and Austro-Hungarian Empires.

Despite the club playing its first-ever match in November 1911 against Korona – a team of Warsaw students whom Denhoff-Czarnocki himself had played for – it was not possible for Polonia to be registered officially that year. The reason was that Tsarist Russia had forbidden registering any new sports clubs, as it saw them as covert tools for the Polish cause.

Polonia became an official club in 1915, deep into the First World War and while Germany was occupying Warsaw. The occupiers proved to be somewhat more liberal than their Russian predecessors – if only in relation to Polish sport – as they allowed new sports clubs to be registered. As a result, Polonia, a club steeped in romantic nationalist ideology, was able to become not only an official entity but a powerful symbol against Warsaw's invaders.

Its nationalist romanticism seemed clear from the club's strip. Although in its first year it played wearing a black-and-white-striped shirt, in 1912 it adopted an all-black kit. This choice was interpreted as expressing grief over the partition and occupation Poland suffered.

The actual story behind the strip chosen is more pedestrian. When buying a new outfit, the top person at the club seems not to have been able to get their hands on black-and-white-striped shirts and chose to buy all-black ones. All the same, the idea developed in the club's collective mindset that the new colour signified Poland's lack of freedom. To underline this nationalist imagery, the ebony shirt ended up combined with white shorts and red socks – two elements that unmistakably denoted the colours of the Polish flag.

For Warsaw residents, this symbolism made Polonia their favourite team – much more so than its arch local rival Legia. The latter club had been founded in 1916 – in the middle of the First World War – out of the Polish legions in the Austro-Hungarian Imperial Army. This would explain why many former soldiers who had settled in Warsaw after the war featured among its supporters.

From 1939, following the German–Soviet Pact and the start of the Second World War, Poland was once again occupied and partitioned by the regimes that replaced its former rulers: Nazi Germany and the Communist USSR.

Warsaw came under German control and its occupiers banned all local sports clubs. The measure naturally affected Polonia, which ceased to exist from 1939 to 1945. Yet, its players stayed faithful to the Polish nationalism characterising the club. They kept playing games but underground, winning the Warsaw championships in 1942 and 1943.

Putting sport to one side, some Polonia members played a more direct role in the fight against Nazi occupation. Several perished on the battlefront, in the concentration or extermination camps, in the Katyn Massacre, in the Warsaw Ghetto Uprising, and during the city rising in August 1944.

During this last episode – the uprising which lasted for 63 days but ended with a Nazi victory and Warsaw's near-obliteration – Polonia's stadium was the stage for a clandestine operation against the German forces. In this a dozen resistance fighters linked to the club were killed, which perfectly illustrates the role played by Polonia during the fight against the German occupation.

With the end of the Second World War, Polonia resumed its activities under the auspices of the Citizens' Militia – the police in Poland's new socialist republic – and on 25 March 1945 played the first game of soccer held in liberated Warsaw.

Before long, the club broke its links with the police, and yet still managed to write what is probably the most glorious page in its footballing history: winning the first free Polish championship in 1946. The league had been played in a Warsaw ravaged by Nazi barbarity and ended with Legia showing wonderful solidarity with its big local rival. Legia allowed Polonia to play its last and decisive match of the season in its stadium, as Polonia's usual home ground had been destroyed by the Nazi forces.

When implementing the communist system, the new authorities sought to erase all traces of the pre-war past. Mirroring the way in which Soviet sport was organised, Polonia was forced to affiliate with a public corporation, in this case the railway company. It was renamed Kolejarz Warszawa – 'kolejarz' meaning 'railwayman' in the local slang.

The railways had much less influence on the power structure than the army or mining industry – to which other sports clubs were linked. Hence, Polonia's sectoral association led it to lose ground. In 1952, despite the club winning the cup final against the Legia's B team – the almighty Polish People's Army club – Polonia was relegated to the second division. This ushered in a truly dire period lasting over four decades and which allowed its main urban rival to assert itself as the capital city's big team.

All the same, the club kept its identity alive and when the communist authorities allowed for modification of the names that the new regime had imposed on clubs in 1955, Polonia recovered its previous name – combining it with to its existing name. It thus became Kolejarz-Polonia.

Two years later, the club dropped any reference in its name to railways to simply become Polonia Warszawa (with Warszawa meaning Warsaw), thus reverting to its original name – the same name its founders had given it when Warsaw was still under Russian control.

The end of communism and of the advantage that clubs like Legia gained from their powerful connections meant Polonia was able to return to top-flight football and add to its trophy cabinet. It picked up the 1999–2000 league title – joining its 1946 win – and the 2001 cup – repeating its 1952 cup victory. Yet despite this, the club has spent recent decades constantly in the shadow of a Legia that took advantage of communism and the early years of capitalism to win the footballing hearts and minds of Warsaw's residents and become the Polish capital's dominant club.

A new chapter in Polonia's tragic history occurred in 2013, when the club went bankrupt and disappeared. Yet it resurfaced soon after, starting from Polish football's lowest division and propelled by fans. Their enthusiasm was akin to that of the students in occupied Poland in the autumn of 1911 who created a club akin to their romantic ideals. The result faithfully reflects Poland's last century.

Ajax Amsterdam
The Jewish identity of a Dutch club with a Greek-warrior name

The Netherlands' capital Amsterdam has historically been a significant city according to the Jewish worldview. Before the Second World War it was seen as the 'Jerusalem of the West' because of the very many Jews living there. This led Egon Erwin Kirsch, Czech journalist and International Brigades fighter in the Spanish Civil War, to characterise Amsterdam as 'the city of Jews and bicycles'. Perhaps this is why the Dutch capital was also known as '*Mokum*' – a Yiddish name that translates as 'the place' or 'the city' – a clear reference to this large urban area's relevance to the Jewish world.

With Amsterdam having such a background, it should come as no surprise that the city's leading club has had close ties with the Jewish community. Created in 1900 and named after the Greek mythological hero who fought in the Trojan War, it quickly became one of the most popular clubs locally. After little more than a decade, the team reached the top flight of Dutch football and soon began winning national titles: the cup, in 1917 and the league, a year later. From then on, the victorious Amsterdamsche Football Club Ajax became the beloved club for Jews living in East Amsterdam – the same area where the club with the Godly fighter's name had settled.

By the 1920s, Ajax was steeped in Jewish culture even though the city's Jews, of whom most were from humble backgrounds, were not a very significant part of the club's fan base (as they rarely could afford to pay the footballing entity's membership fee). In the 1930s, the Jewish facet of Ajax grew steadily. This was largely thanks to its Deer Meer stadium, which opened in 1934, having been built at the heart of the Dutch capital's Jewish quarter, which encouraged more people of this faith to attend Ajax's home matches. There was also growing fraternisation between the local Jewish people and club supporters from other parts of the city. The two would coincide in the neighbourhood hosting the stadium every other Sunday.

Ajax self-identified as being culturally tied to the city's middle and professional classes and was not a specifically Jewish club – unlike other teams in 1930s Amsterdam that were exclusively made up of players from this religion. Yet its establishment in a Jewish area, turned the club into a multi-ethnic one with a significant Jewish presence.

Nazi Germany's invasion of the Netherlands, in May 1940, brought the growth in importance that Jews were acquiring in Ajax to a standstill. The occupation encouraged the darkest side of the Dutch to flourish. Many embraced National Socialist ideology, as illustrated by the country having Europe's second largest Nazi Party – the National Socialist Movement in the Netherlands (NSB) – of which only its German equivalent was bigger.

On 15 September 1940, shortly after Holland was occupied, a decree was passed that forbade Jews from doing any sports. On 23 October, the group was also banned from being members of sports clubs. Jews living in the Netherlands could therefore not be involved in any sport.

Some clubs with a notable Jewish fan base, including Sparta Rotterdam, had pre-empted the decision and revoked club membership to all Jews and banned them from attending the stadium prior to 23 October. For the club, it was a matter of keeping the new occupying authorities happy and acting before anything was formally declared.

Ajax followed Nazi orders, expelling its Jewish members. Many of these would become victims of the Holocaust, which claimed the lives of 100–140,000 Dutch Jews. Among those murdered was Eddy Hamel, one of Ajax's greatest players in the 1920s. He died in Auschwitz in April 1943.

It might seem contradictory that Ajax's Jewish identity was not formed until the post-war years and after most of Amsterdam's Jewish population had been annihilated. It was precisely in the 1950s and 1960s that Ajax was labelled a 'Jewish club' as an insult by its rivals. When playing its Feyenoord rivals in Rotterdam, the most extreme local fans would meet the capital's team supporters with the chant 'Here comes the Ajax train from Auschwitz' or by making a chilling 'ssssss' sound – mimicking that of the Nazi gas chambers that killed millions of Jews.

Despite not being a Jewish club and having few people from this faith in its ranks – only because Jews made up a small percentage of the local population – Ajax reacted to provocations by proudly embracing its Jewish identity. Its reputation was ratified when Jaap Van Praag, a Jew who had survived the Holocaust by going into hiding, became club chairman. As club head from 1964 to 1978, he decisively contributed to building the great Ajax team that ruled over the Old Continent in the early 1970s – when Ajax won three consecutive European Cups (the predecessor to the Champions League title). A splendid player in that team was Johan Cruyff, who came out of the Ajax youth academy and became the best player of that time. Cruyff has traditionally been seen in club circles as 'pro-Jewish'.

Ajax's financial strength, part-aided by Jewish individuals, was a key ingredient in the Amsterdam club's European successes, alongside its 'total football' playing style. The growing association between Ajax and Judaism led its fans to take this to be one of the club's hallmarks. Thus, they cheered on their players with cries of '*Joden! Joden!*' (Jews! Jews!) and displayed Jewish symbols openly in the stadium; particularly the Star of David.

Over the years, even the most feared Ajax hooligans, the F-Side, embraced Jewishness as a key part of the club's personality. Jewish symbols and the Israeli flag became signatory elements used by Ajax fans – alongside the club and city's traditional colours and the face of the warrior the club's name came from.

These developments created a contradiction for those of a Jewish background who supported Ajax. On the one hand, they were delighted to see how the Jewish strand grew within the club's identity. However, they also regretted the trivialisation of the Jewish cause in the stands and the way Ajax's identity fuelled anti-Semitic chants inside the grounds their team played in.

The stadium where the most hatred was expressed towards Ajax's Jewishness unquestionably was, and still is, that of Feyenoord Rotterdam. Besides making the sound of the gas chambers, more contemporary anti-Semitic taunts have been added, greatly hurting Ajax's Jewish fans, and leading them to stop attending their beloved team's matches. Common examples include 'Hamas, Hamas, Jews to the gas' and 'We're going on a Jew hunt': both demonstrating the extreme verbal viciousness which the stands of Dutch stadiums can stoop to when Ajax is their opponent.

Such a situation led a club chairperson at the start of the new millennium to try to drop the club's Jewish identity by encouraging fans to cheer '*Goden!*' (Gods!) instead of '*Joden!*' (Jews!). It was an unsuccessful proposal as it involved rewriting the club's history – one that has been closely linked with Amsterdam's Jewish community.

Hakoah Vienna
Vienna's Jewish power

One of the first steps taken by the German Third Reich after annexing Austria in March 1938 was to ban all Jewish organisations – by which Hitler showed his determination to persecute Jews by eliminating all organisations that could act for them. Among those banned, was Sport Club Hakoah Wien (Hakoah Vienna), which had become an icon for Austrian Jews.

The decision to outlaw it was brought in with immediate effect. All the matches Hakoah was to play in Austrian football's second flight's 1938–1939 season were declared null and void. The club was disbanded and several of its players were tried and murdered by the Nazi authorities.

The German authorities outlawed the club due to the symbolism it had picked up over the years as an embodiment of Vienna's Jewish community. Indeed the outfit had been created by two prominent Austrian Zionists: writer Fritz Löhner and dentist Herman Körner. Their aim was to put into practice Max Nordau's *muskeljudentum* (muscular Judaism), which wanted Jews to do sport (or some other physical activity) to develop the mental and physical strength to change their traditional group image and achieve Zionism's goals.

The setting up, in 1909, of Sport Club Hakoah, which had as its aim 'to give Jewish youth the chance to engage in physical exercise as conscious Jews' defied the Austrian sporting authorities of the era. They banned practising Jews from joining the existing sports clubs.

The name chosen for the new club was quite a statement in itself. 'Hakoah' means 'power' (or 'strength') in Hebrew – making the name clearly associable with Max Nordau's 'muscular' doctrine. And if any doubt remained over the entity's Jewish connections, its crest centrally featured the Star of David.

Despite Hakoah being a multi-sports club, its best-known section was its football team, which soon won the hearts and minds of the thousands of Jews who lived in Vienna at the time. But backing for the club was not limited to the Austrian capital. Being one of the first overtly Jewish sporting entities in the world earned it ardent support from prominent figures of the same faith or who had Jewish roots. For example, the eminent writer Franz Kafka, who had been born to Ashkenazi Jewish parents in Prague when the city was part of the Austro-Hungarian Empire, became a devout fan of the Viennese club, despite being an avowed atheist.

Hakoah's popularity grew steadily among the Jewish community thanks to the club's successes in the early 1920s. After gaining promotion to the Austrian first division, it came runner's up in 1922. This turned out to be the prelude to its first and only championship title in 1925. This was a momentous triumph. For the first time, a Jewish team was crowned Austrian champions.

Just before, Hakoah had shown its sporting prowess by becoming the first foreign team to beat an English club in a match on British soil. This happened during Hakoah's visit to Upton Park in September 1923, when it humiliated its West Ham hosts 5–0. This historic milestone stirred the Jewish community's pride across the world; and it underlined the symbolic side of Hakoah, not just for Austrian Jews but those from elsewhere.

International admiration for the Viennese team led the club to receive many invitations to do sports tours in different parts of the world. A tour worth highlighting was one it did to the United States – where there is a large Jewish population – in 1926. There, the team played a series of friendlies which aroused great interest; as shown by the match against a team of US league players, which drew 50,000 spectators.

The wonderful reception Hakoah players received in the United States, together with the winds of persecution that could be seen nearing on the Old Continent led some of the Vienna club's top players to stay on in New York for fear of their safety.

Among the footballers who chose to settle in the US was Béla Guttmann, a Hungarian Jew and one of the team's biggest stars. He ended up being a central promoter of New York Hakoah, a club created in the image of its Viennese namesake, and which played in the American Soccer League. In 1929, it won the National Challenge Cup (the US soccer cup) – a title demonstrating the quality of the Jewish players in the new club.

Once his North American experience was over, Béla Guttmann chose to go back to the Austrian capital, where he played for the Viennese Hakoah in his last season as a player. Straight after hanging up his boots, however, Guttmann took charge of the team and began a successful coaching career that would take him – over two decades later – to win two European Cups for the Portuguese Benfica. After being sacked there, he predicted that the club would not be the continental champion again for a hundred years, and the curse still haunts the Lisbon team which, since, has lost no less than eight European finals.

After Hakoah Vienna's return from its 1926 US tour, it had to face some particularly turbulent years in European society and politics. These, and the team's loss of talent to the US, greatly weakened Hakoah. From 1928 to 1938, it was a 'yo-yo club' (constantly going up and down); playing several times in Austria's second division.

Despite its reduced ability to compete, admiration for the club remained intact and thousands of fans would flock to its stadium in what was, in the context of Nazism's growing support among Austrians, an unambiguously political act.

It was Hakoah's unmistakable Jewish symbolism that led it to be summarily banned after the *Anschluss* – Nazi Germany's annexation of Austria. This was not the only repressive measure suffered by the club. Some of its key players were imprisoned and then executed. Others were deported or were killed by the Nazis in the concentration camps they were held in. Among those murdered were the remarkable Max Scheuer and Ali Schonfeld, who played at international level, but the list is much longer and includes other players, non-football sportspersons, and club administrative staff. Due to the post-annexation persecutions, some players for the disbanded Hakaoh Vienna opted to emigrate to Palestine – then a British colony – where they created Hakoah Tel Aviv in accordance with the Zionist principles that shaped the Viennese club.

In April 1945, the Soviet Red Army freed the Austrian capital from the Nazis. The nightmare suffered by the Jewish people was over but after having paid an immense price. Out of the nearly 200,000 Jews living in Vienna before Nazism, only 6,000 survived. That June, a group of Jewish Holocaust survivors decided to start up the Hakoah football club again. It began its new journey in the same Austrian second division that Nazism had purged it from in 1938.

During the early years of this new chapter, Hakoah was able to revive the original enthusiasm that had made it a symbol for Jews across the planet, and it once again managed to win promotion to the top tier. All the same, the club ended up disbanding in 1950 after a major controversy within the club over the decision to accept players of other faiths. Gone was a symbol of the Jewish community and a reminder of the Nazi repression in Vienna.

Five decades later – in 2000 – a group of Viennese Jews longing to recreate Hakoah's glory days, decided to buy the land where the club was once based to promote a new Viennese Jewish club. Thus, Maccabi Wien was created and was playing in the amateur flights of Austrian football. This was a far cry from the heights its predecessor once reached – including being the 1925 Austrian champions. In those times, Hakoah was clearly Vienna's true Jewish power.

Christiania SC
The team that'll never smoke alone

Christiana is undoubtedly one of Europe's most unique places. It was originally a Danish army barracks that stopped being used after the Second World War and was left deserted in 1967. It is now a truly free 'town'. It is a district in Copenhagen which has proclaimed independence from Denmark and has its 34 hectares governed according to the principles of equality and total freedom.

The neighbourhood's remarkable history began in September 1971. Then, after the former military land had been neglected for four years, a group of neighbours from the Christianshavn neighbourhood chose to pull down the fences around it so their children would have somewhere to play. This was the first act by which citizens recovered the area. Then, most of the families involved in liberating the space chose to settle there as a self-governed community. Months later, Freetown Christiania was founded.

During the wild 1970s, the self-proclaimed independent Freetown attracted hippies, squatters, and people committed to anarchism or collectivism – in which individual needs were subordinate to those of the collective. Nearly a thousand self-governed people lived together, according to a liberty-based ideology. A new model of society was attempted. Among Christiania's peculiarities, alongside practising collectivism and free love, was a policy that began as a demand from the alternative movement: freedom to take drugs.

Christiania was a space where drug use was permitted, which turned Freetown into a big attraction for its Danish neighbours. The association between the neighbourhood and marihuana and other soft drugs was so strong that Christiania started being popularly known in Copenhagen as the Green Light District. Its main thoroughfare – lined with bars and alternative trading – was nicknamed Pusher Street: a name that does not make it too difficult to guess the main occupation of many of those frequenting the road.

As part of the Christiania inhabitants' quest to build a truly independent 'town', they produced their own flag: red with three yellow circles. The 'town' even acquired its own currency: the *Løn* (the Danish word for 'wage'). All the same, this has never managed to replace the (Danish) Krone in the area – despite efforts from those running Freetown.

Something was missing from the free state, flag, and currency equation: a football team to epitomise the 'town'. This was overcome by creating the Christianshavn Soccer Club (CSC) in 1982. There were naturally some doubts expressed about whether a free and alternative community like Christiania's, in which libertarian and anti-authoritarian ideas prevailed, could handle setting up a football club at a time when the sport was immersed in the unstoppable commodification process that dominates it today. Even so, the CSC easily became well-established, as it came out of the desire that young people in Freetown and the adjoining Christianshavn neighbourhood had to play football while representing their own community.

In its first phase, beginning in the early 1980s, the club was not able to formally adopt Freetown's name and so had to include the name of Christiania's neighbouring area in its official name. This was out of fear that the Danish Football Federation would prevent a club with Christiania in its name from becoming a member due to the federation's right-wing conservatism and fears over Freetown's left-wingers – a perception that accurately reflected the conservatism of the official footballing hierarchy at the time. The club was therefore called Christianshavn Soccer Club until 1994.

Despite its name, CSC was unmistakably the Freetown Christiania team. Eleven years later, it could boast of being one of the most representative clubs in the Danish capital. Its squad proudly wore the red and yellow of Freetown's flag, accompanied by a crest featuring a rainbow – one of the most emblematic symbols of Christiania's diverse, egalitarian, and anti-authoritarian identity.

CSC was not seen as a rarity by Christiania's other inhabitants because it was run in a fully democratic way – like Freetown itself. This is shown by its heads mostly being from the same area and conducting themselves according to the same standards adopted by Christiania's fellow citizens.

A simple example of such is that since the very beginnings of the club, one of its defining features has been some of its members' regular cannabis smoking, which has even been customary in the changing rooms before matches. Maybe this explains why CSC spent its early years languishing in the Danish eighth division.

In the 1990s, the club received a big boost when it won a long-awaited promotion. This led to it leaving the Meadow of Peace: the stadium where it had been playing its home matches and whose distinct name captured the pacifist values prevailing in the free neighbourhood. The club moved to Kløvermarken: a former camp accommodating German refugees in 1945 and that was turned into a sports venue later.

CSC's good progress in the 1990s came to an abrupt halt in 1994 when it was heavily punished for its players' violent conduct and threats, which led to the club being disbanded. The club was re-founded, this time being able to adopt the name *Christiania* Sports Club. That way it kept its CSC initials while at the same time incorporating in its name a reference to Freetown it wished to act for.

The new CSC began its journey in the eighth flight of Danish football. Yet it decided to implement a daring marketing and communication policy aimed at highlighting its links with the Christiania Freetown. This, by then, had become one of Copenhagen's legendary and iconic tourist attractions – being visited annually by nearly a million tourists.

The new club incorporated in its crest the symbols that had appeared in 1982: the Freetown flag and rainbow. But it also added a white dove to underline its staunch pacifism. It was in this new era that the club adopted two of its most successful and characteristic slogans: first, 'You'll never smoke alone!' – an adaptation of the famous line sung by Liverpool and Glasgow Celtic, and which has become the Christiania club's anthem; second, 'Joint the club!' using a play on words and a reference to cannabis-cigarettes to encourage club membership.

Clearly Christiania Sports Club has flaunted the use of marihuana, which has been widely puffed in the stands and dressing room. At least that was the case until recently, when manager and former professional player Michael Ruch Svendsen decided to ban joints in the changing room due to the growing demands for the club to be competitive.

Although this measure limited the club's 'stoner' identity, the fact is that Christiania has remained true to its libertarian and anti-authoritarian principles. A good example of this is the derby regularly played by the Freetown team against the club that became its main rival: Politiets IF – the team of the police.

Matches between CSC and the police club also have a special flavour for Freetown residents, probably because the police have not been welcome there for decades. Yet these games have not usually been accompanied by conflict off the pitch. The simple reason for that is that few Politiets IF fans go to see their team in their rival's heartland.

Despite staying true to its roots, Christiania Sports Club has not escaped the changes that Freetown has undergone. As well as having prohibited cannabis smoking in the dressing room, the club hopes to build a new stadium and become semi-professional. Such ideas have been encouraged by the different sponsorship deals the club has had. These have included that with the Danish Hummels firm which, since 2012, has produced the club kit and wants to turn Christiania into a Danish St Pauli: a professional club with an unorthodox rebel identity. Meanwhile, Christiania's fans will continue to enjoy the football while smoking one joint after another. For good reason, their team is one that'll never smoke alone.

5
The Balkans

Sloboda Tuzla's 1970–1971 team, with a red star and hammer and sickle on their crest, which lost the Marshal Tito Cup final against Red Star Belgrade in May 1971

GNK Dinamo Zagreb
A mirror to present-day Croatia

Few clubs sum up the recent history of their country as well as Croatia's Dinamo Zagreb Citizens' Football Club (Građanski nogometni klub Dinamo Zagreb). Founded on 9 June 1945, just after the Partisan triumph in the region in the Second World War, the new Dinamo carried on the legacy of the previous Zagreb clubs. The new government decreed them banned due to their complicity with the fascist Croat state under Ante Pavelić, which had been a staunch ally of the Nazi occupiers in Yugoslavia.

Those two clubs were Građanski – the Croatian Citizens' Sports Club – and HAŠK – the Croatian Academic Sports Club (linked to the University of Zagreb). The latter outfit had been founded in 1903 by several students wanting to oppose the growing Hungarianisation of Croatian society back then stemming from the Austro-Hungarian Empire's rule over its territory. True to its will to embody Croats' desire for national freedom, HAŠK took on the red, white, and gold colours that symbolised the Croat provinces.

Građanski, the other Zagreb sports club in the early 20th century, had been set up in 1911 to embody Croat national identity by opposing participation by Croatian teams in the Austro-Hungarian competitions. In no time, Građanski became the Zagreb working-class club of choice, being counterposed to HAŠK, which, given its relationship with the city's university circles, had more support among the more affluent classes. Građanski's links with the grassroots nationalist movement became apparent when its stadium was opened by Stjepan Radić, the Croatian Peasant Party's leader imprisoned for his nationalist activity; and when a crest was adopted that reproduced the characteristic chequered red and white Croatian colours.

The Austro-Hungarian Empire disintegrated at the end of the First World War, and the first Yugoslavia was created: the Kingdom of Serbs, Croats, and Slovenes – thus uniting the South Slavs (which is what the name Yugoslavia translates as). From 1923, both Građanski and HAŠK played in the new Yugoslav competitions, where the Zagreb clubs were regular contenders to win the league title. Indeed, they won it on several occasions.

Građanski's success had a European dimension. The same year the new state's league was up and running, the Zagreb club travelled to play in Catalonia and the Basque Country, where it beat both Barcelona and Athletic Bilbao. In 1936, it earned the honour of being the first European-continental team to beat the legendary Liverpool FC.

The Zagreb club's participation in the Yugoslav tournaments came to an end after the Nazi invasion of the Kingdom in the Second World War. The new political situation led all sporting events to be suspended except for those organised by the new independent Croatia; a puppet state run by the Nazis' local allies and consisting of most of present-day Croatia (bar the then-Italian-annexed Dalmatia) and the whole of Bosnia and Herzegovina. Građanski and HAŠK joined the new Croatian league that held championships between 1941 and 1944, for which only two full seasons were played.

It was precisely the Zagreb clubs' decision to play in the fascist independent Croatian league during the war that led to their disbanding once Tito's Partisan guerrillas were victorious and created the new Socialist Federal Republic of Yugoslavia. The only Croatian sports club that was spared dissolution for complicity with Nazism was Hajduk Split, which, as discussed in the following chapter, refused to play in the fascist Croatian league and had during the whole war a political stance closely aligned to that of the Partisans.

Curiously Građanski and HAŠK's last game was a local derby between the two clubs that ended in a 2–2 draw. Two months later, the new Dinamo Zagreb was created, inheriting Građanski's colours. Soon afterwards, the legacy behind the new club became deeper when it acquired HAŠK's stadium – the legendary Maksimir – which has hosted the home matches of the leading Zagreb club to date.

Shortly after Dinamo entered the new Socialist Yugoslavia's sporting competitions, it established itself as one of the new state's major clubs. This was alongside Hajduk and the two biggest Belgrade teams: Partizan and Red Star, which were also formed after the creation of the federal republic.

Thus began the successful history of the Croatian capital's club. It won the first of four Yugoslavian league championships in 1948 and became the first Balkan team to win a cup in Europe – after overcoming Leeds United in the final of the Fairs Cup (later the UEFA Europa League Cup) in 1967.

Despite the policy of 'brotherhood and unity' espoused by the Tito regime, nationalism spread within Croatian society. With that, Dinamo evolved into being a sporting icon fully identified with the Croatian national cause. Thus, the club chose to modify its crest in 1969, reviving the Građanski emblem in the colours of the Croatian flag, yet adding a red star – obliged to do so in keeping with official Yugoslavian identity at the time.

The association between Dinamo and Croatian nationalism strengthened in the 1980s. The most extreme fan group in the Maksimir, the Bad Blue Boys, was created in 1986. It unabashedly identified with the most extreme Croat nationalism.

On 13 May 1990, with Yugoslavia in the throes of disintegration, the same stadium was the setting for one of the preludes to the war that would ravage the Balkans for a decade. In a match between Dinamo and Red Star, the supporters from Belgrade made chants claiming Croatia as Serbian and threatening Franjo Tudjman – leader of the nationalist Democratic Union of Croatia. This was the dominant Croatian political force and days earlier had won a clear victory locally in the first multi-party elections held in Yugoslavia since the end of the Second World War.

The Serbians' slogans angered the Bad Blue Boys and the event degenerated into a pitched battle. It would be a simple preamble to the conflict that the same people – this time wearing military uniforms instead of team shirts and scarves – would wage on the battlefield months later.

The clashes at the match were brutal and went down in history. This was not least because Dinamo captain Zvonimir Boban kneed a policeman who was attacking a Croatian fan during a fight on the pitch. (Ironically, the officer turned out to be a Bosnian Muslim). The Bad Blue Boys protected Boban from the fury of the police, turning him into a true national hero. The player's act earned him a six-month suspension from the Yugoslavian Football Association and legal prosecution. All the same, the footballer justified his actions afterwards, saying: 'Here I was, a public face prepared to risk life, career, and everything that fame could have brought, all because of one ideal, one cause; the Croatian cause'.

That 13 May is etched on Dinamo fans' memory as for many of them it marked the beginning of a violent struggle for national freedom. That is why today there is a monument at the Maksimir gates to commemorate the young fans from the north stand who, from that day, took up arms to fight for a free and independent Croatia.

In 1990, when Croat nationalism won its first elections, Dinamo removed the red star from its crest and began using only the colours of the Croatian flag. This was the prelude to a more dramatic change. In June 1991, after Tudjman proclaimed the new Croatian state, the club was renamed Građanski, as the replacement of this original name by 'Dinamo' was seen as having been imposed by the Yugoslavian communist author-ities. The 'new' Građanski left the Yugoslavian league and immediately joined the football competitions in the recently proclaimed independent Croatia.

As encouraged by President Tudjman, the club made a further change to its name, becoming Croatia Zagreb (CZ). The capital's club became the biggest force in the post-indepen-dence Croatian competitions, establishing an overwhelming dominance over its regional rivals.

Despite most of CZ's supporters being strongly national-istic, as well as the club's triumphs, they never accepted the new name, and forced the club to go back to its historic name, Dinamo Zagreb, in 2000. Since then, Dinamo has continued to build on its history of successes in Croatian football, which it has dominated absolutely. It is a history closely tied to that of its country. A Croatian history.

HNK Hajduk Split
The unconquerable Dalmatians

On 23 July 2011, Barcelona opened its pre-season friendlies with a match in the Croatian town of Split on the beautiful Adriatic shoreline. For the reigning European champions, the game was a discreet affair. Yet for Hajduk Split, the home team, it was everything, as it was celebrating its centenary. A hundred years of rebelliousness and disobedience had shaped the Croatian club, making it one of the teams with the most tumultuous histories in Europe.

Indeed, the exceptional nature of Hajduk was displayed from its very beginnings. The outfit was 'founded' on 13 February 1911 in the legendary beerhall U Fleku, in the centre of Prague – almost a thousand kilometres from the Dalmatian coast in Croatia. This came during a heated discussion among a group of Croat students who had just witnessed a derby between Spart and Slavia – the two main clubs in what is now the Czech capital.

At the time, Prague and Split were both in the Austro-Hungarian Empire. Czech nationalism was commonplace in Czech cities at the beginning of the 20th century and this was reflected in its major soccer clubs. The young Croats decided they also wanted to use sport to defy the occupying power.

Their intentions were made clear by their choice of club name. In the Balkan imaginary, a *'hajduk'* is a romanticised hero who stands up to invader authorities, robbing the rich and sharing out the spoils among the poor. They are a kind of nationalist Robin Hood.

Despite the derogatory meaning that the Ottomans and Austro-Hungarians tried to give to '*hajduks*', those of the 17th to 19th century – guerrilla groups fighting foreign powers – were very popular among local people. This was so with Andrijica Simic, a Croat *hajduk* who was received in Split by an adoring crowd that wanted to pay homage to the warrior's gallantry after a lengthy imprisonment in an Austrian jail.

In case putting Hajduk in the Split club's name was not a clear enough statement, Hajduk founders added 'HNK' (the Croatian initials for Croatian Football Club) and adopted chequered red and white – the country's colours – for the central element in its crest. HNK Hajduk's worldview was from the very beginning closely tied to a rising Croatian nationalism. It was particularly close to the nationalist '*puntari*' faction, led by the People's Party, which called for uniting the two Croat provinces that were ruled by the Austro-Hungarian Empire: Dalmatia, including Split; and Croatia-Slavonia, which included Zagreb. Hajduk's nationalism led it to openly clash with the imperial government, which did not want to hear of a merger of such provinces.

As mentioned, the break-up of the Austro-Hungarian Empire after the First World War was followed by the formation of the Kingdom of Serbs, Croats, and Slovenes – the pan-Slavic dream of uniting the South Slavs held by a significant wing of the Serbian, Croatian, and Slovenian nationalist movements. It was this new state's league that Hajduk joined in 1923.

The Croatian-nationalist nature of the club was again revealed on 6 January 1929. That day, King Alexander I established a dictatorship that abolished the constitution, changed the Kingdom's name to Yugoslavia, and introduced a

Belgrade-centred policy of national unification and standard-isation. Croat nationalism decidedly opposed this, triggering repression in which Hajduk was forced to change the initials at the start of its name. It went from being a 'Croatian Football Club' (HNK) to being a 'Yugoslavian Football Club' (JNK). The nuance was loaded with symbolism.

Despite the club's close relationship with Croatia's national liberation movement, the most glorious chapters in the club's recent history were written during the Second World War after Nazi German and fascist Italian troops occupied Yugoslavia in April 1941, following the country's declaration of neutrality. Several fractions of Croatian nationalism collaborated with the invaders to usher in the pro-Nazi Independent State of Croatia (NDH). Yet Split was absorbed into Mussolini's Italy – like most of the Dalmatian region. Consequently the Italians suggested Hajduk play in the Italian championship but making participation conditional on the club adopting a new name without any pro-Croatian connotations. Staying true to the club's identity and indomitable spirit, the heads of the Dalmatian club flatly turned down the offer.

When fascism fell in Italy in 1943, Split was briefly liberated by the Partisans. Yet the Nazis re-occupied the city in a counter-offensive, handing it to the NDH. The people of Split had enormous misgivings about this. They were resentful towards the *Ustaša*-led government in Zagreb for allying with the Nazis and allowing the partition of Croatia. Thus it was decided not to cooperate. Hajduk showed its rejection of Ante Pavelić's puppet regime by declining to play in the Croatian tournaments – in the same way the club had done to playing in the Italian league.

Split's Croatian nationalists and the Hajduk club were a lot closer to the communist Partisans led by Josip Broz – better known as 'Tito' – than they were to the *Ustaša* government. For that reason, the club's players left Split for the Adriatic island of Vis, where the Partisans' headquarters were located. It was there that Hajduk went back onto a pitch, to play a Partisan team (on 7 May 1944 – Split's patron saint's day). From then, the club took up the Partisan cause itself and played (symbolic) matches along the Italian Adriatic coast against teams made up of soldiers from the Allied armies. In these, Hajduk was treated as the official team of the (Partisan) National Liberation Army of Yugoslavia. To formalise its new role, the army's initials – NOVJ – were added to its name.

The matches Hajduk played against military teams included one in Bari on 23 September 1944 against a pick of players from the British army, which ended in a 7–2 victory for the Brits. As well as being memorable for its big goal difference – a surprise as Hajduk had won almost all its matches up until then – it notably drew over 40,000 spectators – an attendance exceeded by almost no other match during the Second World War.

After the Partisans liberated Split on 26 October 1944, Hajduk was able to exact its revenge. In a match played just after Christmas 1944, which it could now play in its home city, it narrowly beat the same British military team that had defeated it in Bari. The setting was a Split that had been made the provisional Croatian capital, while Yugoslavia's full liberation was pending. The city had become a target for a Nazi German navy that was lashing out as Germany's war effort was in its death throes.

To underline Hajduk's ideological affinity with the Partisan movement, the club added a red star to its crest and wore this during matches. In 1945, when Split had been liberated and the war was in its final months, the club started a Mediterranean tour that took it to Egypt, Palestine, Malta, Syria, and Lebanon to play military and civilian teams.

In Lebanon, Hajduk took on a team picked from the French army stationed in the country. It was on such an occasion that Charles de Gaulle, head of the Provisional Government of the French Republic, gave the club one of the most prestigious titles of its history: Honorary Team of Free France. Through this distinction, De Gaulle wished to acknowledge the Split club's efforts in the fight to free Europe from the grip of Nazism and fascism.

The Partisans won the war, and the Socialist Federal Republic of Yugoslavia was formed, with Tito as President. He advised Hajduk to move to Belgrade and become the official club of the Yugoslavian People's Army. The answer from the unconquerable Split club was a typical 'no'. Hajduk was staying at home. Instead, the army had a new club created for it: Partizan Belgrade, which incorporated in its name that of those who had fought for freedom. Tito, whose father was Croatian, remained supportive of Hajduk despite the club's refusal, and it was one of the few clubs not to be disbanded by the post-war communist authorities.

Despite Hajduk's close Partisan links and having the red star on its crest, the club soon aroused distrust inside the new communist power structure. The *Torcida* supporters' group that emerged in 1950 – making it one of the first in Europe – was seen as having a worldview close to Croat nationalism.

Over the years, the pro-Croatian leanings of club fans became increasingly noticeable. Tito's death, in 1980, revealed the weaknesses of the Yugoslavian project and sparked national tensions that would peak with the Balkan Wars that exploded in the 1990s.

The slope the federal republic was now on was clear in the Croatian stadiums in 1990. As well as the pivotal pitched battle during the match between Dinamo Zagreb and Red Star Belgrade, a match in Split between Hajduk and Partizan

Belgrade saw the death of Yugoslavia acted out when several home fans went onto the pitch and set fire to the federal flag.

On 8 May 1991, Hajduk won its last Yugoslavian cup, beating Red Star Belgrade in another match filled with tension that went beyond the sporting variety. A month later, Croatia proclaimed independence and Hajduk removed the red star from its crest and brought back its original chequered Croatian one.

The Split club has since then competed in the new Croat league, but with its rebelliousness still intact. This is now expressed in opposition to Zagreb centralism as embodied by Hajduk's bitter but close enemy Dinamo. It has kept a strong rivalry thanks to its own history and its unfading non-conformist spirit: one that has helped the Split club remain the unconquerable Dalmatians.

FK Sloboda Tuzla
A working-class team for a working-class city

Tuzla is a unique city. Thought to be one of the oldest in Europe, it has always been an example of diversity. The hills surrounding Tuzla look out over mosques and Catholic and Orthodox churches which all still coinhabit in its old town. All the same, it has not been the minarets or steeples that have most decisively contributed to building the Bosnian city's identity. More vital to this have been the chimneys of the many factories in the working-class hub that was the epicentre of the social revolt that shook Bosnia-Herzegovina in February 2014.

Tuzla is the country's third most populous city after Sarajevo – the federal capital – and Banja Luka – the capital of the Republika Srpska region; and it has always been industrial, having a large proletarian population that has given it a national image of being a 'red' and militant area.

True to such an image was the workers' occupation that took place in 2014 in the Dita detergent factory: one that was once collectivised and jointly owned by workers and the state, and now had its future threatened due to privatisation.

Companies like Dita in a range of industries were the true symbols of proletarian Tuzla throughout much of the 20th century. As was also the sports club which held the affection of the town's working class: Fudbalski Klub Sloboda Tuzla. A team whose name literally meant 'freedom' and which for decades brought together in its crest a five-pointed red star, the hammer and sickle, and an industrial gear wheel. These symbolised the sporting entity's working-class nature – in case there was any doubt.

In fact, the history of Sloboda Tuzla is as old as the city's communist movement, which initially took the form of the Socialist Labour Party of Yugoslavia. Both club and party date back to 1919.

Since sport was then a priority for communists, one of the first decisions made at a conference of the new party in Tuzla was to bring about the forming of a new sports club at a particularly crucial time for the city. The First World War forced it to be incorporated into the new Kingdom of Serbs, Croats, and Slovenes – commonly known as the Kingdom of Yugoslavia; the name which, as previously mentioned, would be officially adopted in 1929.

Owing to this decision, the Maxim Gorky Workers' Sports Club was created in late October 1919. It was named after the Russian socialist poet Maxim Gorky, pointing to the influence of the 1917 Russian Revolution on the international communist movement.

The new workers' sports club had several different sections, most notably its football club FK Gorky – the forerunner to Sloboda. During its first years, its home matches were played at a venue popularly known as the 'Communist Ground' and its fans were all workers who sympathised with such politics. Even so, its most unique aspect was the ethnic diversity of its base, which contrasted with the other Tuzla clubs at the time. Most notably among the latter were Zrinjski, which drew its support from the Croatian community; Obilić, which had the same among Serbs; Bura, supported by the Bosnian-Muslim population; and Maccabi, rooted among the city's Jews.

Unlike these football teams, FK Gorky defined itself as a pluri-national and multicultural club, accepting members from all national and religious communities. It strictly followed the communist ethos which called for unity between workers regardless of their specific ethnic or religious background.

As a communist club, Gorky fell victim to government policies under the Yugoslavian monarchy in 1920 and in the following years outlawed all Marxist-Leninist activities. Consequently, a Yugoslavian court ruled that the Gorky workers' club be banned, an order some of its members disobeyed. This led them to be jailed by the authorities.

The banning of the Maxim Gorky Workers' Sports Club sparked a new communist sporting entity to be set up in 1924. It was called Hajduk after the Slavic guerrilla fighters that had also inspired the similarly named club in the Croatian city of Split. The new sports society had a rather short life as it was banned almost from day one.

Tuzla's communists had to wait until 1927 before creating a new club that could revive the Gorky's club spirit. On 20 November that year, the Sloboda Cultural Sports Society was formed. This had sections ranging from footballing – its central attraction – to amateur theatre and music – including choral singing. Perhaps unsurprisingly the Sloboda footballing section stood out for using red and black (the libertarian colours) for its strip. This was a clear statement of its principles.

Although formally this was a new club, FK Sloboda saw itself to be continuing the legacy and activity of Gorky. This is why the club dates its official founding back to 1919 – the same year the Maxim Gorky Workers' Sports Club was established.

All the same, it should be noted that there were significant differences between both clubs: the main one being that Sloboda was led by social democrats unlike the Communist-Party-led Gorky. Despite this change, Communist Party members still massively supported a club they felt to be Tuzla's only workers' team.

This distinctly left-wing proletarian past allowed FK Sloboda to avoid being affected by Marshall Tito's restructuring of Yugoslavian clubs after the Partisans seized power at the end of the Second World War. It was also the reason the city's team could keep its historic name. Meanwhile, a large majority of Yugoslavian teams, which revolved around ethnic and religious identity and sometimes had been openly complicit with Nazism, dropped off the chart when the Socialist Federal Republic was created.

In the Tito era, Sloboda enjoyed its golden era. It regularly played in the Yugoslavian first division and even qualified for the UEFA Cup tournament in the 1977–1978 season. In the latter, however, it was knocked out in the knockout stage by (the Spanish) Unión Deportiva Las Palmas, which thrashed the Bosnians 5–0 when playing at home in the Canary Islands. This rendered useless the Sloboda's narrow 4–3 win in the first leg.

The Tuzla team won the Yugoslavian second-division championship in 1959 and the same tier in the Bosnian League in 2014. However, its biggest success was reaching the Marshal Tito Cup final in 1971 – even though it ended up losing this to Red Star Belgrade – one of Yugoslavia's footballing giants.

Sloboda's decline began with the unravelling of Yugoslavia. Indeed, the disappearance of Tito and the Partisans' socialist and federal republic was watched with horror from Tuzla – one of its most multi-ethnic cities and one with the largest slice of the population self-identifying as simply Yugoslav (and not according to any minority-national or communalist identification).

Ethnic diversity was one of Tuzla's hallmarks even during the Bosnian War years – from 1992 to 1995. The city managed to survive these while preserving its diverse nature – just, and not without conflicts. After the war ended, Sloboda resumed its sporting activity and did so by playing in the Bosnian League – one of the three competitions organised in Bosnia and Herzegovina between 1995 and 2003. This was despite the country remaining deeply divided along ethnic lines – regardless of the official peace.

An example of this division was how football was organised after the war. Sloboda and the Bosnian-Muslim clubs competed in a league that wished to be all-Bosnian, but they could see that this failed to draw in the Croat teams from the region of Herzeg-Bosnia or the Serb ones from Republika Srpska. Not only did these teams refuse to participate in this tournament but they organised their own parallel tournaments. Fortunately, by 2003, Bosnian soccer made a breakthrough, managing to convince all of the country's clubs to participate in the same top-flight competition: the *Premijer Liga*.

Tuzla and Sloboda are to some extent metaphors for the understanding there can be between the different ethnic groups that together make up Bosnia and Herzegovina now, and formed Yugoslavia before. The city, which lies on the banks of the Sava River, is one of the few in Bosnia where schools do not separate children according to ethnicity. Maybe this is why it still has a statue in memory of Marshal Tito. These features of the city suggest that the city and Sloboda yearn for the good old days: of full employment, industries working in full swing, and Sloboda fighting for Federal Yugoslavian titles and even qualifying for European competitions. Those were very different times from those the city lived through in the 2000s, when its inhabitants had to speak out against the economic model imposed through the Dayton and Washington peace agreements that ended the brutal war (while institutionalising entrenched ethnic divisions). That was a time in which Tuzla and its number-one club once again embodied defiance of the powers-that-be and respect for ordinary people's ethnic and religious diversity. Put simply, it is what Sloboda's founders would have called class struggle.

FK Velež Mostar
Red star of Mostar

The city of Mostar, capital of Herzegovina (the southern part of the state shared with Bosnia), has undoubtedly been one of the key European historical arenas. The *Stari Most*, the long-standing bridge turned symbol for a city that even takes its name from it, has always been thought of as a human and cultural crossing point. To the west of the Neretva River is the Adriatic Sea and Latin civilisation; to the east, Sarajevo and the Slavic and Eastern world. Mostar Old Bridge is therefore a perfect symbol for Mostar's multi-ethnic character.

The other major embodiment of the metropolis' multi-ethnic fabric is its leading football club: Fudbalski Klub Velež Mostar. It is a historic outfit that has united Croats, Serbs, and Bosnian Muslims in perfect harmony, and which Bosnian writer and journalist Alija Kebo dared equate with the very same legendary and symbolic bridge over the Neretva.

Velež is not in fact Mostar's oldest club. That distinction belongs to Zrinjski Mostar, a sporting entity formed in 1905 only from Croatian-nationalist youth. In 1922, with the city having been incorporated into the recently constituted Kingdom of Serbs, Croats, and Slovenes, local communists led creation of a new entity that could circumvent the recent ban by King Alexander I on Marxist-Leninist-aligned parties or associations. Thus was born Velež Mostar, taking for part of its name a mountain near the city, which itself owes its name to the ancient Slavic god Veles.

Velež, unlike its Croat neighbour, was notably multi-ethnic. This was in line with the Yugoslav communists' policies regarding such matters. In fact, Velež began as a workers' club with most of its original members being communist activists who insisted that sport should be part of the revolutionary struggle of the working class.

This overtly political approach led the Yugoslavian monarchic regime to keep a watchful eye on the club's actions. Indeed, the club was even banned from doing any activity in 1940 – just before the Nazi and fascist occupation of Yugoslavia – after members from different sections of the club joined a major anti-fascist demonstration in Mostar.

The decreed ban continued after Bosnia and Herzegovina had been occupied by the *Ustaša* regime and absorbed into the new Nazi-allied Independent State of Croatia. The Croatian-only Zrinjski, went to play in the fascist Croatian league. Yet Velež was blocked from joining it. Even so, it was precisely in those years that the club wrote the most glorious chapter in its history by joining Josip Broz's Partisan resistance.

The price Velež paid due to this was extremely high: 77 sportspersons and 21 club employees lost their lives on the battlefield in the Partisan fight to free Yugoslavia from the fascist yoke. However, they did help achieve the goal of putting Tito at the head of a Socialist Yugoslav federation. This was a real triumph for the communist values and brotherhood between peoples that Velež had acted for so admirably while underground.

After the war ended in 1945, the tables were turned in the city of Mostar – one of the few that had been spared the savage ethnic violence that had ravaged the Balkans during the conflict. The Croatian Zrinjski was banned by the communist

authorities for its complicity with the *Ustaša* regime, while
the multi-ethnic Velež had its legality restored. It became a
vehement supporter of the socialist state and Tito's defence of
'brotherhood and unity' among peoples.

In the following decades, Velež developed into being one
of the central expressions of this policy. The club was almost
entirely made up of players from Mostar or the Herzegovina
region and who embodied the different ethnic groups. So
in Velež there were always Croat, Serb, and 'Bosniak' (Bosnian-Muslim) players – demonstrating the multi-ethnic
nature of the territory. Despite only including local players in
its team, Velež reached the Yugoslav First League in 1955 and
became one of the country's leading clubs, never being relegated from the top tier.

The club's golden era was the 1970s and 1980s. In 1971, it
unveiled a new stadium, Bijeli Brijeg, which had a monument
outside in honour of the club members who died fighting
fascism. Also noteworthy was the club ending runner-up in the
Yugoslav League in both 1973 and 1974 with a team perfectly
epitomising Mostar's multi-ethnicity. The squad was popularly known as *BMV* (the local initials for the luxury BMW
car brand): the initials for the surnames of the team's three big
stars: Bajevic, Maric, and Vladic. The players just happened to
be Serbian, Bosnian Muslim, and Croatian, respectively.

Just before the trio's biggest successes, Velež had been
awarded by Tito – on occasion of his Golden Jubilee – a distinction that went far beyond sport: the Order of Brotherhood
and Unity with Gold Wreath. Among the acknowledged
merits that justified the club receiving such high-ranking
honours was its 'enormous participation and contribution to
the national liberation struggle' and having constant 'spreading brotherhood and unity among our nations' (those in the
Yugoslavian federation).

Velež's trophy cabinets began to sparkle in the 1980s, when the team won two Yugoslav Cups – in 1981 and 1986. A further irony was that Josip Broz Tito was not able to see Velež become champions, as he died in 1980. This was despite Velež being a quintessentially 'pro-Tito' team, and the Yugoslav President even having a holiday home – Tito's Palace – on the banks of the Neretva in Mostar. In the same decade, when nationalisms – particularly Serbian and Croatian – were being stirred up in football grounds, Velež stayed faithful to its original pro-Yugo-slavia approach. Even its most extreme supporters' group, the Red Army – created in 1981 after the club's first cup win and originally called *Crveni Šetjani* (the Red Devils) – embraced the communist cause and the pro-Yugoslavian view that Velež had also championed since 1922.

The spread of Croat nationalism, which culminated in Croatian independence being proclaimed in June 1991, had a major impact on Herzegovina. Most Mostar Croats identi-fied with the new state and began to shun the multi-ethnic Velež. In 1991, Croatian nationalists demanded that the club withdraw from what they dubbed the 'Serboslavian league', as the Croatian and Slovene clubs had done. The Mostar club rejected this course of action, as did the other Bosniak clubs. The decision had serious consequences for Velež. Just before a match against Partizan Belgrade began in August 1991, a bomb went off in the Bijeli Brijeg ground. It had been planted by members of the nationalist Croatian Democratic Union – Franjo Tudjman's party.

The event was the prelude to a tragic period, which saw the end of Yugoslavia and threw Bosnia and Herzegovina into the hell of inter-ethnic conflict. Mostar's diversity – until then seen to be a virtue – turned the city into a permanent battlefield between communities. Serb paramilitaries and the Yugoslav National Army attacked the city from the east, while Croat nationalists strove to turn it into the capital of a 'Republic of Herzeg-Bosnia' – the Croatian Bosnia they wanted to be annexed by an independent Croatia. Meanwhile, Bosniaks fought to preserve the unity of Bosnia and Herzegovina, which by 1992 had become an independent state; leaving a mini-Yugoslavia which the Serb and Croat authorities hoped to divide up among themselves.

With Bosnia and Herzegovina's independence, Velež left the Yugoslav League for good, but the war ravaging the country prevented it from being able to play in an alternative competition. Meanwhile, pro-Croatians re-created Zrinjski Mostar, the city's old Croatian club, and this moved into Velež's Bijeli Brijeg stadium. This was located on the west bank of the Neretva in an area mainly inhabited by Croats.

Mostar's multi-ethnic status was seriously harmed by the Balkan Wars. On 9 November 1993, Croat forces destroyed the *Stari Most* – the bridge symbolising the peaceful co-existence the city enjoyed. Bijeli Brijeg was soon being used as a prison camp for Bosnian Muslims. Thus fell the two big icons of multi-ethnic Mostar: the old bridge and Velež. The latter was now an exiled club; lacking a league, headquarters, and ground; with its fan base being increasingly limited to the Bosniak community – the only one that still believed in peaceful cohabitation between the country's different ethnic groups.

Velež had to wait for the signing of the Dayton Accords that put an end to the Bosnian War before it could play matches again. It then did so in the three football leagues that appeared in the pacified but still deeply divided Bosnia and Herzegovina. While Zrinjski joined the Herzeg-Bosnia league, using the Bijeli Brijeg stadium as its own, Velež had to take refuge in a ground in Vrapčići – a small town near Mostar – where it played its home games in the Bosnian League Championship.

These were years in which Velež, like Mostar, lost some of its hallmark symbols. These included the red star on the club's crest, which it decided to drop in 1994 – during the war. It was seen as too identified with the Serbia-dominated Yugoslavia which Bosnia was fighting against. The five-pointed red star would not be reintroduced for over a decade – happening a year after Mostar's other great symbol – the Mostar Bridge – was rebuilt.

The city on the Neretva began to heal despite its wounds still being open and bloody. An example of the conflict still raging in the city was seen in the first match – taking place in 2000 – between Zrinjski and Velež in the latter's former home that had been transformed through war into the domain of Mostar's Croatian-nationalist team. At the derby, the Velež fans were humiliated to discover that the old monument devoted to its fallen heroes in the war against fascism had been turned into an area honouring Croatian nationalists.

Since then, the matches between the two leading Mostar teams have been true battles between the Croatian chauvinism exemplified by Zrinjski and the multi-ethnic Herzegovina embodied by Velež. While Croats hold up Herceg-Bosnian Republic flags or banners reminding their rivals that they will never return to Bijeli Brijeg, Velež supporters claim the figure of Tito and show their nostalgia for the good old days of Federal Yugoslavia. Velež remains the true red star of Mostar.

Olympiacós Piraeus
Piraeus' red rebels

The sports club Olympiacós Sýndesmos Filáthlon Peiraiós
(Olympic Club of Fans of Piraeus) was created in Piraeus,
Greece, in 1925. From day one, its Piraeus hosts became pas-
sionately attached to it and infused in it the working-class
spirit of a port city characterised by its shipyards and industrial activity.

Since its very beginning, Olympiacós was therefore supported by the humble families living in Piraeus; basically
seafarers, shipbuilders, and proletarians working in the city's
industries. Such a social base made Olympiacós the working
class team – an identity that led it to develop great rivalry with
Panathinaikos, a club formed in 1908 in central Athens, and
which became the sporting flagship for Greece's urban upper
classes.

The social divide between Olympiacós Piraeus and Panathinaikos, which has since diluted due to sympathies developing
for both clubs among different classes, helped to strengthen
the working-class identity of the Piraeus club's fans. Olympiacós took on red and white as its official colours on the
grounds that these stood for honour and purity, respectively:
two traits that were meant to guide the club's sporting activity.

All the same, the red acquired another meaning other than
honour – logically, bearing in mind who made up the bulk

of the Piraeus team's players and fans. It came to symbolise rebelliousness, especially after October 1940, when Mussolini's fascist Italy began an offensive – within the context of the Second World War – to conquer Greece.

The outbreak of this Greco-Italian War paralysed the Greek football league which, despite being dominated at the time by AEK Athens, had been previously won by Olympiacós on six occasions – out of a total of eleven championships. The wartime pause in footballing activity meant that several Piraeus club players briefly hung up their boots to join the Greek army and stand up to fascist invasion from neighbouring Albania – a territory that had been under Italian occupation for a year.

Several Olympiacós footballers went to halt the advance of Mussolini's troops. These included Christoforos Raggos, one of the best of the Piraeus team's strikers in the 1930s, who was wounded in the leg during fighting and never played football again; Leonidas Andrianopoulos, another member of the club's legendary attack, who was nearly killed on the Albanian front; and Nikos Grigoratos, who was injured in January 1941 during the epic Greek capture of the Klisura pass – a crucial battle in the Greek troops' eventual triumph over Italian fascism.

Overcoming Mussolini's forces did not mean an end to combat for Greece's freedom fighters. First, Nazi Germany – supported by its Italian and Bulgarian allies – began an offensive that broke the Greek resistance and put a puppet regime at the country's helm while forcing the Greek government and King into exile.

The Greek people created an underground resistance movement in which, once again, Olympiacós players played a noteworthy role. The start of the war disrupted the national championship, leading it to be suspended until the end of the Second World War. Yet after this, Greek football was able to resume some of its activities – watched over by the occupying authorities.

For that reason Olympiacós was able to renew much of its team after its losses in the anti-fascist war. Its new incorporations included the impressive figure of Nikos Godas, a young Greek refugee who had to leave his Ayvalik birthplace at a very young age after Turkey's victory in the Anatolian War. That conflict ended with a population exchange agreement between Greece and Turkey, which left virtually no Greeks in Ayvalik – a town on the coast of Anatolia (Asia Minor).

Godas had joined the club just as the Nazi occupation began. Through this, he fulfilled his dream of playing for his beloved team. After a long journey, his family settled in Nikaia, an area of Piraeus that had taken in many Greek migrants from Asia Minor. There, the Godas family ran a popular tavern, with their son working there until signing for Olympiakos.

Despite not being able to play in the (suspended) league, the young forward showed his natural talent to his teammates, leading them to nickname him 'the Artist'. Godas was instrumental in Olympiacós' biggest successes under Nazi occupation: most notably winning the 1943 Christmas Cup by thumping its arch-rival Panathinaikos 5–2 in the final.

Besides his performance on the pitch, Nikos Godas shone due to his commitment to opposing the Nazi occupation. The young player joined the ranks of both the Greek Communist Party (KKE) and the armed resistance: the Greek People's Liberation Front (ELAS), which was spearheaded by the KKE and other left groups allied in an anti-fascist popular front.

The Olympiacós striker rose to be a captain in the ELAS and actively fought in several battles, in Nikaia and Piraeus, against the Nazi troops and their Greek collaborators. While fighting in 1944, Godas discovered that one of the players with whom he shared a dressing room, Michalis Anamateros, had died during the battle for Exarcheia in Athens. One of Godas' watermarks was his involvement in the defence of the national electricity company against acts of sabotage by German troops while evacuating after their defeat at the hands of the Greek resistance.

The end of the Nazi occupation did not mean an end to hostilities on Greek soil either. Indeed, Greece was the stage for the first Cold War conflict because of the subsequent clashes between the communist-led resistance – including Godas – and the forces loyal to the exiled King and government. The latter side wished to restore the deposed conservative monarchist regime with the aid of the British armed forces.

In this new fight, Piraeus became a stronghold for the communist resistance and Nikos Godas was arrested there in 1945. The player-fighter was sent to Aegina prison, where he joined a football team consisting of prisoners. On 19 November 1948, after spending three years in jail, he was executed by the royalist Greek army on Corfu island.

Over those years, Godas had repeatedly refused to sign a public apology which would have saved his life. He asked to be slain with his eyes uncovered and wearing the red and white jersey of the Piraeus teams. His last wish: 'Shoot me and kill me with my Olympiacós shirt on, and do not blindfold me, I want to see the colours of my team before the final shot'.

Despite this show of love for Olympiacós, the club did not lift a finger to save him. The reason for this was that, although much of the fan base identified with communist ideas, the club's directors were closer to the royalist government. 'I am dying for my country and my beliefs', Godas wrote to his family just before his execution. The moment he died; the talented 27-year-old forward recalled the Piraeus rebels that shared the same red Olympiacós jersey as he: 'We won! Glory to the champions of socialism! Farewell teammates'.

6

Eastern Europe and the Caucasus

Ramzan Kadyrov joins Terek Grozny players to celebrate the Chechen club winning the Russian Cup in 2004

FC Olt Scorniceşti
Life and death of a dictator's club

Scorniceşti is a small town in the Romanian county of Olt. It is really only known for being the birthplace of Nicolae Ceauşescu; the man who ruled the country with an iron fist from 1967 to 1989. Ceauşescu was born on 26 January 1918, as the son of a humble peasant family whom he helped as a child by doing agricultural work. He was the first Nicolae in the clan, but saw his dad baptise his little brother with the same name, when he was aged 8. Three years later, the elder son left his native Scorniceşti to settle in Bucharest – Romania's capital – where he began working as a shoemaker.

Nicolae soon joined the Union of Communist Youth and, just after, the Romanian Communist Party. He took part in the resistance against Nazi occupation and had a meteoric career that led him to become leader of the party in Bucharest, an MP, a member of the party's Central Committee, Deputy Minister, and party General Secretary. In 1967, after the death of the President of the Socialist Republic of Romania Gheorghe Gheorghiu-Dej, Ceauşescu was himself made President.

While in this role, Ceauşescu did not forget where he came from and tried to turn Scorniceşti into a 'model town' for the 'new man' that socialism promised to forge. In accordance with this modernising obsession, the Romanian dictator ordered the demolition of the conurbation's traditional houses and their replacement with socialist-style housing blocks.

The only exception to this was his family home, which was preserved and turned into one of Scorniceşti's main tourist attractions.

His will to turn his hometown into one of Romania's big cities was reflected in the football club that Nicolae Ceauşescu created to epitomise the town in 1972. Until then, local football was characterised by small clubs participating in very limited regional league competitions. Ceauşescu was anxious to improve the reputation and glory of the town he had been born in, and he promoted creating the poetically named FC Viitorul (Future FC).

The following year, the authorities decided to change this name to Fotbal Club Olt Scorniceşti, thereby incorporating the name of Scorniceşti's county. The aim of the new sports club was very clear: to turn it into one of Romania's biggest clubs and thus compete with the capital's teams, which greatly dominated the country's football. To make this wish come true, the club required the kind of political favours that had already been bestowed on Steaua – the army team – Dinamo – the police team– and Victoria – the club of the *Securitate* (the regime's feared political police branch).

The fact that the country's *conducător* (leader) was 'a local boy' hugely aided the club's development. The dictator built a large stadium called the First of May (after International Workers' Day) with a capacity of 12,000 spectators: more than the number of people living in Scorniceşti at the time. He also invested huge sums of money in the club, which soon paid off in terms of sporting success.

After spending its infancy in regional divisions, Olt Scorniceşti enjoyed a meteoric rise, gaining promotion year after year until it won the all-Romanian third division, sending it up to second-tier football. This promotion was especially controversial because in the last game of the season, in which it became champion on goal difference, it won by no less than 18–0. Years later, players in the opposing team – Electrodul Slatina – acknowledged that they had been bribed to lose by the outrageous score line. It is likely that this was using the money Ceaușescu had awarded the Scornicești Club.

In the following season – 1978–1979 – Olt Scornicești achieved its big goal: reaching Romania's first division. Yet it should be mentioned that there were suspicions throughout that championship, over favourable refereeing benefiting the apple in Ceaușescu's eye. The club also benefited from collaboration with the two biggest Romanian clubs, Steaua, and Dinamo, who also had close links with the powers-that-be. FC Olt received several of their players on loan, which significantly raised the level of the team's game.

Such help seems to have been strengthened while FC Olt was in top-flight football in the 1980s. To give one example, the club struggled to stay up in its debut season there and eventually only a point separated it from the relegation zone – a suspect position which only fuelled rumours over biased refereeing benefiting the all-powerful club from the President's birthplace.

The next few seasons were Olt Scornicești 's glory days. In 1981, it finished the season in seventh place, and the following, fourth – the highest place it has reached in Romanian league football in its history. It ended only behind Dinamo București, the champion and qualifier for the European Cup; and Universitatea Craiova and Corvinul Hunedoara, which both qualified for the UEFA Cup.

In less than a decade, FC Olt had gone from playing in the regional leagues to taking on the big teams from the capital. Indeed, it now ended up above Steaua, the other team that had always been given an official helping hand and was indeed headed by the dictator's son – Valentin Ceaușescu.

The Romanian *conducător* had achieved his goal of making his hometown team one of the championship's greatest. Yet, all this depended on corrupting referees and discretionary capital injections that disturbed the normal development of the country's footballing competitions.

For the rest of the 1980s, Olt Scorniceşti always managed to stay in the top-flight *Divizia A* but without equalling its 1982 success. Among fans of 'the beautiful game', the rumour spread that Olt would never be relegated thanks to the protection Ceauşescu afforded the club, which was behind the assistance given to the club by referees however well-hidden this was.

In 1988, Romania's President went even further in helping the sporting entity. As part of a renewal programme for his hometown, he decided to build the club a new stadium, the *Stadion Viitorul* (Future Stadium) – taking on the name the club had been christened with back in 1972. This would have room for 25,000 fans – almost double Scorniceşti's population at the time.

Nevertheless, Olt was not able to enjoy its new footballing shrine for long. While the stadium was still only half built, a popular uprising began on 22 December 1989 to Nicolae Ceauşescu's surprise. It ended up putting an end to over 20 years of totalitarian rule by the so-called 'genius of the Carpathians' (mountain range). On Christmas Day that year, Nicolae Ceauşescu and his wife Elena were executed after being arrested trying to flee the country and given a summary trial.

The outbreak of revolution that led to Ceauşescu's death and brought down his regime left FC Olt exposed. The new authorities expelled it from the league and ordered it to disband. This was not the only case of its kind. The *Securitate*-linked Victoria Bucureşti was also removed from the league and dissolved. Both clubs were accused of having received favours during Ceauşescu's rule.

Fotbol Club Olt Scorniceşti therefore had a short history – not having lasted two decades when it disappeared in 1990. It was superseded by CS Olt 90, a new club that sought to represent the county by breaking with all past associations with the tyrannical Ceauşescu family. Yet this project was also short-lived, as it disappeared soon after due to its financial difficulties.

In 2003, FC Olt Scorniceşti was re-founded; now staying clear of any Ceauşescu-family linkages. It has been playing in Romania's lowly fourth division. A new club which – beyond its name – had no relation to the life and death of an entity that was merely a dictator's whim.

FC Dynamo Kyiv
When Dynamo acted as the Ukrainian national team

Fixtures between FC Barcelona and Dynamo Kyiv have become a European clash of the titans. Yet before this came about, the two sides met in a continental competition for the first time on 6 March 1991: in a European Cup Winners' Cup quarter-final. The geopolitical context was completely different then than it is today. The club was called Dynamo Kiev (with 'Kiev' being the Russian name for the city of Kyiv), it played in the Soviet league, and Ukraine was still part of the USSR – although decomposition of the Soviet state was already accelerating.

That day, Dynamo went onto the pitch at the Republican Stadium (today's Lobanovsky Stadium) in Kyiv wearing a yellow shirt and blue shorts: displaying thus the Ukrainian national colours. The strip, which substituted its traditional white one from 1990, sought to show Dynamo's commitment to the growing Ukrainian nationalism that had no qualms about demanding independent statehood.

The bicolour Ukrainian flag had been banned until the USSR began its *perestroika* and *glasnost* reform processes (to bring about greater institutional openness and transparency), which in practice lifted the ban on some historical national symbols of different republics within the USSR. It had two bands: a light blue one which signified the sky; and a yellow one, symbolising the country's fertile wheat fields. The flag had first been used during the 1848 Springtime of the Peoples (European revolutions); and later became the official flag for the short-lived Ukrainian People's Republic that was pro-claimed following the October Revolution in Russia.

It was not the bicolour banner that flew over the Republican Stadium on that day in March 1991, however, but the Soviet Union's one. Displayed with this were the St Andrew's Cross, honouring the Scottish referee David Syme; and a Spanish flag. (The latter was mistakenly the version from the Franco era, which includes an eagle, which embarrassed the Iberian diplomats in the guests' box.)

The Ukrainian flag could only be seen by looking at the pitch, where the Dynamo players effectively formed it with their kit; or by watching the stands, where many of the almost 100,000 fans wore it to cheer on their team on that cold Kiyv evening. But this did not stop *Barça* winning (2–3) and sealing a place in the Cup Winner's semi-final (which it lost against Manchester United after a 1–1 second-leg draw at Barcelona's *Camp Nou*).

Although Dynamo became a flagship for Ukrainian identity, earlier in its history it had been closely linked to the USSR's secret police – like the other '*Dynamo*' clubs across the Soviet Union. When Dynamo Kiev was established in 1927, it was the team of the *Cheka* (secret police) – created by Felix Dzerzhinsky; and later it was the club of the feared KGB. Such police units aimed to hound Ukrainian nationalism, seeing it to be counter-revolutionary and anti-socialist.

A reason for the changes to Dynamo's colours can be found in the internal transformation the club went through in 1989, when it became an independent sporting organisation and therefore able to make decisions that were not to the liking of the Soviet authorities. These included changing its kit to embody the historic Ukrainian national flag for the 1990 and

1991 seasons, which oddly enough turned out to be the last in which the club played in the USSR championship.

In those seasons, the Kyiv club became the territory's true national team, taking onto the pitch the patriotic zeal being expressed in the streets and that would take the country to independence. While Dynamo wore the Ukrainian colours in both the Soviet league and European competitions, the country was taking firm steps towards full sovereignty. Independence was declared on 24 August 1991 by the Ukrainian parliament which was created on that same day by (and to replace) the Supreme Soviet of the Ukrainian Soviet Socialist Republic.

The declaration was ratified in a referendum held on 1 December, in which 84 per cent of Ukrainians voted and 90 per cent of these voted in favour. That month Ukraine became an independent state with its own fully sovereign football federation, which a few months later was confirmed as a full member of the major international footballing bodies.

The newly created Ukrainian national team took on the same strip that Dynamo had been using in 1990 and 1991. This prompted the Kyiv team to return to its traditional white and blue. The reason was simple: although Dynamo was still a much-loved team for very many of the country's football fans, Ukraine now had a national team that could play in the big international competitions.

Yet the Kyiv team's peculiarly nationalist character certainly did not begin in the early 1990s. When Ukraine was still in the USSR, and particularly in the post-war period, the Dynamo Kiev team emerged as a truly national symbol for Ukrainians.

Its rivalry with the Moscow teams, particularly Spartak, ended up mirroring the tensions between the USSR's epicentre of power and Ukrainian nationalism. The fact that Dynamo defied Moscow's might by winning nine cups and 13 league titles – more than any other club in the USSR – and was the first Soviet team to win a European competition – the Cup Winners' Cup and Super Cup in 1975, and the former trophy again in 1986 – made the club a source of national pride for Ukraine; so much so that even the Ukrainian authorities saw Dynamo as the national team.

Its winning team in the 1970s and 1980s was managed by Valeriy Lobanovsky, who went on to coach the USSR squad. The backbone of such a team was formed by Dynamo players, which produced not a few contradictions for Ukrainian nationalists. On the one hand, it was proud of its players' successes; on the other, it loathed that this took place under the Soviet flag and not the Ukrainian national colours.

Soviet repression against nationalist symbols meant that – before *perestroika* – displaying the Ukrainian flag was limited to actions carried out by Ukrainians in exile. A very eloquent example took place during the 1976 Montreal Olympic Games, during the semi-final of the soccer tournament, which pitted the USSR against East Germany. Many Ukrainian exiles in the stands called for freedom for their country, while the young Danylo Mygal jumped onto the pitch to wave the banned flag while doing the *hopak* – a major Ukrainian folk dance. Besides calling for Ukraine's freedom, Mygal wished to highlight the fact that the USSR's Olympic team was basically formed by Ukrainian footballers from Dynamo Kiev.

The Ukrainian nationalism, as well as anti-communism, of many of its supporters did not abate after Ukraine became independent, set up its own national squad, and Dynamo reverted to its original strip. However, the creation of an independent Ukrainian league saw average attendance at the Dynamo stadium plummet: from 50,000 in 1987–1988 to 2,000 in some of the first Ukrainian championship seasons. In the new league contest, the Kyiv team showed an obscene degree of domination, winning nine out of the first ten tournaments.

Despite independence, the tensions that have persisted between Russia and Ukraine, and which have their clearest example in the Donbas conflict or the war stemming from this that began on 24 February 2022, have kept Dynamo's nationalist symbolism alive. This was illustrated by the war against the Russian forces involving the club's most extreme fans, who also identify with far-right nationalism. It is a nationalist symbolism that once made the club, at a turbulent time in its country's history, the national squad of a Ukraine striving for independence.

FC Shakhtar Donetsk
Shakhtar as a byword for the history of Donbas

Donetsk is the unofficial capital of Donbas, a mining basin situated between the Sea of Azov and the river Don and the epicentre of the biggest war in the world today. As with most mining regions, Donbas' identity has been deeply shaped by the central economic activity that has traditionally taken place there. As a good example, its leading football club, Shaktar Donetsk, has a name starting with the word for miner and wears black and orange, inspired by coal and fire – the two quintessential mineworking symbols.

The association with mining was present when the club was set up under Soviet Ukraine, when the club was called Stakhanovets. The name referred to miner Alexei Stakhanov, who had been working in a Donbas mine since 1927 and made a legendary record in the amount of individually dug coal in 1935. In the eyes of the Soviet state, his capacity for work and self-sacrifice made him a model for other workers. A year later, the club was created.

The Donetsk Stakhanovets played under such a name for a decade until they were renamed Shaktar, like its stadium until then, which was also a nod to the area's mining activity. The new Shaktar incorporated players from different Donbas mining firms. With time, this demonstrated its potential, becoming one of the biggest teams in Soviet football.

Mirroring the engine that the Donbas mining area was for the USSR's economy, Shaktar became one of the few teams able to compete with the big Moscow clubs and the Ukrainian Dynamo Kiev. This was shown by its triumphs in four USSR Cups – in 1961, 1962, 1980, and 1983 – and the 1984 Soviet Super Cup (played between the winner of the first division and the USSR Cup).

This background helped Shaktar become one of the leading clubs in the new Ukrainian football championship created in 1992 after the country won independence. Yet in the first decade of the new league, the club played in the shadow of an all-dominant Dynamo Kyiv, which was champion in ten out of the first eleven seasons.

Nonetheless, the Donbas team's trajectory was impressive and was closely associated with that of its directors, who had clear links with the kind of illicit activities that were common in Ukraine after the fall of communism. For instance, in October 1995, the then-club-chairman, Akhat Bragin, a businessman linked to the local mafia, was killed in a bomb attack during a match at the Shaktar stadium, together with six bodyguards.

The event changed the history of the miner club as it was put in the hands of a new chairperson: Rinat Akhmetov, another controversial businessperson linked to mafia activities. Akhmetov invested heavily in Shaktar until it became the dominant club in 21st-century Ukrainian football.

Shaktar Donetsk won its first domestic league in 2002 and can now boast of having a total of 13 leagues and 13 cup trophies in its cabinet. As well as these national trophies it picked up the UEFA Cup in 2009, making it only the second Ukrainian team to win a European title – having picked up the baton from Dynamo Kyiv which had won the Cup Winners' Cup and European Super Cup but during the Soviet period.

The years between Akhmetov becoming club head in 1996 and the outbreak of the Donbas conflict in 2014 were Shaktar's golden years in which the club grew on every level. In 2009, the club opened a new and luxurious stadium, the Donbas Arena, which was the best equipped in Eastern Europe. As well as having been a stage for Shaktar's sporting achievements, the new stadium hosted several matches in the Euro 2012 championship that was jointly organised by Ukraine and Poland.

There were political differences between the mainly Russian-speaking and pro-Russian Donbas region and the rest of Ukraine, which were expressed in the rivalry between the Donetsk team and clubs such as Dynamo Kiev or Karpaty Lviv – who have fans closely associated with Ukrainian nationalist movements. Yet few could have imagined that the stadium that was the setting for the European Football Championship would, two years later, bear witness to a war that would directly affect the ground.

During the club's glory days, Shaktar was associated with its chairman's politics. Akhmetov was a leading figure in the pro-Russian Party of Regions, a now-banned organisation that had strong roots in Donbas and reached national office under Victor Yanukovych. Again, however, the course of history influenced the leading Donbas club. The triumph of the 2012 Maidan Revolution, which was led to a considerable degree by far-right activists in Ukrainian football's big fan groups, led to the Donetsk and Luhansk regions' estrangement from the Kyiv hierarchy and to the outbreak of war in 2014.

Oddly the last title Shaktar won before the Donbas War was the United Tournament: a 'super cup' pitting the best Ukrainian and Russian teams against each other. This was only held in 2013 and 2014 when the Kyiv government was run by the pro-Russian Party of the Regions. Shaktar won the last United Tournament, which was played in Israel in 2014 – just two months before the Donbas war broke out.

The conflict pitted the Ukrainian army aided by nationalist militias such as the infamous Azov Battalion, created from far-right supporters of the Metalist Kharkiv football club against pro-Russian separatists who proclaimed Donetsk and Luhansk to be People's Republics. The war forced Shaktar to leave Donbas Arena and play its home matches at Arena Lviv – on the other side of Ukraine. However, there it hardly drew any spectators due to Western Ukraine's dislike for the country's Russian-speaking areas.

At first, Shaktar refused to clearly align itself with the Kyiv government, refusing to wear before its matches a shirt bearing the slogan 'Glory to the Ukrainian Army'. However, the fierceness of the growing war ended up splitting the club. While it was officially moved to the area controlled by the Ukrainian government, several players chose to stay in the People's Republic of Donetsk and recognise the related government's authority over the territory. Such a government, which was not recognised by either Kyiv or the international community, helped set up the People's Republic of Donetsk Football Federation in 2015. Interestingly it was headed by Ihor Petrov, a former Shaktar player who got to be captain of the Ukrainian national squad.

The new federation set up a local cup and league competition as well as a 'national' team, which played several games from 2015 to 2018 despite failing to receive official recognition. These were against teams from the People's Republic of Luhansk or the self-proclaimed (ex-Georgian) Republic of Abkhazia.

As the Donbas conflict spilt over into the current war, the political stance of Shaktar's chair has undergone a notable change. Rinat Akhmetov has gone from being accused of funding pro-Russian separatists in the region to giving financial aid to the Ukrainian army and their families, while calling for Ukraine's borders to be respected and to include Donbas and the Russian-annexed Crimea.

The most telling example of this was Akhmetov giving 25 of the 100 million Euros Shaktar received for transferring to Chelsea its young star Mykhailo Mudryk to the army or the families of the soldiers who were killed or wounded fighting the Russian military in Mariupol. And during these battles, the businessman allowed the mentioned Azov forces to bunker up in the Azovstal company he owns. Akhmetov has even declared that if football has survived in Ukraine, it is precisely thanks to the soldiers fighting to defend it.

Mudryk's transfer created quite some controversy as Chelsea paid far more for him than his 'market value', leading several analysts to see the transaction as including covert aid for Ukrainian-army weapons purchases. The deal was made with Chelsea's new owner, US businessman Todd Boehly, after the Russian magnate Roman Abramovich was forced to sell the club due to the sanctions Britain applied in response to the Russian–Ukrainian War.

After the transfer was formalised, Akhmetov announced he wished for Shaktar to host a friendly against Chelsea at the Donbas Arena. Since 2014 and while the consequences of war were hitting hard, the Donetsk club stadium has been used as a humanitarian aid centre and dubbed the Arena of Mercy. Another reason why Shaktar has become a byword for the tragedy that Donbas has suffered for almost a decade.

FC Karpaty Lviv
Footballing bastion of Ukrainian nationalism

Lviv had a multicultural and cosmopolitan past as the capital of Galicia-Volhynia – a medieval principality part of the Kingdom of Poland and, later, the Austro-Hungarian Empire. Yet despite this, the city – the largest in Western Ukraine and with the Latin name Leopolis – has become a bastion for Ukrainian nationalism. This has been so much the case that although the Town Hall is governed by pro-European liberal conservatives, the far-right Svoboda party is strongly embedded locally and commands significant electoral support.

Most of Ukrainian society has embraced nationalism in recent years. This was spurred by the war in Donbas in 2014 – a conflict in the Donets river basin in which pro-Russian rebels have been trying to free themselves from Kyiv's gove-nance. Furthermore, pro-Ukrainian sentiment has deepened since the Russian invasion in February 2022. It is now totally pervasive in Lviv and has in FC Karbaty Lviv – the city's football team – one of its main exponents.

Founded only in 1963, Karpaty has become a sports team closely linked to the region it grew out of: the Carpathian Mountains – from which the club takes its name. It emerged from another club named Selmash – the same as the local arms manufacturer that employed some of the workers who founded it.

From the outset, Selmash Lviv gained the affection of most people in the city. This was because the main club until then had been SKA Lviv – the Red Army Sports Club. As this was a sports entity tied to the Soviet Union – to which Lviv had been annexed after the Second World War – its best local players were often sent to Moscow to play for CSKA – the Soviet army's biggest club.

Selmash achieved success right from its first year: winning the regional league and cup championships it played in. This earned it a place in the USSR's third football division, a leap to the 'national' level, which led it to be re-founded in 1963 under the name Karpaty. This was seen as a more suitable one for the federal tier the team would now compete in because it allowed identifying the club's geographical origin.

Soon after being officially constituted, Karpaty won its biggest sporting milestone yet: the 1969 Soviet Cup. In a packed-out Lenin Stadium in Moscow, the Ukrainians beat the Rostov army squad to become the first club in Soviet footballing history to win the cup while in the second division.

One significant political aspect of the event was the patriotic songs that rang out from the stands: most notably 'Cheremshyna' – a romantic Ukrainian-language ballad that was popular at the time. The singing of it during the event confirmed that Karpaty had truly become a symbol of the Ukrainian nationalist movement, which ardently celebrated that victory for the club. Karpaty's subsequent promotion to the Soviet Top League strengthened its symbolic status. The Soviet authorities reacted by merging the club with the other city club: SKA, thereby putting the team under the control of its army.

This development meant that the legendary club that had won the 1969 cup wearing a green and white shirt – the colours of Lviv's region – now had to wear red and white: the colours of an army that many club fans saw as foreign. The fusion came at a time when Lviv was emerging as one of the counter-cultural hubs against Kremlin policies and many young people supporting the club were also involved in the first big anti-Soviet protests organised in the city by the pro-Ukrainian movement. Not surprisingly, the club merger was unpopular among fans.

In fact, one of the demands pro-Ukrainians now raised was to restore Karpaty's autonomy; allowing it to play in its original colours and be rid of any links with the Soviet army. The call was met in 1989, when the club and SKA were separated, thus strengthening the already marked Ukrainian nationalist symbolism of the club.

Karpaty regaining full sovereignty was the sporting prelude to Ukraine being made an independent republic in 1991. After the latter took place, the Lviv club freed itself from Soviet competitions to join the new Ukrainian national league. Its stadium, until then called *Druzhba* (i.e. Friendship – referring to Ukraine's relationship with Russia) but now renamed *Ukraina*, hosted the first league-championship final in the newly created republic.

Since Ukrainian statehood was proclaimed, Karpaty fans' nationalism has become stronger, and far-right groups' influence among them has grown. Chants and banners celebrating figures who collaborated with the Nazis in the Second World War are commonplace in *Ukraina*. This is to such an extent that the biggest local fan crew is named 'Banderstadt' ('Bandera City'). This is the (belittling) label which Red Army officers gave the city due to its inhabitants' sympathies for the likes of Stepan Bandera, a Ukrainian nationalist leader who allied with Nazi Germany to fight Soviet troops.

The historic links with far-right bigotry have meant Karpaty's most hardcore fan base has become a recruitment ground for parties such as Svoboda, as well paramilitary organisations such as Right Sector and the Azov Battalion. Club members also actively participated in the rebellion against the pro-Russian Party of Regions government in late 2013 and early 2014, as well as in the resistance against the invading Russian troops from February 2022.

Despite the above, the club has paradoxically been chaired by someone closely linked to the Party of Regions – the party of former President Viktor Yanukovych. This was Petro Dyminskyi – club chair between 2001 and 2020 – who was one of the many tycoons who amassed a fortune thanks to the privatisations that took place after communism.

Dyminskyi, who is from eastern Ukraine and was once a footballer for his city Kryvyi Rih – one with a significant Russian-speaking minority – is a notorious figure. Since 2017, he has been a national fugitive after causing a traffic accident in which a young woman, Natalya Trila, was killed. This has not stopped him from being seen at different Karpaty matches outside Ukraine, whether in Poland or Turkey.

Despite Karpaty's chief's political leanings, the club's association with Ukrainian nationalism is very clear, as is shown by the club adopting for several seasons a red-and-black away kit. The colours were those used by the Organisation of Ukrainian Nationalists and its military wing, the Ukrainian Insurgent Army: in other words, Stepan Bandera's pro-independence movement and Nazi-collaborationist movement.

If any doubt remained over the true meaning of these colours, the club chose to dispel them when it presented the new jersey in front of the monument the city of Lviv created to honour the nationalist fighter. This was quite a statement which showed that Lviv and Karpaty had become the stronghold for the most belligerent stances against any concession to the mainly Russian-language regions in Ukraine's east. In short, they both had become true bastions of the Ukrainian nationalist right.

The stronghold has only hardened its attitude since the Russian occupation: a war that has turned Lviv into the destination for many Ukrainian refugees fleeing the same war fronts where Lviv nationalists are arriving to take up arms against the Russian army.

FC Stroitel Pripyat
The tragic fate of the club born under the wing of Chernobyl

On 26 April 1986, Ukraine witnessed the biggest nuclear accident in the history of humankind. That tragic spring day and during a safety test, reactor number four of the Chernobyl power plant blew to smithereens.

Blown up alongside the reactor was the development model that characterised the Soviet Union in the 1970s, with nuclear energy being one of its central foundations. The Chernobyl plant was indeed often presented in the USSR as a symbol of the nuclear power and modernity of the workers' state that had been ushered in thanks to Lenin (which had led the complex itself to be officially named Vladimir Ilyich Lenin Nuclear Power Plant). It is no coincidence that the plant began being built in the early 1970s in a small Ukrainian town 100 kilometres to the north of Kiev (Kyiv). This was accompanied by the creation of a new closed city – *atomgrad* in the Russian vernacular at that time – which was to house the new plant's workers and their families.

Thus the town of Pripyat came into being, inaugurated in February 1970 – almost seven years before Chernobyl began operating – as one of the most modern urban areas in the Soviet Union. Within a few years, the new Pripyat, located only 2 kilometres from the plant, went from being a simple project to having 50,000 inhabitants and receiving many accolades for being one of the most welcoming and advanced *atomgrads* in the whole of the USSR.

The services and leisure activities the local authorities provided the new residents naturally included a football team, as soccer was the most popular sport in the Union. FC Stroitel was consequently created, in the mid-1970s, with a name translatable as 'FC Builder'. The club had a pro-worker feel to it, as best suited to the working-class character of the city hosting it.

Initially, Stroitel was a team that rooted itself well in the local community. It was made up of youngsters from Pripyat or failing that, from the neighbouring town of Chistogalovka. The latter had much more history to it than the new closed city, as well as its own team which had performed very respectably in regional competitions. It goes without saying that FC Stroitel received the full support of the Chernobyl plant, both to run the club and in the strictly sporting arena. Many of the firm's employees played in the club's jersey.

With backing from a city such as Pripyat and a plant like Chernobyl, Stroitel quickly became one of the strongest teams in local competitions. In 1981, this led the club to decide to compete in the fourth tier of the Soviet amateur championship – then organised by the Football Federation of the Ukrainian Soviet Socialist Republic.

Stroitel's biggest success in this new division took place in 1985, when the team narrowly missed out on promotion, prompting it to consider becoming fully professionalised. Consequently, the following year Stroitel tried to positively transform itself as a club. Besides the discussion over turning professional, it had a new ground built as the increase in match attendance had made the one 'the builders' had been playing in until then too small.

In early 1986, Pripyat saw its brand-new stadium completed with a capacity of 5,000, which, alongside being the venue for Stroitel's home games, was used for athletic competitions. The ground, which was christened *Avanhard* ('Vanguard' – another name with a clear ideological connotation), never got to be officially opened. Stroitel played several games in it in what was expected to be its breakthrough season. Yet the atomic city's heads had reserved 'May Day' 1986 as a symbolic date to formally open the sports venue by hosting a significant event.

Tragically the official celebration at the *Avanhard* never took place. A week before Workers' Day (1 May), the fourth reactor of the Chernobyl power plant blew up, forever trans-forming the history of Pripyat and its people.

The nuclear explosion on 26 April of that year turned what had previously been one of the Soviet Union's model 'atom' cities into a ghost town. The communist authorities ordered Pripyat to be completely evacuated 36 hours after the tragedy – too late some argued. Among the first to find out that the town was to be cleared were the FC Borodyanka players who were due to play in the Ukrainian-regional cup semi-final against Stroitel at the *Avanhard* stadium on 27 April – the day after the accident. The match was naturally suspended, as was the Chernobyl club's involvement in the Soviet amateur fourth division.

Stroitel's players never went back to the ghost town, except those who helped out as 'liquidators' in the heroic tasks attempting to seal Chernobyl's fourth reactor and prevent an even bigger catastrophe. Like most of Pripyat's population, the club moved to Slavutych, a town founded soon after the Cher-nobyl disaster to become the new home for the atomic town's refugees. Once there, the club took on the name of FC Stroitel Slavutych and played for two seasons in the same fourth division as its Pripyat namesake had done. Yet the new club had a short life, it too disappearing, in 1988. It was a victim that could be added to the tens of thousands that the Chernobyl accident had caused.

The old stands of the *Avanhard* have since become overgrown with vegetation confirming the ground's desertedness. What is left of the ground, and the memory of those who used to support the club, are still witnesses to the fact that once Pripyat had a team. A team that, like its fans, saw its dreams dashed by the nuclear tragedy at the Chernobyl nuclear plant – the very one under whose wing it grew.

Klub Oktyabrskoi Revolutsii (Lokomotiv Moscow)

The October Revolution Club

On the night of 7 November 1917 – recorded in history as 25 October because Russia then used the Julian calendar – the Bolsheviks stormed the Winter Palace. This act began what is known as the October Revolution, which celebrated its centenary in 2017. Headed up by Lenin, it led to the building of the first socialist state.

The Bolshevik government overthrew the Russian Empire, transforming the territory from top to bottom. Russia pulled out of the First World War – a step that the bourgeois government that had come about thanks to a previous (February) revolution had not dared take, leading to its downfall. In addition, there were changes to all spheres of life; including sport of course. There was a notable impact on Russian football that had developed embryonically in the late 19th century in Tsarist Russia's few industrial centres, thanks to the arrival of foreign capital and businesspeople.

The first soccer competitions were limited to being local affairs, as was the case of the St Petersburg Championship that started being held in 1901 and involved several clubs. The city was home to the Tsar's palace at the time.

Despite Russian soccer's weak roots, it made remarkable progress during that decade, leading to the founding of the All-Russian Football Union in 1912. That same year, the Tsarist Football Federation became a FIFA member and Russia took part in its first international tournament: the 1912 Stockholm Olympic Games. At these it suffered two humiliating defeats: first against Finland which then was still part of the Russian Empire; and second, and even more embarrassingly, losing 16–0 to the German Empire, which the Russians would soon be fighting on the battlefield in the Great War (the First World War).

The war's outbreak brought Russian football to an almost complete standstill; a paralysis that would persist after the October Revolution. Indeed, the institutions that initially emerged from the revolutionary uprising were against any revival of sports activities that had taken place in Tsarist Russia.

The country then suffered a Civil War, pitting the Revolution's supporters against those wishing to bring back the previous regime. For this reason the sporting structures put in place by the Bolsheviks were primarily geared towards military training. Yet some revolutionaries involved in the *Proletkult* institution championed the need to develop a new proletarian culture and eradicate all traces of bourgeois society in the new socialist state. They consequently advocated putting an end to bourgeois sports such as football, which furthermore had reached Russia thanks to foreign capitalists and was deemed too competitive an activity to embody communist values.

In keeping with *Proletkult*'s view of the sport, soccer was banned from many of the 'gymnastics' events held after the October Revolution. However, their perspective was far from being a majority in the revolutionary movement. This would be revealed when football received the backing of the Bolsheviks in the Supreme Council of Physical Culture, the body which began overseeing sport in the new Soviet Union.

The Council was more practical than *Proletkult* and started allowing competitive sports – including football. This decision coincided with the end of the Civil War and therefore to a degree of being able to return to normality for a country that had suffered back-to-back wars since 1914.

This prompted the setting up of the first soccer clubs since the revolution, which replaced the football societies created at the end of the 19th and beginning of the 20th century. These, like the All-Russian Football Union, had been disbanded after the revolutionary triumph as they were seen to be spreading the Tsarist values the Bolsheviks wished to eradicate.

The first of the new clubs inspired by the Soviet doctrine, and which still exists today, was oddly enough not in Moscow but in the remote Caucasian city of Vladikavkaz in North Ossetia. This was Unitas, created in 1921 – before the Civil War was over. Two years after being founded, it was renamed Vladikavkaz International Communist Youth.

This was followed by sports clubs emerging in the country's biggest cities. One of the pioneering clubs in the new Soviet football was popularly known as Moscow Kazanka, while its official name was the Moscow-Kazan Railway Footballers Circle. The name originated from the train line that linked the Russian capital with Kazan, the main city in Tartarstan, which thanks to its increasing industrialisation had become a revolutionary centre during the 1917 uprising.

Kazanka made its debut on 23 July 1922 in the lower tiers of the Moscow league, thumping Izmaylovo – a club in one of the Russian capital's eastern suburbs. It had a short life under its original name as in 1923 it was officially renamed as the October Revolution Club (*Klub Oktyabrskoi Revolutsii*, KOR).

The fact that Kazanka was made up of rail workers, thereby epitomising the proletarian values behind the October Revolution, was a key reason why the Soviet authorities chose to change its name to that of KOR. It happened at the same time as other Moscow teams appeared that would go on to be the

best known and most successful. These included Dynamo –
linked to the Cheka secret police; CSKA – associated with the
Red Army; and Spartak – originally created as the Moscow
Sports Circle and associated with the public-sector union.

The October Revolution Club only had this grandiose name
for eight years. Perhaps because the authorities did not want
the revolution and its values to be exclusively associated with
a single club, the heads of Soviet sport ordered it to change: in
1931 KOR became Moscow Kazanka. And that name did not
last long either, as in 1936 it was changed again to Lokomotiv,
thus acquiring unmistakable railway overtones.

That year, the first USSR football competitions were established. In May, the first Soviet League Championship began,
opening with a match between Dynamo Leningrad and
Moscow Lokomotiv.

Creating competitions involving teams from all over the
Soviet Union marked the triumph of the Supreme Council of
Physical Culture's approach over that of *Prolekult*, who had
been planning to ban sports they deemed as competitive and
bourgeois. Those in charge of proletarian culture in the early
days of the revolution could hardly have imagined that not just
would soccer stay in the Soviet public arena but that it would
feature a club named after the October Revolution. A club
with an unmistakable working-class nature, like the uprising
that inspired it.

FC Akhmat Grozny
A Chechen club at the Kremlin's service

Today, the Republic of Chechnya is an integral part of the Russian Federation. All the same, the Chechen people's desire for national freedom is still alive and well and makes the region one of the biggest headaches for those in the Kremlin. Indeed, the Chechens have been characterised by their rebellious spirit since Russia occupied their land in the 17th century. Since then, people's revolts have been recurring and even led, in the late 20th century and early 21st, to two brutal wars that ended up with Russian sovereignty being re-imposed despite Chechens' struggle for freedom and independence.

For the last three decades, Grozny – Chechnya's capital – has been the site of intense fighting between pro-independence rebels and forces loyal to Moscow. Clashes were particularly fierce during the First Chechen War – from 1994 to 1996 – which ended in a rebel victory after a battle for Grozny that left the city in ruins; and in the Second Chechen War – between 1999 and 2000 – which put an end to the effective independence the Chechen Republic of Ichkeria had enjoyed since its victory in the first war.

It was while Grozny was being devastated in the summer of 1996 that a team emerged that in the decades afterwards would become the main ambassador of Chechen football: Football Club Akhmat Grozny, as it is called today. The name was given to the club in 2017 to honour Akhmad Kadyrov, the

President of both the Republic and the club who was killed in a rebel attack in 2004. Before that, the club was known as FC Terek – after the river that feeds the Chechen capital – yet it had actually been founded as Dynamo Grozny. This was in 1946 and amid Stalinist repression of the Chechen people, who suffered mass deportations after being accused of having collaborated with the Nazis in the Second World War. This was nothing but a smokescreen to stamp out Chechens' nationalist aspirations.

Like all other similarly named clubs in the Soviet Union, the Chechen capital's Dynamo was linked to the regime's secret police. Such a relationship came to an end in 1948 when the team spent a decade with the name Neftyanik: Oil Worker, tying itself to the oil industry. In 1958, it began being called Terek – a name it kept for half a century.

In its early decades, today's FC Akhmat played without fanfare in the lower divisions of Soviet football. This changed with the break-up of the USSR, which had a big impact on Chechen society. In 1991, while the erstwhile all-powerful state was fragmenting, pro-independence Chechens led by General Dzhokhar Dudayez – a former Soviet army officer – proclaimed the Chechen Republic of Ichkeria. Although this independence was never recognised by the new Russian Federation, which made every effort to hold on to its sovereignty over the Caucasian region, the Chechen rebels exercised effective control over much of the territory.

The shift in in the region's geopolitical situation had some effect on Terek Grozny which, despite the declared Chechen statehood, left the now-defunct Soviet regional leagues to play in the Russian second division. There was a simple reason for this small change: while the rebels claimed full sovereignty, they did not control the Chechen capital, enabling the local club there to continue to compete at the Russian federal level.

To regain full control of Chechnya, Russian President Boris Yeltsin decided in December 1994 to deploy Russian troops in the country. This invasion sparked a devastating war between rebel and Russian forces, which lasted until the summer of 1996 and ended when the pro-independence side spread its control across the whole country – including Grozny. The First Chechen War had significant consequences for local soccer, as Terek practically ceased to exist from 1995 to 2000 due to the instability in the region, which was under constant attack from Russian troops.

With Putin now in the Kremlin, the Second Chechen War in 1999 saw the Russian Federation pushing the tide back to regain its hold over the rebel territory – even if a further decade was needed to pacify the region. The battle that took place between December 1999 and February 2000 prompted the United Nations to consider Chechnya's capital 'the most destroyed city on Earth'. After Russia retook control of it, the forces loyal to the Kremlin helped set up a new football club to be the heir to the historic Terek. For that reason it adopted the very same name.

At the root of the club's re-founding was the will of the new Chechen authorities loyal to Moscow to present a degree of social and political normality in a land in which, despite the apparent defeat of the rebels, guerrilla warfare was still being waged. Pro-independence rebels had taken refuge in the mountains and continued to enjoy widespread backing from local people.

The new authorities were led by the formerly pro-independence Akhmad Kadyrov. During the Second Chechen War, he had switched sides to give his services to the Kremlin – a move Putin rewarded by appointing Kadyrov as head of the pro-Russian administration in 2000. He would later (in 2003) be formally proclaimed President of the Chechen Republic within the Russian Federation.

The new Terek was formed under the auspices of the pro-Russian government and its chairman was Kadyrov himself. The revamped club was undoubtedly an instrument to help such a government normalise Russian sovereignty over Chechnya and was almost its head's personal project. This meant the new club was not very popular among local pro-independence supporters who derisively labelled it 'Terek Kremlin' to highlight its pro-Russian stance.

The new Terek started out in the southern group of Russia's third division, but it soon won promotion to the second. Its truly golden season came in 2004, however, when it achieved two historic feats: winning the Russian Cup and securing promotion to top-tier football. Two milestones that were all the more impressive considering the team was unable to play home games in Grozny due to a lack of safety in the Chechen capital, which was constantly subject to pro-secession guerrilla attacks.

Yet Akhmad Kadyrov, the inspiration behind the club, was never able to enjoy 'his' Terek's cup triumph or promotion to the first division. The club and national head fell victim to a rebel bomb attack in May 2004. This was at a soccer stadium in Grozny and while presiding over a military parade commemorating the Day of Victory (when the Soviet Union triumphed in the Second World War). The man responsible for the attack was Shamil Basayev, the pro-independence guerrilla fighter who oddly enough was also a football man and had been President of the Chechen federation for the sport in 1998, when the Republic of Ichkeria was in place.

Kadyrov's death had a profound effect on Terek, which stayed in his family's hands all the same. His son Ramzan followed his father's steps: combining taking over the chairmanship of the club with becoming President of the pro-Russian Republic of Chechnya from 2007 onwards as a member of Vladimir Putin's United Russia Party.

The cup final held on 29 May 2004, just three weeks after President Kadyrov was assassinated, was a huge event in both Chechnya and Russia. Even the pro-Chechen fighters – the same that accused Terek of being a tool at the Kremlin's service – put down their rifles for a few hours to follow the match pitting the Grozny team against Krylia Sovetov Samara, a Russian Premier League club.

The Chechen people had mixed feelings about the match. On the one hand, it was hard to support a team without a Chechen in its ranks and which was clearly linked to the institutions legitimising the occupation. On the other, it was the first time that a Chechen club was competing for a federal title. Furthermore, it was doing so in Moscow against a Russian team.

Despite the ongoing war in the country, almost 8,000 Chechens travelled to the Lokomotiv stadium in Moscow to experience first-hand a final held under the strict security conditions imposed by the anti-terrorist police force. Those same fans displayed images of Akhmad Kadyrov in a stadium dominated by a huge banner bearing the slogan 'Death to Chechen terrorism!'. The match was preceded by a minute's silence in memory of President Kadyrov, while his son Ramzan in Terek's executive box watched his team win by a single goal – scored by Andrei Fedkov in the dying moments of the match.

The Russian striker dedicated his goal to 'the Chechen people' aware of the happiness his winner had given the people of a region hard hit by war. While celebrating the title on the Lokomotiv stadium's turf, the Terek players held up a portrait of Akhmad Kadyrov and offered the trophy to his son and current club chairman. The triumph in the Russian

Cup and then promotion to the Premiere League prompted a brand-new stadium to be built in Grozny; the Akhmat-Arena – named in honour of its former chairman – which opened in 2011.

The club's complicity with the Kremlin was such that during Terek's first season in the top Russian division, the club sent a letter to Putin to protest referees' mistreatment of the club and calling for his intervention. Putin did not respond but the mere fact that they dared to send such a letter revealed the closeness and trust there was between the club and the Russian government. This proximity was understood as being politically motivated. The current affairs magazine *Russky Newsweek* even wrote, 'each day that Terek plays in the Russian first division is another day that the Kremlin can boast of stability in the region'.

Perhaps this is why after spending only one year in the Russian Federation's top tier, Akhmat Grozny managed to win promotion back to it two years later and has since remained there. A spot that provides a central argument to the claim that the country has returned to peace and normality. A club with a marked political character turned puppet of the Kremlin and the Kadyrov family to justify Russia's dominance over the ever-rebellious Chechnya.

Qarabağ FK
The exiled club that left behind a ghost town

One of the most dramatic consequences of war, as well as the number of dead and wounded, is that of people being forced to leave their homes. The war in the autonomous province the Soviets named Nagorno-Karabakh, and which pitted Armenia and Azerbaijan against each other, pushed over a million people into exile. It is a figure that reveals the full extent of a conflict that has had an impact way beyond the upper Karabakh region – as this area only had a population of under 200,000. This shows how the war forced out most Azerbaijanis living in Nagorno-Karabakh and Armenia at the same time as doing the same to the Armenians in Azerbaijan.

We must add to these million refugees a whole football club: Qarabağ Futbol Klubu, which was originally from the Azeri city of Aghdam but was forced to leave its hometown in the summer of 1993 when the Armenian offensive conquered Nagorno-Karabakh and its neighbouring areas. After fleeing the Armenian troops, the club took refuge in Baku, the Azerbaijani capital, where it made a new home and has played its home matches there ever since.

Although the Nagorno-Karabakh war did not officially begin until 1988, when the Armenian Soviet Socialist Republic formally claimed sovereignty over the region, the fact is that the whole Karabakh region has always been at the centre of disputes between Armenia and Azerbaijan. The two neighbouring countries, which formed part of the Soviet Union until 1991, have competing religious identities: Christian in the Armenian case and Muslim in the Azeri. This has turned their border into one of the world's many East–West conflicts.

Contemporary dispute over upper Karabakh – a region that is now the Armenian-controlled independent republic of Artsakh – began with the establishment of the domestic borders within the USSR that came into being in 1922. The USSR initially planned to incorporate the region into its Republic of Armenia, but this decision was reversed as a result of the anti-Soviet uprisings in Yerevan in the early 1920s. Thus, despite Nagorno-Karabakh having a 94 per cent Armenian population, the area became an autonomous province of the Socialist Republic of Azerbaijan when the USSR was officially formed. Under Soviet rule, the Azeri government developed an aggressive demographic policy which eventually reduced the percentage of Armenians to 75 per cent by the early 1980s, while reinforcing the idea that the historical land of Karabakh, whose territory extends beyond that incorporated in the autonomous province, was an integral part of Azerbaijan.

One of the historic Karabakh cities touching the autonomous province was Aghdam. It was here that today's Qarabağ FK was created, in 1951, albeit originally with the drab Azeri name of *Mehsul* – translatable as 'Product'.

The new club spent its first decades playing in the local Azerbaijani league, where it had ups and downs and even temporarily disappeared as a club. In that period it adopted a myriad of names – all Soviet-inspired. In 1987, however, it adopted the name Qarabağ FK – associating thus with the historic Karabakh region – influenced by rising Azeri nationalism.

The new name was unmistakably political, claiming the Azerbaijani identity of Karabakh at a time when Armenia's attempt to regain sovereignty over its upper territory was gaining momentum. It brought luck to a club which won the Soviet Azeri local league championship for the first time in 1988. But this was also for the last time, as the championship stopped being played after Azerbaijan declared independence in November 1990, which was recognised the following year.

Around that time, the former Nagorno-Karabakh autonomous province was embroiled in an open war between Azerbaijan and Armenia – also independent since September 1991. It was a conflict that split across the province's borders, leading to the population being mobilised for the war in both states. It particularly affected the rest of historic Karabakh – including Aghdam.

The city's strategic importance made it one of the Azeri forces' strongholds and consequently a key target for the Armenian troops they were fighting. The wartime atmosphere in the city did not prevent its leading club from being instrumental in launching independent Azerbaijan's first league competition in 1992.

Yet Qarabağ's home matches at its Imaret stadium were often played against a background noise of shelling that was even known to have landed on the pitch. Such a situation, together with the unstoppable advance of Armenian troops in Nagorno-Karabakh, eventually led to figures linked to the club joining up with Azeri militias to defend Aghdam.

A special role in this defence was played by Allahverdi Baghirov, one of Qarabağ's legendary figures – as he had not just played in its jersey but was later its head coach. In 1988, he championed creating self-defence groups in the city, and he later became a key person in the Azerbaijani Popular Front, the nationalist coalition that fought for Azeri independence from the Soviet Union. Baghirov commanded the troops that fought the Armenian forces for sovereignty over Nagorno-Karabakh.

Many Qarabağ players wanted to follow in his footsteps but Baghirov himself stopped this, arguing that their job was to keep playing football so that the people of Aghdam could think about something other than the war they endured daily. As the highly respected Azeri Commander Baghirov, he featured in one of the most iconic images of the war when during a prisoner exchange with the Armenian army, he hugged one of his enemies just before freeing him, explaining that they had played football together for years and expressing his desire to not have to fight against him again on the battlefield.

Baghirov could not lead his troops for long as in June 1992 he was killed when an anti-tank mine exploded in his path. The former Qarabağ player became a national hero and was even respected by the Armenian commanders who told off their soldiers for 'not having saved a man like that'.

In practical terms, the definitive end of the war in upper Karabakh came in 1993, when Armenian troops reached Aghdam in a final offensive. Despite the city's agony, that same year paradoxically saw Qarabağ have its best season to date: winning both the Azeri league championship and cup.

The semi-final for the cup competition was the last match the club would play in the city that gave birth to it. This took place on 12 May 1993. That day, the Aghdam team took its first step towards qualifying for the final in Baku (Azerbaijan's capital) on 28 May, which it won. Two weeks later, the Battle of Aghdam started.

For a month and a half, Armenian forces laid siege to the city until it surrendered – on 23 July 1993. This was only five days after Qarabağ celebrated its victory in the league championship. It was obviously a triumph with more than a bitter aftertaste. The league trophy went to Aghdam but the city was on the way to becoming a ghost town. No-one greeted the champions, who, in no mood to celebrate their historic win, put their energies into trying to find their relatives among the survivors.

Aghdam was seen by the Armenians as a strategic strong-hold to protect Nagorno-Karabakh. In no time, it was razed to the ground. Faced with such destruction, the city's 40,000 inhabitants fled, leaving it deserted. Some say it has become the biggest ghost town in the world.

Like the population, Qarabağ FK also had to leave the city, leaving the Imaret ground in ruins. Thus began its long exodus as an exiled club which led it to first play its matches in the town of Quzanli, where many of the Aghdam refugees had settled. Eventually Qarabağ settled in Baku, where it became the dominant team in Azerbaijani football in the early 2000s.

Despite the desperate situation the club was in due to these moves, Qarabağ managed to survive thanks to the refugee identity it took on, which made it a symbol for the thousands of exiles that Azerbaijan had taken in because of the armed conflict in upper Karabakh. This identity was shown in every home match that the club played in the Tofiq Bahramov National Stadium. The ground is probably one of the only ones on the planet to be named after a referee: that of the controversial Azeri assistant referee in the 1966 World Cup final. The linesman's name replaced those of Lenin and Stalin. It should be noted that Qarabağ left the Azeri national ground in 2015 when construction of its new Azersun Arena stadium was completed.

After some difficult years, Qarabağ became one of the country's top clubs – the only one able to take on the historical Baku clubs. This is partly thanks to being sponsored by the food producer and exporter Azersun – the same conglomerate that paid for the new stadium to be built. It was also due to having hired Gurban Gurbanov – a former Azeri football star – as coach.

Gurbanov introduced a playing style similar to that of (Barcelona and later Manchester City manager) Pep Guardiola. Under Gurbanov's stewardship, the refugees' club has won six league titles in a row and has established itself as the powerhouse of Azeri football, earning it the nickname '*Qafqazin Barselonas*' (the 'Barcelona of the Caucus'). The name stems from the good football that Gurbanov was able to instil in the club but also from Qarabağ being (like *Barça*) more than a club.

One of the club's recent big successes, beyond its titles and the beauty of its game, has been its repeated appearance in European competitions. This has allowed its fans to internationalise their cause. Indeed, Qarabağ FK was the first Azeri team to reach the group stage of the Champions League when in the 2017–2018 season it was put in the same group as three historic European teams: Chelsea, Roma, and Atlético de Madrid.

Qarabağ's continental matches, which have also included frequent matches in the (second-tier) Europa League, are ideal to showcase its Azeri identity and links with Turkey with which it shares a long-standing confrontation with their Armenian neighbour. Maybe that is why in 2009, in its first European match for three seasons, Qarabağ asked UEFA to hold a minute's silence in memory of the victims of the Aghdam occupation. The match was held on the same 23 July that the city was conquered by Armenian forces 16 years earlier.

Those in charge of European football refused to heed the request. Yet this did not stop the match from becoming a show of Azeri nationalism in a stadium presided over by a banner bearing 'We shall never forget. 23-07-1993'.

The club's strong identity also often gives rise to counter-reactions. When Qarabağ visited Borussia Dortmund's Westfalenstadion for a Europa League match, the *Südtrib-*

une's 'yellow wall' (south stand supporters) waved several Armenia flags to support this republic's sovereignty over Nagorno-Karabakh.

Despite such reproaches, the triumphant Qarabağ club still has a dream: to stop being a refugee club and one day return to an Aghdam that is no longer a ghost town.

7

The Middle East and Central Asia

Amman New Camp: the Palestinian refugee camp in which the Al-Wehdat club was formed

Erbil SC
Iraqi Kurdistan's flagship team

On 25 September 2017, Southern Kurdistan (the Kurdish territory under Iraqi sovereignty) voted overwhelmingly for independence in a referendum set up by the regional government against opposition from Baghdad. The high turnout, together with the easy win by the pro-independence vote, seemed to make the region an embryo of a future Kurdish state – a dream that decades ago would have been unthinkable for Iraqi Kurdistan's citizens.

Despite the clear outcome, in which around 93 per cent supported full Kurdish sovereignty, the poll did not go beyond being merely symbolic and without practical effects on the Iraqi Kurdish autonomous region. This was due to both a lack of international support for the referendum and military intervention by the Iraqi Federal government, which ruled out any prospect of separate statehood. Nevertheless, the referendum showed that Iraqi Kurds had widely shifted towards a pro-independence stance.

An indisputable role in this process was played by football, which mirrored recent Kurdish history and had been a key component in the development of related nationalism.

One of the pillars of this footballing nationalism and the biggest club in Southern Kurdistan is Erbil Sports Club, a multi-sports club in the similarly named capital of the autonomous region that fans often label 'Hawler' (ھەولێر) – the

Kurdish name of its home city. Erbil SC was created in 1968 in the context of the Kurd national revolution in Iraq, which prompted armed conflict between nationalists in the Kurdistan Democratic Party (KDP) and the Iraqi state forces. The struggle went on throughout the 1960s and ended with a timid recognition of Kurdish autonomy by the Iraqi authorities, which had been led by the pan-Arab socialist Ba'ath Party during all of Erbil SC's existence.

Despite originating out of political upheaval and emergent autonomy, it is worth noting that Erbil from its very beginnings had to face a repressive offensive against expressions of Kurdish identity such as that epitomised by the club. This persecution worsened in 1979, when Saddam Hussein came to power, and the bloody war began that pitted Iraq against Islamic Iran.

During Hussein's rule, the Kurdish people lived under harsh conditions. Its members were systematically persecuted and excluded from any influential circles. This was reflected in football by the Kurdish players being excluded from the Iraqi national team.

Ironically, it was during these years of greatest repression against the Kurdish people that Erbil SC scored its biggest sporting success to date: earning a historic promotion to the Iraqi first division in 1987. Until then, the flagship team for the Kurds of Iraq had only competed in the lower leagues of Iraqi football.

Fate had it that this success coincided with the biggest repressive operation the Hussein government had ever led against the Kurdish people. This was the military campaign named 'Anfal' in which Iraqi forces used poison gas, killing thousands of Kurds from 1986 to 1989. The architect of this was General Ali Hassan al-Majid – better known as 'Chemical Ali' and 'the butcher of Kurdistan'.

Erbil was not spared from persecution either. Its unmistakable Kurdish identity meant that during its matches against Arab teams, its players were subjected to all kinds of insults from opposing fans. Such a situation was exacerbated after the First Gulf War, in 1991, when US-led international military intervention left Kurdistan as an autonomous territory with its own regional government.

As a result, when Iraqi league matches resumed after the wartime disruption, rival supporters would make chants increasingly meant to offend Erbil fans. It is worth mentioning that these included ones labelling the Kurds 'Iraq's Jews'.

These constant taunts only reinforced the club's Kurdish identity. On a symbolic level, Erbil had already included the Kurdish language on its crest. In 2001, however, it renamed its stadium, Franso Hariri. By doing so, it paid direct homage to the former Erbil governor and KDP leader who was a leading figure in the 1960s Kurdish Revolution. In September 2017, the ground hosted the largest-ever rally held in Iraqi Kurdistan during the pro-independence referendum campaign.

The relative prosperity that the Iraqi Kurd territory enjoyed as a result of its autonomy allowed Erbil to establish itself as one of the leading clubs in the Iraqi league championship. Indeed it led the competition when games were halted again due to the American-led military assault in 2003.

That invasion ousted Saddam Hussein from power but created much instability. Iraqi Kurds were able to take advantage of this to consolidate their regional autonomy and government. The Kurdish territory consequently became, in a twist of fate, the safest area in the whole of Iraq. It was this that enabled Erbil to emerge as one of the top teams in the newly organised Iraqi championship. It was able to sign the best Arab players who preferred to live in a peaceful Erbil instead of a conflict-ridden Baghdad.

Resultingly, in 2007, the Kurd club managed to end the Baghdad teams' dominance in the championship, which led them to win every league trophy since 1990. Southern Kurdistan's flagship team not only managed to wrest the title from them, but did so for three seasons in a row, signalling a transformation in Iraqi football which was completed by Duhok – another Kurdish team – winning the 2010 championship and the Erbil team again being victorious in 2012.

This period coincided with the Iraqi national team also shining and picking up the 2007 AFC Asian Cup thanks to a team made up of Arab and Kurdish players – a victory much celebrated in Kurdistan. However, the recent boom in support for independence has distanced the Kurds from the Iraqi squad, which led few of them to celebrate the victory of Iraq's Under-21 team in the 2014 Asian Cup.

Kurds prefer to support their own Iraqi Kurdish national team: a team created in 2006 and which, despite not being officially recognised, played from 2008 in the Viva World Cup – an alternative world cup bringing together federations that FIFA does not recognise. In 2012, this unique cup was played in Southern Kurdistan itself and saw the host nation crowned as champions – the squad's first big international triumph.

This team, which since the September 2017 referendum has hoped to become a fully fledged member of FIFA and officially recognised, is comprised of players from Iraq's leading Kurdish clubs – led by Erbil and Duhok. Indeed, the role that football has played in developing Kurdish national identity must be borne in mind. This has happened through the Kurdish national team but also Erbil Sports Club itself – a team that has become the main ambassador of Iraqi football by reaching a continental final. In 2012, Erbil faced SC Kuwait in the AFC Cup – the second biggest competition in Asian football – at the Franso Hariri stadium. It ended up having to mourn being defeated. However, the club still made use of the platform the tournament provided to make the political statement that 'Kurdistan is not Iraq'. This was the slogan its fans shouted while packing out the stadium and waving Kurdish flags.

Reaching the AFC Cup final again in 2014 was the last major milestone for Erbil (despite being defeated for a second time). In the latter years of the 21st century, it was plagued with financial difficulties. It also has been on the receiving end of growing hatred from Arab clubs – especially Shiite ones – which accuse it of being complicit with Islamic State despite the Kurdish *peshmergas* (military forces) having been on the front line of the fight against Daesh. An example of the abuse suffered were the chants heard at the home ground of Al-Najaf, a Shiite Baghdad club, in the 2016–2017 season: 'Erbil and the *peshmergas* are Islamic State'.

It was actions such as this that prompted the Iraqi Kurdish capital's team to pull out of the league championship after playing only twelve matches. This decision led it to be automatically relegated to the Iraqi second division: a tier from which the Kurds hoped to pull out of if the independence voted for in the referendum on 25 September 2017 was implemented.

As those hopes were dashed, Erbil played in the Iraqi second division in the 2017–2018 season, for which it ended up champion and promoted to the first division. It has played in the latter ever since, awaiting the arrival of an independent Kurdish state. With that, it would be able to play in the league it always wanted: that of a free and united Kurdistan.

Al-Wehdat SC
Palestine's footballing voice

Before FIFA eventually recognised the Palestinian national team in 1998, after a long fight for official recognition that took over three decades, the main footballing embodiment of the Palestinian national cause was Al-Wehdat Sports Club. This was a modest team that had been formed in the main Palestinian refugee camp in the Jordanian city of Amman.

The camp was one of the consequences of the first armed conflict between Arabs and Jews for sovereignty over Palestine that broke out at the end of Britain's colonial mandate over the land. The 1948 war ended with the proclamation of the state of Israel and the mass flight of Arab citizens in what the Palestinians termed the '*Nakba*': the catastrophe that drove them from their homes due to the birth of a state that sought to be the exclusive national home of the Jewish people.

Many of the hundreds of thousands of Palestinians forced into exile sought sanctuary in neighbouring Jordan. This led to the forming of the Amman New Camp, a refugee camp commonly known as '*al-Wehdat*' (also *al-Wihdat*) – an Arabic name meaning 'units' and that referred to the precarious housing it consisted of.

Al-Wehdat had been built and was run by the UNRWA, the United Nations' Relief and Works Agency for Palestinian Refugees created after the 1948 Arab–Israeli War to care for Palestinian nationals who had fled their homes because of the war. It quickly became the biggest camp for Palestinians in the country.

Among the activities that the UN agency promoted at the *al-Wehdat* camp was physical exercise among the exiles. In 1955, this led it to create and manage a multi-sports club which would represent the camp and encourage the refugees being housed in the camp to do sport.

Al-Wehdat Sports Club quickly became a very popular institution among the large Palestinian diaspora in Jordan. The fact that it had the same name as the main centre taking in such refugees helped its football section – the best known in the club. Its football team participated in Jordanian championships, attracting thousands of fans. Furthermore, these were not only from the *al-Wehdat* Camp but from all over Jordan. A further wave of forced migration into Jordan (on top of that produced by the 1948 war) had been in response to the 1967 Six-Day War, in which Israel occupied Gaza and the West Bank.

In September 1970, armed Palestinian militias clashed with the Jordanian army in fighting that ended with the Palestinian Liberation Organisation (PLO) being expelled from the country it had been exiled to. These events sowed discord between Jordanian citizens and Palestinian refugees.

From then on, matches pitting al-Wehdat against Jordanian teams became political platforms for the growing Jordanian–Palestinian confrontation to be played out. Such tension ratcheted up in 1975, when al-Wehdat earned a long-awaited promotion to the Jordanian first division.

Five years later, the refugee club won its first top-division title – once again cheered on by thousands of Palestinians. This was after a dramatic clash on the last match day with al-Ramtha, the Jordanian team which came runner's up. During the match, serious battles between both sets of supporters took place.

Despite the incidents, the team's success was widely celebrated in the streets of the *al-Wehdat* camp. So too, in the main streets of Palestine's West Bank and Gaza Strip – occupied Palestinian lands which in the absence of local or national football teams to stand for them had adopted al-Wehdat as their standard bearer.

Palestinian flags and their colours tended to fill the stadiums the club played in, leading the club to adopt them for its own kit. And, in keeping with the sporting embodiment of Palestinian nationalism that history had bestowed on it, al-Wehdat also included in its crest the Palestinian flag's colours, accompanying these with an image of the al-Aqsa mosque. This was a clear demand for *al-Quds* – the name Arabs use for Jerusalem as the capital of Palestine.

Al-Wehdat's nationalist symbolism heightened its rivalry with al-Faisaly, the biggest Jordanian team and also from Amman. Games between the two featured real pitched battles between fans in which the police would always side with the Jordanians. The unrest that often accompanied al-Wehdat matches was the excuse used by the Jordanian sporting authorities to heavily punish the club in 1986. Concretely the club was forced to change both who ran it and its name. The authorities even went as far as demoting it to a lower division – although that was never carried out.

Since then, the Jordanian Ministry of Youth took over al-Wehdat, renaming it al-Difftayn. The name conjured up a union between the two 'Jordans': 'Trans-Jordan' (Jordan) and the Palestinian 'Cis-Jordan' (the other name for the West Bank). The aim of the club's new management was to bring together Palestinian and Jordanian supporters alike. It did not come to fruition as the club's faithful was still almost exclusively from the Palestinian refugee community in Jordan.

The club's new name had an obvious nationalist meaning, alluding to an alliance between Arabs from both 'Jordans' (which from the angle of Palestine could also be interpreted as the coming together of Cis-Jordanian Palestinians and Palestinians in Jordan). Yet club fans flatly opposed the change, never seeing the Jordanian–Palestinian union as their own.

In the Amman ground stands, fans still referred to the club as al-Wehdat, as figuring in one of the most popular chants from that era: 'March! Move! All the people will move with al-Wehdat from the Amman stadium to Jerusalem!'. This also expressed Palestinian refugees' desire to set foot again on a land having *al-Quds* as its capital.

The relaxation of the Jordanian regime that took place in the late 1980s led to the holding of the first parliamentary elections, in November 1989. Although political parties were still banned, many independent candidates linked to the pan-Islamist and conservative Muslim Brotherhood did stand. The electoral success of the Islamist candidates, who were particularly sensitive to the Palestinian issue, eventually spurred a parliamentary discussion on al-Wehdat which led to the return of the club's original name and management to be handed back to the refugee-camp representatives that had originally created it.

Yet despite this, the rivalry with al-Faisaly only increased. The trading of insults between the Jordanian and Palestinian sets of fans was commonplace in any match between the two football clubs. The fans of al-Faisaly – Jordan's dominant club until al-Wehdat started being able to rival its game – even popularised a chant in its ground calling on Prince Abdullah, who was made King in 1999, to divorce his wife Rania – referring to the Palestinian origins of the future Queen.

In 1995, as the peace process between Israelis and Palestinians was unfolding, al-Wehdat was finally able to travel to Palestinian territory. There it played several matches in the West Bank and Gaza in front of large crowds. It was during this emotional tour that the team was received by Yasser Arafat, the celebrated leader of the PLO who became the first *Rais* (President) of the Palestinian National Authority that emerged from the peace process. During the unique meeting, Arafat addressed leading club figures with the words, 'Once, when we [Palestinians] had no voice, al-Wehdat was our voice'. By doing so, the *Rais* was explicitly recognising the symbolic significance of al-Wehdat for Palestinian pride.

The club, for its part, stayed faithful to its Palestinian identity. In 1996, it refused to play Israeli teams in international competitions. It therefore stood up to a state that had forced most al-Wehdat supporters into exile, and which was refusing to acknowledge their right to return even in the middle of peace talks.

In the last decade of the 20th century and the first years of the next, al-Wehdat became a successful club, winning many titles over three decades, and challenging al-Faisaly's long-term grip over Jordanian football. This was helped by its fans' allegiance to the club, even when it was the victim of persecution and bans, which conclusively proved the Jordanian authorities' dislike of the club.

Besides the reprisals following the 1970 Black September conflict, fans of the refugee-camp club saw the Jordanian government try to prohibit Palestinian flags in its matches. The measure was to no avail and only increased the popularity of a team which on the pitch was constantly bringing joy to those barely in a position to speak out. As Arafat had said, al-Wehdat helped break the silence for a Palestinian community that mostly lived a long way from what had been its home.

Al-Wehdat's crowning year came in 2009, when it won all four of the Jordanian competitions it entered: the league, cup, league cup, and super cup. This was unprecedented and was very widely celebrated both in the *al-Wehdat* camp and the occupied Palestinian territories, whose streets have become used to celebrating the club's (numerous) triumphs since then.

This is the clearest sign that al-Wehdat still has a special place in the hearts of organised pro-Palestinians, even though the country now has a national team to stand for it internationally and in its own domestic competitions – both in the Gaza Strip and West Bank. All the same, the Palestinian refugees' club in Amman will always be a footballing representative of the Palestinian people's struggle for freedom.

Sheheen Asmayee FC
Kabul's Falcons

Afghanistan's capital, Kabul, is a city that has spent much of the last two centuries in ongoing conflict. Peaceful periods have been few and far between from the First Anglo-Afghan War in the 19th century to the international invasion that overthrew the Mullah Omar regime protecting Osama Bin Laden and the Taliban retaking of the capital in August 2021, and they have always heralded new armed conflicts.

Under such continual tension, actions such as playing football become a symbolic statement of the people's will to establish at least some normality to defy such frequently disruptive violence. That was the logic behind the Afghan authorities' decision to help create the first major national sports competition in the country: the Afghan Premier League. This is also known as 'Roshan' after the company sponsoring it – the biggest telecommunications company in Afghanistan (as happens in the big domestic competitions across the world). Curiously the authorities' plan came to fruition in 2012, coinciding with the beginning of the international forces' gradual withdrawal from the country.

Creating this new competition was a significant step forward for Afghan football. The sport had been brought to the country in the 1920s, but this was the first time that a league had been created that aimed to involve teams from the whole territory. Until the last decade, the main football competition had been the Kabul League, created in 1946 and limited to clubs from the capital. The league has been subject to many interruptions as a consequence of the many changes the country has suffered since then, with the war against Soviet Russia and the subsequent Civil War that ended with the Taliban taking power as the main episodes in this tragic history.

One of the main irregularities of the new Afghan league was the agreement made for the competition to consist only of eight clubs who each would play in the name of one of Afghanistan's equivalent number of regions. This led to eight new teams having to be formed which were then tasked with being the footballing standard bearers for their respective areas.

The greater Kabul area – the one with the longest football tradition – saw its representation fall to the newly founded Shaheen Asmayee Football Club – or Asmayee Falcons. Asmayee is the name of one of two mountains in the centre of the city (popularly known as 'Television Hill' as it is home to many TV broadcasting antennae). The mount also includes a fortress, control of which had been the aim of heavy fighting during the various Afghan wars.

Aside from its structure, the new Afghan league was also unique in how the squads of the teams playing in it were put together. A considerable number of the players forming teams like the Asmayee Falcons were picked through a reality TV show called *Maidan-e-Sabz* ('Green Field' in the Pashto language). The aim of this was for viewers to choose some of those making up the team for the viewer's region.

This extraordinary step, which resulted from an agreement between the Afghan Football Federation and the Moby Media Group, was popular among the public and helped hook several regions where football had very little roots. Of course, the agreement also gave the mentioned media group the rights to broadcast matches – a practice imported from the major

European and North American competitions, where TV revenue forms a substantial share of the football business.

Even so, the purpose of the Afghan Premier League went beyond the sporting and business arenas that characterise the main soccer competitions on the planet today. Those championing the new league aimed to unite the country through football, which was a tough mission, given Afghanistan's cultural and linguistic diversity and particularly the violent conflicts that have taken place between different ethnic groups over recent decades.

Despite the difficulty of meeting the challenge, the footballing initiative was much applauded by institutions such as the Afghan High Peace Council. This was a body created when Hamid Karzai was the national President and aimed to negotiate peace with the Taliban. It saw the setting up of sports contests such as the Afghan Premier League as a chance to bring stability to the country.

The permanent conflicts in Afghanistan led those creating the new league to opt for a modest format. The championship lasted just a few months – from August to October – was limited to 18 matches, and was exclusively played in Kabul – due to the unsafe conditions in the rest of the country. The venue for most matches in the Afghan league, and which drew respectable numbers of spectators, was the Ghazi Stadium (Hero Stadium). This had been built in 1923 during King Amanullah Khan's reign and was named as it was to refer to the King's role in the Afghan victory in the third war against the British, which led to the recognition of the Kingdom of Afghanistan's full sovereignty.

Yet the stadium's hosting of matches contrasted with the fact that it had been used under the first Taliban government – between 1996 and 2001 – as its favourite setting for executions. Indeed these were often carried out during half-time of sports events.

The first Afghan Premier League, played in 2012, was won by Toofaan Harirod (Storm of the Hari River) – the club playing for the country's western region. Yet since then, Kabul's Falcons have dominated the competition, picking up five league titles (in 2013, 2014, 2016, 2017, and 2018) and only missing out on three (when it ended as runner-up).

Particularly politically relevant were the last matches in the 2016 and 2017 seasons as they pitted the club from the Kabul region, and therefore the symbolic heartland of power and government, against that of De Maiwand Atalan (the Maiwand Champions): the team playing for the south-eastern region that was one of the Taliban's biggest strongholds at the time, and a hub of anti-government insurgency. The regions (and therefore clubs) therefore symbolised completely opposed stances on the Afghan political spectrum. Political readings to one side, the two finals between the teams from these regions were held without incident, and the Falcons' win was widely celebrated on the streets of the capital.

These streets have, since August 2021, gone back to being controlled by the Taliban, who took power on the eve of the final withdrawal by international troops, led by the United States, which had been the true authority in the country since invading it in 2001. The Taliban's return to power poses an obvious threat to the Afghan Premier League, a competition that was formed under the mantle of a government that was bitterly fought against by the insurgents who are now the country's lords and masters.

Whether or not Kabul's Falcons will be able to continue fighting to dominate Afghan football is unclear; what is clear is that the images of women watching the Afghan capital's club games or young women footballers playing in a league will be a thing of the past under the Taliban government. An administration that suggests that the city of Kabul will, alas, continue to pulsate to the rhythm of war.

8
Africa

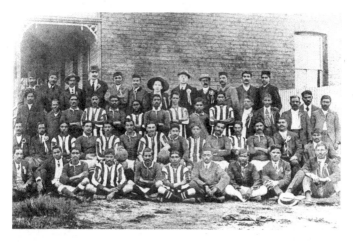

Picture of the Passive Resisters SC family where 'Mahatma' Gandhi can be identified sixth from the left, in the back row

Racing Universitaire d'Alger
Camus' and French-colonial Algeria's club

There is only one soccer club that can boast of having had a Nobel Prize winner for Literature in its ranks. Indeed, it seems that traditionally – bar a few honourable exceptions, including renowned figures such as Eduardo Galeano and Manuel Vázquez-Montalbán – football and writing books do not mix well. This is not so with Racing Universitaire d'Alger (RUA), a club created at the university that gave it its name, which not only had many university students in its ranks but also Albert Camus, the 1957 Winner of the Nobel Prize for Literature, who was goalkeeper for its youth team.

Although Camus' time in the RUA was rather short-lived, as a tuberculosis infection he acquired at the age of 17 thwarted his sporting career and stopped him from one day being Racing's first-team goalkeeper. Yet he would later say, 'Everything I know about morality and the obligations of men, I owe to football. It was at Racing Universitaire d'Alger where I learned it'.

Simply recalling the memory of RUA was for Camus a reminder of his colonial childhood in a French Algeria in which the university team had become quite a symbol. Indeed, Racing Universitaire Algérois – the name the club originally adopted, and which later had the adjective ('Algérois') replaced by the noun ('Alger') – had been created in 1927 out of a merger between two clubs. These were first Racing Club d'Alger, which wore a jersey with white and sky-blue horizontal stripes, like its Parisian equivalent and as now adopted by RUA; and second Club Sportif Alger Université, which played in a violet shirt – the colours of the University of Algiers that the new club also included in its crest to reflect its university connection.

The merger had the sporting goal of creating a club able to compete against the capital's big clubs – in particular, the mighty Gallia Sport. It also had a political one, as it had been instigated by a group of people closely linked to the commission responsible for organising the centenary for the French colonisation of Algeria, which was to be celebrated with great fanfare in 1930. Thus, from its inception RUA's identity was determined by two elements: being a university club and being linked to prominent figures in colonial Algeria.

Once Racing Universitaire was formally established, it was incorporated into the Algiers League – the body that ran football in the French *département* (region) of Algiers and was dependent on the French Football Federation. It was in 1932 – just two years after its founding – that Albert Camus joined the university sports society's youth team. He had already started out as a footballer, playing for Monpensier Sports Association, another Algerian colonial team from the poor neighbourhood of Bab el Oued. This was despite Camus living in Belcourt – one of Gallia Sport's bastions.

His time at Bab el Oued was fleeting because, as Camus himself explained, he was embarrassed at his high school by the fact that, being so gifted at writing and hoping to go to university, he was not goalkeeping for the new Racing Universitaire d'Alger. So it was that the future Noble Prize winner ended up in the Algerian university team where, as mentioned, tuberculosis thwarted his footballing dreams.

The 1930s was Racing Universitaire's golden age. The team quickly established itself as one of the strongest in the Algiers League's *Division d'Honneur* and was champion in 1934, 1935, 1939, and 1945. It was in that period that the colonial-origin university team developed a rivalry with the city's big Muslim popular-class team Mouloudia Club d'Alger. Enmity went beyond the strictly sporting because it played out the confrontation between the Islamic identity of native Algerians with the French identity of the settlers. To fight the notably increased politicisation of sport in the colony – particularly in football which aroused the greatest passions – the French authorities introduced different measures from 1928 to 1936 purportedly to fight against 'communalism'. Their real intention was more to eliminate any non-French identification with a sports club from the region.

The first of these provisions was to force all teams with any 'Muslim' reference in their name to also incorporate the word 'French'. As an example, Union Sportive Musulmane Blidéene (with 'Musulmane' meaning Muslim) became Union Sportive Franco-Musulmane Blidéene. Yet, the step not only failed to stop the club from having an Islamic character, but actually strengthened such, as the name change was seen as an affront.

Given the tense atmosphere felt during matches pitting colonial teams, such as Racing Universitaire, and Algerian ones stirring up revolt among the native population, the next rule the authorities brought in was to force all Muslim squads to include a minimum quota of settler players. This was initially a third of all players and later, half. Additionally, there had to be French people on each club's board, and clubs could be disbanded if they failed to comply with such rules. Despite the harshness of these regulations, none succeeded in their goal of detracting from the symbolism of the Muslim clubs, whose clashes with settler teams continued to be seen as a political battle.

Despite its clearly colonial side, it is also true that Racing Universitaire d'Argel included among its players the children of the indigenous Algerian elites – the same who were able to study at the University of Algiers (even if in tiny numbers). Rumour had it that even Ferhat Abbas, a prominent leader of the movement for Algerian independence who later became Prime Minister of the Provisional Government of the Algerian Republic, had passed through its ranks when he still advocated recognising Algeria's own identity without the land defini-tively breaking with the French state. Abbas having been in the Racing changing room may have been no more than gossip, but involvement in the club by leading players of Algerian origin is well-documented. This included Hamid Hadjadj, President of the post-independence Algerian Football Fed-eration, and Abdelkader Ben Bouali, who played for France and was a 1937 French league champion for Olympique de Marseille.

Even though these indigenous additions gave a mixed feel to Racing Universitaire, Albert Camus' club remained a colonial icon that almost exclusively attracted support from Europeans living in Algiers. It was these very Europeans that most ardently celebrated RUA's triumphs in the North African Football Championship – the colonial competition pitting against each other the winners of the Algerian, Tunisian, and Moroccan leagues, while each country was under French control. Twice, in 1935 and 1939, Racing Universitaire was crowned North African champion by winning the *Challenge Steeg* (named after Théodore Steeg, the 1921–1925 Governor General of Algeria and highest authority in the region).

RUA's colonial symbolism was also highlighted when in the middle of the battle for Algiers, during the country's war for independence, one of the matches the club played was the target of a bomb attack by a commando unit for the Algerian National Liberation Front (FLN). This was at the El Biar stadium and against Sporting Club Universitaire on 10 February 1957 (and it was accompanied by another at the stadium where Gallia Sports was playing). Among those killed in the attack was Émile Lambert, a member of *Allez RUA* – Racing Universitaire's fan club.

The bombing was but a prelude to the fateful end that Racing Universitaire met. In 1962, with Algerian independence being declared, the club put a halt to all its activity, as did all other colonial teams. The Algiers League was replaced by a new national competition for independent Algeria. Albert Camus never got to see this as he died in 1960.

The former goalkeeper for the Algerian university team had moved to France during the war for independence and had become a fan of Racing Club de Paris simply because its players wore the same colours as his beloved Racing Universitaire d'Alger. Camus discovered that his cherished new team did not just don the same colours as RUA but had a similar playing style. 'Both play in a scientific manner and scientifically lose matches they should win'. Maybe this is because, despite some people's insistence otherwise, football will never be a science. Fortunately so.

Club Atlético de Tetuán
The Moroccan Atlético

The FIFA Club World Cup is played between the different continental champions, but also includes the league champion from the tournament's host country. For this reason, the 2014 Cup, which ended with Real Madrid crowned as the best team on the planet, included the winner of the Moroccan League. This was none other than Moghreb Atlético Tétouan, the footballing entity that embodies colonial Morocco's history like no other. It was originally founded under the Spanish protectorate (of the very north and south of Morocco) and under the name Athletic Club de Tetuán. It was the first African club to play in the top tier of a European league.

The inclusion in the Club World Cup of Atlético Tétouan, which has some joint history with Atlético Madrid, as well as still sharing close ties and a similar kit, made the competition more interesting and not only because it was the local public's favourite team. The reason was simple: the Tétouan side had the chance of coming up against Real Madrid and exacting 'Atlético' revenge after the nail-biting end to the Champions League Final in Lisbon just six months earlier. In that, Real Madrid won its tenth such cup in extra time, denying its local rival Atlético Madrid's long-awaited European glory.

In the end, a fixture between the Moroccan Atlético and Real Madrid never took place as the Tétouan team was knocked out in the preliminary stage by New Zealand's Auckland City. This meant no repetition of one of Atlético de Tetuán's landmark matches held in the 1951–1952 season – the only one in which the club competed in the Spanish first division. In the match Atlético de Tetuán managed to draw 3–3 against a Real Madrid which was already on its way to becoming the mighty team it soon became.

The roots of today's Moghreb Atlético Tétouan can be traced back to the beginning of Spanish colonial control of northern Morocco in the form of a protectorate in 1913. This development brought football to Tétouan (*Tetuán* in Spanish) thanks to the posting there of thousands of Spanish soldiers. It was they who created the first teams in the area, often in their own barracks. Standing out among the many conscripts who played soccer in the protectorate was Rafael Moreno Eranzadi – better known as '*Pichichi*' (Top Scorer) – who did his military service in the town of Tetuán itself.

Two of the first clubs to spring up in Spanish Morocco were Sporting de Tetuán and Hispano-Marroquí, which merged in 1922 to form Athletic Club de Tetuán (ACT). After a brief initial existence, ACT was revived under the auspices of a group of Atlético Madrid fans in the Spanish army. It is worth recalling that, as mentioned in an earlier chapter, the 'Mattress Makers' had already severed ties with Bilbao's Athletic Club – of which they had been a subsidiary until 1907. The group's liking of Atlético Madrid led them to adopt a crest and red-and-white-striped shirt that clearly came from the similarly named Bilbao club.

At first, Athletic Club de Tetuán was a colonial club with which native Moroccans would find it hard to identify. Indeed, the club's founding coincided with a local anti-colonial rebellion that was savagely put down by the Spanish troops (the Rif War). The Tétouan club spent its first decades in the lower divisions of Spanish football in the Moroccan colony. The

North African team played in the Spanish Moroccan regional championship – a tournament whose winner gained the right to compete in the *Copa de España* (Spanish Cup); and in the *Copa de su Alteza Imperial el Jalifa* (His Imperial Highness the Khalifa's Cup) – named as such after the main domestic authority under the Spanish regime.

The side from Tétouan – a city in northern Morocco – gained its biggest opportunity after the Spanish Civil War, a conflict that had brought footballing activity to a complete standstill in the protectorate. Soon after the fascists won the war, Spanish football was restructured and the decisions the authorities took greatly affected the team from the Maghreb.

In 1940, the Franco dictatorship forced football clubs to Hispanicise their names. Thus Athletic Club de Tetuán officially became Club Atlético de Tetuán. The measure brought with it the incorporation of the teams in the Moroccan protectorate into a relaunched Spanish third division.

This decision soon enabled Atlético de Tetuán to win promotion to the 'silver' tier of Spanish football, thanks to its sporting prowess. At that time, the second division was split into two groups but Atlético had a memorable 1950–1951 season in its group, ending with its promotion to top-flight soccer in Spain. For the North African team, this was a historic feat which made Atlético de Tetuán the first and only club from Africa to play in the first division of a European league.

The Moroccan Atlético's performance in the Spanish first division in 1951–1952 was unremarkable. In fact the club has the second worst record in first-division football history – a record only surpassed by Cultural y Deportiva Leonesa. Naturally Atlético was relegated after its first season there. Yet it did play some memorable matches at its La Hípica stadium – built by the architect Márquez de Varela in 1913 (the early days of Spanish colonisation), making it one of the oldest grounds in

Africa. These included a 4–1 victory over Atlético de Madrid – the club's most prestigious result – and the aforementioned draw against Real Madrid.

Despite its squad basically being made up of Spaniards, Atlético de Tetuán gradually introduced Moroccan players, which helped it increase the local population's identification with the club. A crucial time in Atlético de Tetuán's history was 1956, when Morocco gained independence from Spain. The different sections of the club experienced this very differently: while its Spanish members resented the transformation and only grudgingly accepted that full Moroccan sovereignty would stop the club from being able to compete on a Spanish level, the Maghrebi section enthusiastically promoted having a team that played in the state's newly created league at the same time as preserving Atlético de Tetuán's legacy.

Independence therefore split the club into two. On the one hand, the club's Spanish management and players moved to the nearby city of Ceuta, which remained under Spanish rule. There, 'Atlético de Tetuán' merged with the local club Sociedad Deportiva Ceuta. The resulting team formally inherited Tetuán's right to compete in the Spanish league and acquired its Spanish second-division place from before Morocco became independent.

On the other hand, Atlético's native members soon founded a new club which also sought to take up the baton of the colonial North African team: Moghreb Atlético Tétouan. The heavy influence of Moroccan nationalism was shown in the name 'Moghreb', which literally means 'Morocco' in Arabic.

This new club adopted practically everything from its predecessor: colours, stadium, fans, name … Even so, it wanted to make very clear that from then on, Atlético Tétouan was a Moroccan entity. As such, it joined the Royal Moroccan

Football Federation and played in the competitions it organised.

The Tétouan side was slow to make a name for itself in Moroccan football and for several decades mainly played in the second division, winning only the occasional promotion to top-flight soccer. Yet over time, the Tétouan team's competitiveness, financial resources, and fan base have all grown, and it became Moroccan champion in 2012. This title was won on a nerve-wracking last matchday when its fans formed the largest delegation of away fans in Moroccan footballing history and literally invaded Rabat.

Moghreb Atlético's victory in the domestic league showed it was becoming one of the country's big clubs. To a large extent, this advance was due to the financial resources put into it by its then-chairman, tycoon Abdelmalek Abroun, who helped move the club into a new era. At the same time, he signed a partnership and cooperation agreement with Atlético de Madrid, in 2007, thereby also remembering the club's origins.

When the tycoon stepped down as chairman in 2018 after 14 years in the post, he had turned the former Spanish colonial club into a winning Moroccan-league team. This was shown when it won the championship for the second time in 2014 – the title that gave it the right to play in the FIFA Club World Cup that year.

In a way, the history of Atlético Tétouan is itself a metaphor for Morocco in the last century. It was a colonial club created by Spanish soldiers who fought a revolt by the native population. Over time, it became a Moroccan footballing force thanks to the dirhams of a magnate who symbolised the emergence of a new Morocco. A Morocco that even dared to organise the Club World Cup with FIFA's full cooperation.

JS Massira

A club for legitimising the Moroccan occupation of Western Sahara

From the moment that Morocco stopped being a colony subject to the will of France and Spain, its King – Mohammed V – was obsessed with building 'Greater Morocco'. This is an age-old nationalist notion that includes laying claim to the Western Sahara – at the time under Spanish colonial control – as an integral part of the Moroccan state.

Mohammed V died in 1961, without having achieved his dream. Yet his son and successor to the throne, Hassan II, took the venture upon himself. Western Sahara was occupied thanks to the Green March: a series of demonstrations in November 1975 in which thousands of Moroccan civilians and soldiers invaded Sahrawi (Saharan) land, claiming it for Morocco, while Spain was discussing how exactly to leave its colony.

The United Nations brokered an international agreement to decolonise Western Sahara, which recognised the local people's right to self-determination. Yet Spain agreed that Morocco and Mauritania would take over administering the previously colonised territory, thereby thwarting pro-independence Saharans' hopes of forming a new republic.

In 1979, after Mauritania relinquished the Saharan territory it had been claiming until then, Morocco forcibly spread its occupation to cover the whole of the former Spanish colony.

This forced into exile most of the inhabitants remaining loyal to the Sahrawi Arab Democratic Republic declared on 27 February 1976.

From 1975, Morocco also developed a strategy to 'Moroccanise' all social life, including sporting activity, in the occupied land. Thus, the Sakia Hamra Youth Club was created in Laayoune – capital of Western Sahara – in 1977. The sports club was named after the region in which Laayoune was situated, and, from the start, took part in Moroccan national competitions, with the obvious political aim of underlining that it belonged to Morocco.

Sakia Hamra Youth had its biggest sporting success in 1984, when it won promotion to the Moroccan first division, in which it would stay for three seasons. This development greatly helped Rabat and the Alawi monarch's official discourse, in which the Sahara is deemed inseparable from Moroccan national territory. Despite the footballing entity's political importance, the team was relegated in 1987, and spent the following seasons in the lower flights of Moroccan football.

The fact that Western Sahara – or 'the Southern Provinces' as Moroccan nationalists insist – did not have a club in the country's top flight became an issue. This was so because of the 1991 UN-sponsored agreement between Morocco and the Polisario Front (Sahrawi National Liberation Movement) which obliged a local referendum to be held over the sovereignty of the land in February 1992.

Despite the UN being commissioned to organise this vote, in practice the Saharan people's right to self-determination was denied. Meanwhile, Morocco took advantage of the situation to send greater numbers of settlers to Western Sahara to give the territory a stronger Moroccan identity; that way altering the census of those who would decide the region's future.

In 1994, when Sahrawi self-determination dominated polit-ical discussion in the country, the royal authorities did their utmost for Sahara to be popularly associated with Morocco (and thus seen as belonging to the Moroccan nation). One of the many initiatives taken was to end the lack of a Saharan team in the first division – the symbolic importance of which had not escaped the Alawi rulers.

Accordingly, the Moroccan sporting authorities decreed that the military club, Auxiliary Forces, from the small town of Ben Slimane in the country's centre, relocate to Laayoune. The club had just won promotion to the first division – for the first time since 1990 – meaning it would now represent the 'Southern Provinces' at Moroccan football's highest level.

That was how the Ben Slimane military club, created in 1977, left its birthplace to resettle in the Sahara, where it was renamed Jeunesse Sportive d'El Massira (JS Massira). It thus became a political tool at the service of the Moroccan occupa-tion after its debut in the kingdom's top tier in the 1994–1995 season. JS Massira stayed up for the next 18 seasons, giving it great symbolic value for the Rabat authorities.

But Jeunesse Sportive d'El Massira's inclusion in the top flight was not uncontroversial. From the beginning, the team had to make long trips to play clubs that were mostly in the north of Morocco. In 1997, the club returned temporarily to Ben Slimane, where the squad lived and trained, and only went to Laayoune to play official games. This confirmed that the decision to move the club to the Sahara was merely politi-cally motivated and had no sporting justification.

Another big issue was its suspicious 18-year unbroken spell in the first division (which was renamed the *Botola Pro*). The way by which on several occasions it miraculously avoided relegation created misgivings over whether it was receiving outside aid to further the political goal of having 'the Southern Provinces' in the top flight.

After a disastrous 2011–2012 season, JS Massira was finally relegated from the *Botola Pro*. This helped the newly pro-fessionalised Moroccan League gain credibility after the accusations that the Laayoune club had benefited from many years of political favouritism.

Yet despite being in the second division, the club's role in legitimising the Moroccan occupation continued. As a result, virtually no pro-independence Sahrawi supports the former Ben Slimane team, which they accuse of having set up in Western Sahara in the same way as the Moroccan settlers did. Native Saharans prefer supporting the Sahrawi Arab Demo-cratic Republic's national team, which despite not being able to play at home or in official international competitions is seen as truly representing their country at football.

This is an unsurprising stance considering the close links binding Jeunesse Sportive d'El Massira and the Moroccan powers-that-be. As an illustration, the sporting entity's chairman is Hassan Derham, a former Sakia Hamra Youth player, social-democratic MP in the Moroccan parliament, and present-day head of Atlas – the biggest fossil-fuel corpo-ration operating in Western Sahara.

A key figure in local politics who has been vying for the club chairmanship is Hamdi Ouid Rachid, Laayoune mayor for the conservative Moroccan-nationalist party Istiqlal. The policies he has advocated for the outfit include free entry to the Sheik Mohamed Laghdaf Stadium to watch JS Massira matches. The idea is to fill the sports ground – with a capacity for 20,000 people – to show local people's identification with a club sym-bolising the Moroccan occupation.

One of the clearest examples of political exploitation of football by the authorities in the Sahara took place in 2015, when the Laayoune stadium hosted a match featuring old glories from world football – including Diego Maradona, Rivaldo, and George Weah. The game was to commemorate the 40th anniversary of the Green March that invaded Sahrawi lands. It was further proof of how football and initiatives like Jeunesse Sportive d'El Massira have helped give respectability to Rabat's occupation of Western Sahara.

Hafia FC
A tool for the African Revolution

In the 1970s, during the rise of pan-Africanism and the revolutionary movement that demanded a radical break with the continent's colonial past, there was a football club that represented this desire for liberation like few others. This was Conakry city's Hafia Football Club, which did sport and politics at the same time, thereby following the injunctions of Ahmed Sékou Touré – the first President of independent Guinea and one of the key pan-African leaders of that era.

Hafia's history is closely related to the social and political evolution of Sub-Saharan Africa. The club was in fact founded in 1951 under the name Conakry II, the administrative denomination given to the neighbourhood of the Guinean capital in which it was created. In its early years, while Guinea was still under French rule, Conakry II lived in the shadow of the big colonial clubs in Guinea – Racing Club and the Sports Society – which were winners of the first championships organised by the French authorities.

Conakry II's fans, like those of Conakry I, were sympathetic towards the political stance of the then-young Sékou Touré. He had co-created the pro-independence Democratic Party of Guinea (PDG): the local branch of the African Democratic Rally (RDA), which called for the de-colonisation of the black continent. In those years, Touré became an MP in the French National Assembly and mayor of Conakry, and through such offices he spread his anti-colonial ideas. These made such headway among the Guinean people that on 28 September 1958, the colony's citizens voted in a referendum to scrap both union and collaboration with France. This laid the ground for independence, which was proclaimed on 2 October 1958, with Sékou Touré becoming President of the new state.

The arrival of full Guinean sovereignty radically transformed the country's football. The old colonial clubs vanished, giving way to the teams created under the auspices of the native population. Among such was Conakry II of course. The restructuring of national club football began after the Democratic Party of Guinea (PDG) Cup was set up in 1960. The PDG – also headed by Sékou Touré – had already become the country's single party and had started introducing a Marxist-inspired programme that included nationalising the main foreign firms operating in Guinea during the colonial regime.

This new cup was for its first few years almost the exclusive property of the two Conakry clubs (I and II). In 1965, it was replaced by the newly formed independent Guinea league, whose first consecutive four seasons were won by Conakry II.

This, combined with the importance that the Sékou Touré regime attached to the sport, helped lay the foundations to turn the club into a fighting tool for the African Revolution. In keeping with this, Conakry II became Hafia Conakry after a lively debate initiated by the revolutionary authorities over two possible names of unambiguously pro-African symbolism.

The name 'Hafia' that eventually prevailed corresponded to the historic name of one of Conakry's northern districts and meant in the country's native language 'rebirth' or 'good health'. The other option considered was 'Kakimbo', the name of the Guinean river that according to the local imaginary feeds a mythical forest. Conakry I was turned into AS Kaloum Star.

The new name and, admittedly, the favours the club received from the Sékou Touré regime heralded a real revolution at Hafia which won all the Guinean league championships in a row between 1971 and 1979. The club was seen by the Democratic Party of Guinea as another tool serving the African Revolution. In a speech, President Sékou Touré declared it to be 'the interpreter and image of Guinea's democratic and Africa's revolutionary youth'.

Even so, the Hafia legend was not built out of its national titles but from its big continental successes. Sékou Touré had a particular interest in spreading his doctrine among Guinea's African neighbours. Hence, he attached strategic importance to Hafia playing in African competitions. This was especially so with the Kwame Nkrumah Gold Cup; the forerunner to the African Champion Clubs' Cup – named so after the Ghanaian President, who was another ardent pan-Africanist.

In 1972, Hafia began to cement its sporting glory by winning the first of its African Cups against the Ugandan Simba FC. Sékou Touré saw that victory as his own and focused all his efforts on developing a team that would make its mark on the continent and era.

Hafia Conakry won the continental title again in 1975 with a team built around Suleiman Chérif – the only Guinean to have been awarded the African *Ballon d'Or* (three years earlier). The following year, it looked like the Guineans might win their third African trophy after beating Algiers' Mouloudia Club 3–0 in the first leg of the continental final. This was played at home in the *Stade du 28 Septembre* – a stadium named as such to commemorate the day Guinea began to build its independence by rejecting any links with colonial France in a referendum. Hafia lost the second leg of the final, however, after Mouloudia did the seemingly impossible: beating the Guineans 3–0 and winning the tournament on penalties. That match was played in Algiers' 5 of July 1962 Stadium, whose name honours the date full Algerian sovereignty was proclaimed.

This surprising defeat angered Sékou Touré, seeing the defeat as a 'national disgrace inflicted on the Democratic Party of Guinea'. After the second-leg match, he dismissed the Minister of Youth and Sports, his ministerial staff, the Guinean Football Federation officials who had travelled to Algeria to watch the match, and the two players the President thought were the main culprits of the fiasco. They were accused of 'being those responsible for having violated the Revolution's honour, having ruined Hafia, and having trampled on the dignity of the Republic of Guinea'.

Among the responses that Sékou Touré chose to adopt to regain the African soccer crown was to expand the Hafia squad from 18 to 30 players to increase competition at the club. His measures had an effect and the following year, in 1977, the Conakry outfit again reached the final of the African Champions Cup, this time beating Ghana's Hearts of Oak. The second leg of this final, in which Hafia clinched its third continental victory – an unprecedented feat in African football at the time – was played at the *Stade du 28 Septembre* under the President of the nation's watchful eye.

Once Hafia were announced as champions, Ahmed Sékou Touré went onto the pitch to celebrate, doing several laps of honour around the stadium in his convertible presidential vehicle while offering the title to the local fans. He interpreted the success in political terms, certifying this in his post-match remarks; proclaiming euphorically, 'This is a worthy victory for the Democratic Party of Guinea and its Revolution!'

This third continental win enshrined Hafia as one of the legendary African teams and allowed it to hold onto the Nkrumah Cup for good. This, Sékou Touré took to be a great honour as the trophy was named after a Ghanaian leader with whom Touré shared a deep pan-Africanism as well as friend-ship. Indeed Sékou Touré took in Nkrumah and even made him Guinean Vice-President, when the Ghanian was driven from power in a coup d'état.

After this triumph, Hafia had a further chance to deepen its mythical status after reaching the 1978 African final, but it lost this to Cameroon's Canon Yaoundé. Conakry club's decline logically happened coinciding with the end of Sékou Touré and his party's reign.

The death of the pan-Africanist leader in 1984 and the end of his regime, which was accompanied by the disbanding of its single party, hit Hafia hard. It only managed to lift the national league trophy in 1985 and since then has languished, gaining no more glory than the four domestic cup titles it has won since the 1990s. With Sékou Touré's passing saw the slide of one of African football's greatest symbols: a Hafia Conakry that not only played football but tried on the pitch to serve the African Revolution.

The Passive Resisters SC
The peaceful civil disobedience clubs

'*Mahatma*' Gandhi was one of the 20th century's most significant figures. It is widely known that he played a crucial role in India's struggle for independence from the British Empire. Mohandas Karamchand Gandhi was the ideological father of the strategy to win Indian sovereignty based on peaceful civil disobedience as implemented in the fight against the British occupying authority.

What is less well-known is that Gandhi developed his philosophy while living in another British colony: South Africa. During the two decades he was there – from 1893 to 1914 – he had stood out for his fight against the racist laws imposed there by the Empire. It was then that Gandhi instigated one of the least known episodes in his life: the Indian lawyer's use of football as a tool to spread his doctrine among the South African masses who had enthusiastically embraced the new sport.

Gandhi had become acquainted with football while studying law in London – the heart of the colonial empire his native India was forced to show allegiance to. Ever since, Gandhi showed a particular affinity for a sport he considered to have more popular roots than the elitist cricket – another British-origin sport that had gained a strong foothold in India.

Once Gandhi graduated and qualified as a lawyer, he returned to his home country. Yet the twists and turns of his professional career led him to work as a lawyer for an Indian company that also operated in South Africa, which was then home to a large Indian-origin diaspora.

It was in colonial South Africa he was sent to where Gandhi's ideological beliefs took shape. His great sensitivity towards social issues was sharpened soon after reaching the African country, when during a train journey in 1893, the inspector forced him to leave the first-class carriage he was seated in. Racist laws reserved such carriages for white passengers only.

Gandhi refused to move from his carriage to third class where, by law, black and Indian citizens had to travel, and was thrown off the train. The incident was his first act of peaceful civil disobedience. Gandhi refused to comply with laws he saw were unjust and opted to resist them non-violently.

This life event led Gandhi to promote peaceful civil disobedience against racism, colonialism, and social injustice. Inspired by Henry David Thoreau, a 19th-century North American philosopher who advocated disobedience against unjust governments, and by Leo Tolstoy, the Russian philosopher and novelist who also championed peaceful resistance, Gandhi developed a campaign among his fellow countrymen and women in South Africa to non-violently resist discriminatory laws that treated them as second-class citizens.

Thus was created 'satyagraha' – a Sanskrit concept that can be translated as 'truth force'. This was nothing but the peaceful civil resistance that would eventually lead India to independence, and would later be revived in South Africa, which had witnessed India gaining its statehood by Nelson Mandela in the fight against the racist apartheid regime.

Once working on this strategy, Gandhi quickly understood that sport could have a fundamental role in spreading his ideas, as it aroused the passions of the social groups his discourse was aimed at. 'Mahatma' Gandhi paid particular attention to football, the sport that had fascinated him during the years he was in England, not due to personal liking but because it was so popular among the main recipients of his message: South Africa's Asian and black communities.

The Indian lawyer aimed to use football as a tool to raise awareness about the racial discrimination and social injustices suffered by those most deprived. To this end, at the beginning of the 20th century, he spearheaded setting up three football clubs of the same name in the trio of biggest South African towns: Durban, Pretoria, and Johannesburg. Thus were born the Passive Resisters Soccer Clubs, which as their name suggested, explicitly shared Gandhi's peaceful civil disobedience approach.

The Passive Resisters clubs did not play in any league, as organised football in South Africa was still at an embryonic stage. All the same, the clubs played multiple friendlies at which Gandhi would give a talk to participants at half-time and anti-racist and pro-resistance leaflets were given out to spectators. Besides strictly political aspects, Gandhi's clubs also promoted the moral values that he wished to get across to his community. Consequently being upright, showing fair play and good teamwork also featured strongly in his speeches in the changing rooms.

The Passive Resisters' quintessential natural environment were the pitches introduced at Phoenix – an Indian settlement next to Durban – and the Tolstoy Farm – named after the disobedient Russian author – in Johannesburg. It was in fact the latter that was the setting for one of the Passive Resisters' most memorable matches: one in 1910 pitting the Resisters teams from Johannesburg and Pretoria against each other in a derby that turned into an act of protest over the imprisonment of a hundred Indian rebels who had opposed the racist laws. Clearly the matches played by the Passive Resisters went beyond being strictly sporting affairs to become political acts that promoted peaceful disobedience against injustice and oppression.

The Indian diaspora in South Africa keenly followed the three rebel teams and copied their example by creating several football clubs for their community. In 1903, these came together – supported by Gandhi – to form the South African Indian Football Federation; an umbrella body bringing together small and fledgling provincial leagues that the Indian clubs in the country had begun to organise.

The rapid spreading of Gandhi's ideas and disobedience strategy attracted the attention of the emerging Indian bourgeoisie which was increasingly adopting nationalist and anti-colonial stances. It was this group that eventually persuaded Gandhi to go back to India and implement his peaceful disobedience approach there, which eventually won independence for his country in 1947.

By returning to India, '*Mahatma*' Gandhi had to drop involvement in the Passive Resisters, whose activity gradually dwindled until the clubs disappeared in 1936. All the same, the Hindu leader stayed interested in South African Indian football. This was reflected in the blessing he gave the Christopher's Contingent; an Indian outfit in South Africa championed by Albert Christopher – a comrade in arms during Gandhi's civil disobedience years in the country – when its team toured India in 1921–1922.

Gandhi's South African footballing legacy was revived by the rebels who fought *apartheid* and spearheaded the creation of clubs and federations free from any racial discrimination. Hence, the Indian Football Federation of South Africa that he had helped form in 1903 became a key influence in the birth of the South African Soccer Federation (SASF), the multi-racial association that took on the racist South African Football

Association (SAFA). Another example from history of how football with a Gandhian spirit has been a tool to combat discrimination and injustice.

9

The Americas

A miner greets CD Cobresal players going onto the pitch for a 1986 match at the Cobre stadium

New York Ramblers
Multi-colour soccer against homophobia

Despite many football clubs' working-class roots and links with progressive political stances, soccer stadiums around the world have historically been incredibly homophobic places. As the bulk of fans of the sport have been men and the game has been associated with very masculine values, one of the most commonly heard insults chanted in stadiums refers to the opponent's supposed homosexuality.

Few clubs have been spared from being tarred by such behaviour at some point in their history – even those that can boast of having fans thought to be left-wing. Only the transformed 1980s St Pauli, which had an openly gay and gay-activist chairman, as well as the most politically aware supporters on the planet, seems to have avoided the homophobia that has traditionally ruled in the footballing world.

One of the historic events that revealed the hostile environment in this sport was Justin Fashanu's suicide in 1998, after the footballer was charged with a sexual assault alleged to have occurred while on a date, which he and the LGBT movement have always said was consensual. Fashanu, an English player of Nigerian origin, was the first professional to go public about his homosexuality. This was an unheard-of step in a world shaped by homophobia.

It was precisely to break out of this atmosphere in which one cannot be open about one's sexual orientation that the first gay football team was created in history: the New York Ramblers. This brought together homosexual football buffs who hung out in Greenwich Village – New York's quintessential LGBTQI+ neighbourhood – to be able to play amateur matches in the part of Central Park known as 'the Ramble'. It was this precise meeting point that gave the name to a club that still exists to this day and has become the doyen of gay football clubs.

The New York Ramblers' example quickly led new clubs to be set up that followed the same philosophy, which was none other than to put together amateur players who need not conceal their sexual orientation in an environment as anti-gay as that of soccer. At first, the growth of gay football was limited to the United States which hosted the first LGBT Olympics ever in 1982. These were the Gay Games held in San Francisco. In these, two football clubs – one from Denver and another from the Games' Californian host city – played the first-ever official match exclusively comprised of gay players.

The increased number of clubs following the New York Ramblers' approach led to the forming, in 1992, of the International Gay and Lesbian Football Association: an organisation that aimed to associate gay players across the planet and encourage the normalisation of homosexuality through playing football. The new association took charge of coordinating the soccer tournament taking place during the Gay Games, which was repeated every four years after the first event in San Francisco, as well as holding an annual gay and lesbian football championship.

Thanks to having an association aiming to globalise LGBT football, the phenomenon spread to Europe. In 1994, a team from outside the US – Cologne's Cream Team – won the gay club world cup for the first time. The German team's success led the next championship to be organised in Berlin, and for the baton to later be passed to several other European capitals.

Gay football has also spread to Canada, Australia, and some South American countries including Argentina and Mexico, which hosted the 2007 and 2012 club world cups. Yet the big challenge is still to reach the places where homosexuality is most persecuted. This is hugely difficult because that same repression makes it practically impossible to officially create teams defined by any gay orientation of their members.

Not everyone in the LGBTQI+ community sees events such as the Gay Games and the creation of homosexual teams as such a big step forward. The criticism made is that they do not normalise homosexuality in sport but create gay-only sporting ghettos. What therefore would be needed would be to make gayness a day-to-day feature of football and sport in general, rather than create initiatives separating the homosexual and heterosexual communities. This is probably right but it is hard to implement in practice due to the homophobia that persists in the footballing world.

One of the initiatives that has tried to break this prejudicial atmosphere has been the Queer Football Fanclubs that group together specific clubs' LGBTQI+ supporters. The association was created in Germany, as an initiative of one of St Pauli's gay fan crews, and spread to include dozens of German club crews, which were later joined by more and more fan clubs across Europe.

The Queer Football Fanclubs have devoted much of their activity to denouncing any kind of discrimination in the footballing world and to positively welcoming diversity – whether of skin colour or sexual orientation. Furthermore, the fan clubs actively collaborate with the International Day against Homophobia in Football held every 19 February – precisely the day that Fashanu, the first 'out' professional player, took his own life.

The road to eradicating homophobia from the world of soccer is still a long one, as is also true of wider society. Yet the fact that an environment as traditionally anti-gay as football's is doing its bit to end this scourge should bring us hope.

SC Corinthians Paulista
Corinthian democracy

Throughout the 20th century, dictatorships were a phenomenon sparing few places in the world. Brazil – a regional power in South America – was no exception. A military coup took place in the country in 1964 – aided by the CIA – which ended the brief democratic experience under President João Goulart.

The new regime was a right-wing dictatorship openly supported by the United States. Like almost all totalitarian systems, the Brazilian dictatorship sought to tightly control football and make it a tool to serve the interests of the powerful.

In Brazil '*o jogo bonito*' (the beautiful game) is like a religion. It became the pretext by which many opportunistic employers with government connections became rich by building dozens of new stadiums – commissioned through an obscene degree of real-estate corruption.

Meanwhile, the regime applied its nationalistic principles to introduce contracts that locked in footballers to their clubs for life, creating a near-feudal relationship between players and the sporting entities. Besides the aim of stopping Brazilian footballers from being transferred to foreign clubs, and thus weakening the Brazilian championships, a consequence of the measure was to condemn a great number of players to a life in poverty, as they would earn wages often lower than the national minimum wage.

Clearly the dictatorship was not acting in the interests of national players but those of Brazilian club directors, most of whom were in league with the authoritarian rulers.

This disgraceful setup continued through the rest of the 1960s, the 1970s, and peaked in the early 1980s. By then, the dictatorship had a full grip over Brazilian football, as exemplified by the presidents of the Brazilian Football Confederation and the National Sports Council being two military officers – Heleno Nunes and Jerônimo Bastos, respectively.

Despite this, Brazil won all its matches in the 1970 World Cup and was crowned world champion. Ironically this historic victory was under a coach, João Saldanha, who was a committed leftist and member of the underground Communist Party of Brazil.

The national team's international success was not enough to keep Saldanha in his managerial job after powerful circles hounded him due to his political stance. Likewise, the World Cup triumph did little to ease the plight of Brazilian footballers who continued to be prisoners of the lifelong contracts the regime had imposed. The exploitation players suffered clearly affected their performance on the pitch, and frequently sparked clashes between them and management.

One of the places where this was most obvious was Corinthians Paulista: a club which, because of events it went through in the 1980s, would end up being a benchmark for both people's football and freedom in the sport.

In fact, Sport Club Corinthians Paulista already had a working-class character. It had originally been created in opposition to the first clubs that were formed in Brazil in the early 20th century which had close and exclusive links with the country's wealthiest classes. This was ironic because today the beautiful game is the popular classes' biggest passion.

To oppose this situation, on 1 September 1910, a bunch of workers returning by tram to their Bon Retiro neighbourhood – a working-class area of São Paulo – decided to set up a club for the city's poorer classes. Their choice of name for it – Corinthians – was curious and coincidental. While discussions on the club's name were taking place, a London team called Corinthian FC just happened to be touring Brazil. That coincidence inspired the promoters of the new workers' club, which they named Corinthians Paulista.

Corinthians soon began its successful history. In 1914, the club won its first São Paulo regional championship, thereby defying the biggest teams in the state – such as São Paulo Athletic Club and the Paulistano. Both of these were supported by the dominant classes.

However, Corinthians's high point as a free-minded, democratic, and working-class club came under the harsh conditions of the military dictatorship in the early 1980s. Despite having a squad including players of the calibre of Sócrates, Wladimir, and Zenon, Corinthians were relegated to the Brazilian second division in 1981. This occurred after a long-running and public conflict between the club's players and management.

Due to the poor results, the chairman of the club until then, Vicente Matheus, decided to step down – to be replaced by Waldemar Pires.

The new head then took a step that would change the history of the team: he put Adilson Monteiro Alves in charge of running the club. Monteiro Alves was a 35-year-old sociologist who had been actively involved in the student movement against the dictatorship and had even been imprisoned for this political activity.

The sociologist's arrival completely transformed the way the club operated. After meeting with the players to resolve the crisis at Corinthians, Monteiro Alves led the introduction of a radically different way of managing the club. This was aimed at involving the players in the process. Crucially for his purposes, he managed to obtain the support of Sócrates and Wladimir – the club's two biggest sporting figures.

What they and Adilson did was straightforward: democratise the running of the club. Squad members stopped being merely paid employees to become managers on an equal footing to the existing ones. Thus began one of the greatest experiences in self-management of a football club, as both players and staff freely decided how Corinthians would function and shared out equally the proceeds from ticket sales and TV rights.

The self-management of the squad even extended to key sporting decisions. In 1982, Corinthians' players democratically elected their manager, picking Zé Maria. Maria was a pro-democracy activist, as well as having been a player for Corinthians and in the legendary national team that won the 1970 World Cup. The choice could not have been better, as Corinthians then won the São Paulo regional cup twice in a row – in 1982 and 1983.

The success of a football club governed democratically in a totalitarian state run by military dictators was not missed by anybody. As a result, Corinthians became a symbol for the whole of the Brazilian democratic opposition, which saw the *Paulista* club as a political model to be followed.

As Sócrates himself stated, the 1982 and 1983 sporting successes were fundamental for the democratic movement ('*democracia corinthiana*') that had developed at the club, as they showed that Corinthians could be champions at the same time as practising self-management. Indeed, Sócrates and his teammates' example looked set to spread to other Brazilian teams. Palmeiras and São Paulo – Corinthians' biggest regional rivals, and clubs associated with the wealthiest classes

– tried to adopt its model, but its directors quickly headed off its players' initiatives.

Once the Corinthian players' wages and other labour demands were won, they set for themselves more ambitious goals, including in the political arena. Sócrates described this as such:

> To begin with, we wanted to change our working conditions; then the politics of sports in our country; and finally, we wanted to change politics, pure and simple.

Because of Corinthians' urge to change Brazilian politics, the club did not hesitate to include boldly ideological messages on its jerseys on occasions. While other Brazilian teams had begun to wear the names of their sponsors on theirs, the São Paulo team's shirts were used to call for people to vote in the first elections (applying universal suffrage) that would choose the São Paulo state governor, to be held on 15 March 1983. The club's shirt read 'On the 15th, vote!' – an unambiguous message of support for an electoral process that was the first sign that Brazil was moving away from dictatorship.

In the regional championship final that year, the Corinthians went onto the pitch holding a banner with a new pro-democracy slogan: 'Win or lose but always in democracy!' It would seem that the slogan lifted the team as Corinthians ended up winning the trophy against its arch-rivals São Paulo. This was after a goal by Sócrates, a player who had obtained a doctorate in medicine and had become a true icon of the struggle for democracy in Brazil.

Because the Corinthian Democracy Movement won one of its central demands, overturning the contract system that locked in its players for life, Sócrates was able to leave Brazil in 1984, signing for the Italian club Fiorentina. The country he was leaving behind entered a full democratic transition. In 1985 – the year after he departed to Italy – Sócrates saw from Florence the return of civilian rule to Brazil, with the social-democrat José Sarney elected as national President.

Democracia corinthiana was one of the opposition movements with the most public support and which had most effectively questioned the dictatorship. It was contemporary to some of the big political opposition movements that also emerged in the 1980s. These included Lula da Silva's Workers' Party (PT) – founded in 1980 – which was joined by some of the most emblematic Corinthians players: Sócrates, Wladimir, Casagrande, and Luis Fernando.

Ironically the arrival of democracy in Brazil saw the end of Corinthian Democracy. The movement had already been greatly weakened by the transfer of its central icon to Italy but the final nail in its coffin was in 1985, when the former Corinthian heads took back control of the sporting entity and forced out its rebel players.

So, the turn to democracy was (ironically) accompanied by the end of *democracia corinthiana*: a unique experience in freedom and self-management that shattered the myth that Brazilian footballers were simply individualistic and lacking any social conscience. For that reason, Corinthians has become an eternal symbol of free and democratic people's football.

CD Cobresal

A mining club in the middle of the Atacama Desert

In April 2005, Club de Deportes Cobresal (Cobresal Sports Club) won Chile's *Clausura* league tournament. This prestigious victory led many Chileans to look up where El Salvador was on a map, the mining settlement in which Cobresal was set up in 1979 and which today has less than 9,000 residents.

It should be mentioned that El Salvador is still one of the most out-of-the-way places in Chile. Located in the middle of the Atacama Desert – near the Andes and at an altitude of 2,300 metres – the town was created in the 1950s as a settlement to house the workforce for the region's copper mines. The name of the town (translatable as 'The Saviour' or 'Our Saviour' in English) came from the discovery nearby of new ore deposits that helped rescue mining in Atacama from crisis.

The El Salvador settlement's golden age was in the 1970s and 1980s when its total population surpassed 15,000 inhabitants. The town was then given a significant boost with the creation of healthcare, educational, and recreational facilities and services that improved people's well-being.

In 1971, the Popular Unity government headed by Salvador Allende nationalised the El Salvador mines, which until then had been run by North American firms. This change was not reverted after the coup d'état perpetrated by General Augusto Pinochet on that fateful 11 September 1973. Not only that but the regime decided that all Chilean copper mines, including those in El Salvador, would be placed under the control of the state-run National Copper Corporation of Chile (Codelco).

The projects that Pinochet's military dictatorship implemented were influenced by the desire to decentralise the country to harness regional support for his new totalitarianism. Football – one of the most popular activities in Chile – became a key component in this scheme. The military authorities, very aware that the sport could provide pro-regime propaganda and help control society, set up professional clubs in the country's different provinces. This was done in particular in those areas, such as Atacama, that were far from Santiago and the epicentres of Chilean power.

The state mining corporation played a very significant role in this new sporting policy as it was the company itself that promoted the creation of two new professional clubs. The first was CD Cobreloa, set up in 1977 in the city of Calama in the northern region of Antofagasta. With time, this has become one of the leading clubs in the country and one of the few clubs outside Santiago able to compete with the capital's big clubs. The second was CD Cobresal, created in 1979 in the small El Salvador settlement in Atacama – also in Chile's north – which soon became one of the few entertainments available in the area.

Starting up these clubs had a twofold purpose. On top of the popular game's role in national decentralisation, the military dictatorship sought to use it to pacify the rebellious mining communities. We could say that the decision to create such clubs was the Pinochet regime's version of 'bread and circuses'.

As already stated, Cobresal began its life in May 1979 under the auspices of Codelco, the public mining enterprise run by one of Pinochet's trusted generals. The aims of the club were naturally to be a distraction for El Salvador's miners and encourage an emotional attachment to their firm, with the hope that this would ensure avoiding any workers' protests.

Funding for the new club was jointly raised by members and the Codelco firm's local division. Indeed, the regime managed to involve union reps in Cobresal through an initiative known as the '*política 1+1*' whereby for each fee paid by a new member, Codelco undertook to give the club a contribution for the same amount.

El Salvador's small population and therefore difficulty in acquiring many members meant that in practice Cobresal totally depended on Codelco. Indeed, it was the mining company itself that built the *Estadio El Cobre* (The Copper Stadium), in 1980, which allowed the sporting outfit to comply with the requirements to be able to play professional football.

Unlike Cobreloa (the other Cobresal-sponsored club), which was based in an area with a much bigger population and therefore social base for the footballing outfit, Cobresal found it hard to establish itself among the elite Chilean clubs. Even so, in 1984, it achieved promotion to top-tier football – four years after starting to play in the second division.

Thus began the golden era for the miners' team, which was runner-up in the 1985 league championship and thus earned a ticket to play in the *Copa Libertadores* (South American club cup). This was after beating its sister club Cobreloa – then the Chilean champion – in one of the greatest moments in Cobresal's history.

This play-off marked the beginning of a rivalry between the two Chilean mining clubs, whose duels have since been dubbed 'the copper derby'. This is despite being a very unequal contest, bearing in mind the demographic base of each team.

Cobresal's classification for their first-ever *Libertadores* had important consequences for the club. South American Football Confederation regulations forced the club to upgrade

El Cobre, which was expanded to hold up to 25,000 spectators. That figure was almost double El Salvador's population at the time. As a result, *El Cobre* became ironically labelled 'the biggest stadium in the world' as it was practically impossible to fill (despite the multiple steps Codelco took to encourage its workers to go to matches).

Despite being knocked out of the competition in the group stage, Cobresal's run in its first *Libertadores* was a success. The miners' team did not lose a game, which until 2016 made it the only club in the continent to have played in the competition and never lost a match. This record only fell when the club played in the tournament for a second time and, that time, chalked up its first defeats.

The good work done by the miners was demonstrated in 1987, when Cobresal won its first-ever title. This was winning the Chilean cup competition after beating the almighty Colo-Colo – the biggest club in the country's capital Santiago. A key role in the cup campaign was played by Iván Zamorano – probably one of best players ever to don a Cobresal jersey – who was the tournament's top scorer with 13 goals. The triumph was a big event for El Salvador's inhabitants, who put themselves behind their team like never before, along the way strengthening the ties between the club and local mining.

Hence, while Codelco helped its employees attend Cobresal matches, it also encouraged the El Salvador squad to become familiar with miners' working lives. Therefore, it took the players to see the mines and the work of those who were the club's most fervent supporters. Cobresal's mining identity permeated all aspects of the club. Its crest was based on the symbol for copper, imitating Codelco's logo, and included a miner's helmet. Likewise, the main colour of its shirt is copper orange – another statement.

The link between mining and Club de Deportes Cobresal has been so strong that the El Salvador team went into crisis at the very same time as the mines that had given it its strength also suffered the same. At the end of the last century, Cobresal was on the rise and played several seasons in the second division. Yet the club's future was seriously threatened when, in 2005, the head of Codelco announced the coming closure of its El Salvador section due to the high cost and low profitability of the mines.

The announcement was a huge blow to the city, which had been losing population since the 1980s and now saw its main source of income endangered. The seemingly imminent mine closure also affected Cobresal, which began considering the future option of leaving El Salvador to set up shop in another copper-extraction area.

So far, such a move has not been necessary. In 2010, the then-President of Chile, Michelle Bachelet, announced that Codelco's own studies endorsed extending the El Salvador mine's operating life until at least 2021. The resulting extension guaranteed, for a time at least, the survival of the mining settlement and its 30-year-old club.

The decision proved a lifeline for the club which, soon after, wrote the greatest pages in its history by winning the *Clausura* trophy in April 2005. Ever since, Cobresal has been able to boast of having a Chilean league trophy in its cabinet. The club saw this victory as having a social significance going beyond the strictly sporting. As Codelco had allowed its staff to go to the match where Cobresal became champions, this helped the Copper Stadium start improving its general match attendance, which – at around a thousand spectators – was the lowest in Chilean football.

The league triumph was full of mine-related symbolism. Cobresal won the title with a magical 33 points – the same figure as the number of miners who became (famously) trapped while digging for gold and copper in the San José mine – also in the Atacama region. The win provided new hope to the arid Atacama region. The area had also been badly hit by the major March 2015 storm, leading the *Estadio El Cobre* to be shut for a month – only opening its doors for the historic match that saw Cobresal win its first league title.

The El Salvador settlement celebrated with great pomp the victory of the mining club created in 1979 under Pinochet to divert its workers' attention away from any desire for social revolution. Yet the partying took place under the constant threat of mine closures. A fate that still seems inevitable and that makes CD Cobresal's triumph even more epic and poetic.

Colo-Colo
Pinochet's long shadow

Whenever the fans of Club Universidad de Chile, Colo-Colo's big local rival visit the latter club's *Estadio Monumental* (Monumental Stadium) in central Santiago a chant repeatedly rings out: 'We are going to tear up, we are going to tear up Pinochet's stadium!'. With such, Universidad supporters are thus recalling one of the darkest chapters in Club Social y Deportivo Colo-Colo's long history: its relationship with General Augusto Pinochet's dictatorship. This is the tyrant who even promised during the October 1988 referendum campaign to continue his military regime to fully fund rebuilding the *Monumental* – the same ground that Colo-Colo's bitter rivals say they will destroy.

The truth is that the funding Pinochet promised never materialised as the vote went against the dictator and he had to step down as President of the Republic in 1990. Therefore, the 300 million pesos Pinochet had guaranteed the directors of the club never arrived. This is despite the idea having persisted among the Chilean people that the stadium was revamped and finished thanks to a financial donation by the dictatorship.

This *Estadio Monumental* anecdote is a good illustration of the importance the Pinochet regime gave to football. Like many other despots around the world, such as Italy's Mussolini, Portugal's Salazar, and Spain's Franco – to cite just a few examples – the Chilean dictator understood that the popularity of a sport such as football could be very useful in legitimising his power.

Augusto Pinochet had led the coup d'état against President Salvador Allende at a very special time for Chilean football. Just before the tragic 11 September 1973, when the Moneda Palace was occupied by Pinochet's army, Colo-Colo had attained its biggest sporting achievement thus far: reaching the final of the *Copa Libertadores* – the top South American club tournament.

As if that were not enough, the Chilean national team was just a step away from qualifying for the 1974 World Cup, a goal that it went on to achieve when Pinochet was in power. This was helped by the Soviet Union refusing to play at Santiago's National Stadium, which the dictatorship had turned into a camp for detaining and torturing regime opponents in the months immediately after the coup.

Although this made Chile's qualification for the finals shameful, Pinochet took advantage of the enthusiasm Chileans felt over returning to the world stage to conceal the country's ills. The general thought that while the Chilean people talked about football, they would not be discussing repression, torture, restrictions on civil liberties, and a long list of excesses committed by the regime. Perhaps for this reason, the general quickly understood the role that the country's leading sport could play under his rule.

Although Pinochet's footballing sympathies originally lay with Santiago Wanderers, from his home city of Valparaiso, Colo-Colo's popularity fascinated him, and he sought to take advantage of it. The club was the country's biggest; both in terms of the number of supporters and trophies won.

The fact is that before the Pinochet coup, Club Social y Deportivo Colo-Colo was already a Chilean institution. The Santiago club had been created in 1925 as a splinter group

from Deportivo Magallanes; a sports society with an unambiguously colonial name.* The breakaway club's long history
started in a tavern in the Chilean capital, one poetically nicknamed 'Drowns Sorrows'.

The football club quickly became a national symbol, and
the name it gave itself contributed to this. This was unquestionably nationalist as Colo-Colo had been a wise indigenous
(Mapuche**) leader who had led a hard-fought guerrilla war
against the Spanish colonial conquest of Chile in the 16th
century.

The new club's identification with the Chilean nation was
also unmistakable from the colours of its crest: red, white,
and blue – those of the Chilean flag. The crest was completed
in the 1950s with the addition of a Mapuche profile, which
remains its identifying feature today.

The elementary nationalism that Colo-Colo symbolised
decisively contributed to increasing its popularity, quickly
taking it to be the most popular sporting entity among the
Chilean people. This status was not lost on a certain Augusto
Pinochet who also wished to champion nationalism as an
element to legitimise the overthrow of Salvador Allende and
his Popular Unity government. Incidentally Allende was an
avowed fan of Colo-Colo; a club which he was a member of
and had received with full honours at the presidential Moneda
Palace after the club came runner-up in the 1973 *Copa Libertadores* tournament.

As soon as he came to power, Pinochet courted Colo-Colo,
aware that a club with the background it had could help make
the new dictatorship popular. The ideal chance to take control

---

* Translator's note: Magallanes was the Portuguese explorer who 'discovered' South America's Pacific coast.
** Translator's note: The Mapuches were the largest (indigenous) group
in the land at the time of the invasion.

of the club came in 1976 when elections were held to pick the chairperson for the club. The contest pitted Héctor Gálvez, who was heading the club when the coup took place, against Antonio Labán – a former chair backed by Tucapel Jiménez, a trade unionist and Radical Party member who stood out for his staunch opposition to the military regime (for which he was murdered in 1982).

Such a scenario provided an opening for the opposition to the regime to take command of the club, leading the dictatorship to suspend the vote for the new head. It dismissed all the club's directors and handed over control of the entity to a financial holding led by the Banco Hipotecario de Chile (Mortgage Bank of Chile). The ridiculous pretext offered for the government interference was alleged irregularities in the club's management. Wiping out Colo-Colo's internal democracy was accompanied by an act that was probably the biggest stain in the history of a club deeply rooted in the Chilean popular classes: Augusto Pinochet being awarded an honorary chairmanship – a post the dictator held from 1976 to when he relinquished power.

Such developments made it clear that Colo-Colo was the regime's club even though the Santiago team did not play at its best during the dictatorship years. All the same, government aid came and in various forms. One was by facilitating the return to Colo-Colo of Carlos Caszely, one of the best Chilean players at the time, and who had been playing for Barcelona's RCD Espanyol. This was very ironic as Caszely had stood out for his opposition to the dictatorship, even daring to refuse to salute Pinochet during a reception the latter held for the Chilean national squad.

Yet the most memorable helping hand the regime gave the club came four days before the above-mentioned vote on Pinochet continuing as President. To garner votes from among the fans of the biggest Chilean club, the dictator promised a large sum of money to complete the modernisation of Colo-Colo's stadium. As mentioned, the millions never came because of Pinochet's referendum defeat and stepping down as President.

All the same, the blot on the history of Chile's leading club – due to its association with the dictatorship – could not be erased. Indeed, even after being forced out, Pinochet did not shy away from voting in the elections for Colo-Colo's chair-person held in 1994. The despot who had suspended the 1976 elections and never allowed Chileans to choose who governed, had the cheek to say, 'As a Colo-Colo fan I am really pleased to participate in these elections, which I think are not just impor-tant but also intriguing'. A real act of cynicism by someone who had been characterised by his phobia of democracy and his merciless persecution of dissidence.

If Colo-Colo's big sporting success in the pre-Pinochet era had been coming runner-up in the *Libertadores*, its main one in the post-dictatorship period was precisely to win the biggest South American trophy in June 1991. It is a quirk of history that what Pinochet had wished for with all his might – that 'his' Colo-Colo would win an international trophy – only came when he was no longer in power.

Colo-Colo's rivals still bring up the relationship the club had with the dictator. Maybe for that reason, the '*Cacique*' (Chief) – the popular name given to the Santiago team – strives to erase Pinochet's imprint on it. In the club's history on its official website, the dictator receives no mention and his death in 2006 went unnoticed in the *Monumental* stadium, where no minute's silence was held in his memory. Even so, the dictator's long shadow is present every time Club Universidad de Chile plays in its stadium and its fans express their desire to tear the place down.

Mushuc Runa SC
The Quechuan dream

According to law, Ecuador is a multi-ethnic and multinational state that must respect and stimulate the development of the different languages and cultural identities it is comprised of. At least that is what is laid out in the constitution of a country in which indigenous people are a quarter of the population and mixed-race people, half. All the same, indigenous culture and identity are far from being accepted as normal in most areas of society.

A very telling instance of this is in football, a sport that was brought to Ecuador in the early 20th century by a group of young Ecuadorians who had studied in England. Despite the passion that the sport arouses among all layers of Ecuadorian society, the descendants of the territory's original inhabitants had never had a club representing them in top-flight football until Mushuc Runa Sporting Club's promotion in 2013. The long-running absence of indigenous people in Ecuadorian football was just another indication of the exclusion this section of the population had suffered in all walks of life throughout the last century.

The origins of Mushuc Runa can in fact be traced back to the creation of the same-named cooperative in 1997 by Luis Alfonso Chango – a member of the (Quechuan) Chibuleo people in the Sierra Central region and now the club's Honorary Life President. The original Quechuan-speaking people of this region, which has been the cradle for many uprisings demanding indigenous rights, have always suffered economic discrimination. The banks systematically ignored them or refused them loans to run their own businesses. Chango (and others) responded by creating the Mushuc Runa Savings and Credit Cooperative, which tried to ensure that autochthonous people could access bank loans. Its name reflects its Quechuan roots: '*Mushuc runa*' means 'New Man' in the Quechuan language (which itself is known by its speakers as '*Runasimi*' or 'the People's Language').

The cooperative's success led Luis Alfonso Chango to set the new goal of spreading indigenous 'normalisation' to his other passion – alongside finance – namely soccer. That was how Mushuc Runa SC came about. It is an unmistakably indigenous football club, which started out in 2002 playing in smaller local and regional championships.

The new club took inspiration from one of the few footballing initiatives for Ecuador's original inhabitants that came before it: Club Imbayas. This was set up in the country's northern Imbabura region in the 1940s. Yet, despite its long history, it never qualified to play in a championship above the regional level.

One of Mushuc Runa's most notable differences with the historical Imbayas was that it became a fully professional club – in 2007. Furthermore, it had a meteoric rise through the different flights of Ecuadorian football to become the first indigenous team to play in the *Serie A* – the country's premier division.

The first time in the top division for the 'New Man' – a name full of symbolism – lasted three seasons, until the club went down to *Serie B* in 2016. Yet it stayed down for only two years as in 2018 the Quechuan team (once again) topped that league and won its second promotion to top-tier football.

However, to get to play among the footballing elite, Mushuc Runa had to overcome many adversities. The first was the Quechuan-speaking population's reluctance to play football, which many members of this community thought was a sport for layabouts and idlers. Indeed, many original-inhabitant peasants had kept their children from playing it, seeing it as a distraction from their main occupations – nothing less than providing for the family, tending to the land and livestock, and selling their family's produce.

Chango and the club managed to overcome this initial resistance, and the community was soon enthusiastically behind Mushuc Runa as the club's triumphs gave the Quechuan people something to cheer about. Yet the club still had to tackle the traditional discrimination the ancestral communities suffered in Ecuador despite having a legal framework that was supposed to protect them.

By reaching the Ecuadorian second division in 2011, the club greatly helped indigenous peoples to be seen as an integral part of Ecuadorian life. Since then, Mushuc Runa has earned the respect of most of Ecuadorian society and has become a source of pride for the original communities – particularly Quechuan. For this reason, the sporting entity promotes its indigenous identity and unreservedly claims to be a model for Aboriginal inhabitants' participation in the public arena.

This is why the symbolism associated with Mushuc Runa is unambiguously indigenous. Among the many names used for the club, alongside the grandiose 'Ancestral Race Team', is the popularly used '*El Ponchito*' (the Small Poncho). This originated from the traditional attire donned by the footballer on its crest, which itself was inspired by that worn by Quechuans in Sierra Central. The clothing has been adopted by its fans as a badge of identity and is usually also worn by the club's squad when celebrating sporting triumphs.

Despite Mushuc Runa's indigenous identity meaning that at first its players were only of Quechuan ethnicity, nowadays its first team has few Native Americans – because of the club's professionalisation and having gone up to the top Ecuadorian divisions. Nevertheless, one of its main goals is still to train indigenous players from a junior level to help them reach the first team and, in particular, strengthen the Ecuadorian national team – thereby helping make it a true representation of the country's complex ethnic mix.

Despite the limited presence of indigenous people among the club's players, they clearly dominate the management and organisation of the club. This makes it possible to speak unreservedly of Mushuc Runa being an indigenous club, and more so because the way the club has been managed has been central to the team's successes.

As an example, Mushuc Runa is one of the few Ecuadorian clubs that has not gone through a serious financial crisis in recent times. Unlike most of its rivals, the indigenous team can boast of having a stable financial situation that has led it to become a model of rigour, order, good work, and contract compliance.

These principles have helped it avoid the excesses that have characterised most football-club administrations around the world. They have been made possible by the club's cooperative spirit and by applying to sports management the ideals that have historically defined indigenous societies, and which are none other than responsibility, equality, and solidarity; in other words, values that seemed to have been forgotten in the footballing world.

As if promotion and playing in Ecuador's first division was not enough, Mushuc Runa added another milestone when in 2019 it made its debut in the South American Cup – the continent's second biggest club competition. Its run there was short-lived, as it was knocked out in the first round by Unión Española de Chile. Yet this was after drawing 1–1 in both legs and only losing on penalties, and the mere fact of playing in an international competition was an unprecedented success for the Native American team. A club that has filled the Quechuan community with pride and that represents it on the pitch in a sport which, until Mushuc Runa's birth, few of Ecuador's original inhabitants felt to be their own.

CD Euzkadi

When the Basque national team almost won a domestic championship

A contradiction of history: the Basque national team has not been officially recognised by FIFA despite its long fight for international acknowledgement, and its national squad is the only one that can boast of very nearly winning a domestic championship. This was in the Mexican league's 1938–1939 season, in which the Basque team took part under the name Club Deportivo Euzkadi – 'Euzkadi' being the Basque-language name of its respective country, as spelt at the time. It ended with a highly commendable runner-up place. CD Euzkadi was only beaten by the Asturias Football Club – now defunct but one of the biggest Mexican clubs of that era – which was made up of Asturians (from the similarly named region in Spain) who had emigrated to the originally Aztec country.

The reason why the Basque national team ended up in the Mexican league was none other than the Spanish Civil War, in which fascism was fought in the Basque country by the *gudaris* (soldiers) in the *Euzko Gudarostea* (army created by the Basque government that was part of the Spanish People's Army of the Republic). In the midst of the struggle against fascism, the Basque Prime Minister (*lehendakari*) José Antonio Aguirre set up a Basque national team to do an international tour with the aim of raising funds and promoting solidarity with the Basque and republican fight. He was a former Athletic de Bilbao player and a member of the Basque Nationalist Party (PNV), and was well aware of the political role that a sport like football could play and how it could aid war propaganda.

The Basque team Aguirre organised a renewed attempt to create such a national team following two previous attempts in the 1920s and 1930. In the first, Basque footballers split from the North Team that mixed them with those from neighbouring Cantabria for Spanish regional competitions. In 1930, the Gascony team was created (covering a large part of the Basque lands), forming the embryo of a Basque national football team. The team promoted by the *lehendakari* in 1937 was christened Euzkadi and wore a kit based on the colours of the Basque flag (*ikurriña*), which had just been recognised by the Basque autonomous government as its official flag.

The new national team's debut took place in Paris in April 1937. It was a big sporting success as Euzkadi won by a comfortable 3–0 against Racing Club, who were no less than the French champions at the time. The pre-match atmosphere was laden with symbolism. The Basque national team were welcomed at Austerlitz station by Rafael Picabea, the Basque government's representative in Paris. It then chose to visit the Tomb of the Unknown Soldier under the Arc de Triomphe to pay homage to the French citizens who had died in the First World War by laying an *ikurriña* as a tribute.

Despite the excellent result, Euzkadi's debut was marred by an event that took place a day later in the Biscayan town of Guernica. Spanish fascism's allies – the German Condor Legion and Italian Legionary air force – bombed the town, sowing terror among the population and causing many hundreds of deaths. The Paris match was the first game in a European tour that would go on from the French capital to other towns in the country. They were games shaped by mourning over the Guernica massacre and by condemnation of the fascist attack against the Basque people.

The tour of the Old Continent took the Basque players from France to Czechoslovakia and later Poland, the Soviet Union, Norway, and Denmark. Their aim was always to encourage solidarity with the Basque and republican struggle against Franco. From a sporting angle, the trip was a complete success given that the Basque team won 14 out of its 20 matches and lost only four times. From among the many historically relevant anecdotes the tour produced, it is worth highlighting the suspension of the match that was to be played in the Polish capital Warsaw. This was due to violent incidents caused by Catholic extremist groups who associated the Basque national team with communism and could not understand how avowed Catholics, such as most PNV members, fought against Franco and in defence of the Republic. Quite the opposite happened when the Basque sporting delegation went to the USSR, where the communist authorities gave it a warm welcome, showing them comradeship and support for the anti-fascist and republican cause.

This first voyage – limited to Europe – and particularly the political acts of solidarity with the republican struggle which were held alongside the games received a backlash from FIFA. This international body tried to ban the Basque national squad from playing friendlies against official national teams and clubs, which Euzkadi had been doing since 1937. This prohibition had been prompted by Franco's Football Federation, which was soon accepted as a full member of FIFA.

Despite the pressure from FIFA, the Basque squad managed to continue with its activity. In June 1937, shortly after the fall of Bilbao to Franco's forces, Euzkadi sailed across the Atlantic to begin a new tour in the Americas. This journey first took it to Mexico – one of the countries that was giving the most support to the republican struggle – and then Cuba. In May 1938, the Basque team took part in an act that clearly expressed their identification with national liberation. This was when they paid homage to José Martí – the leader of the Cuban struggle for sovereignty (against the Spanish Empire) – by laying a tribute before the island's monument to independence.

The Euzkadi players' third stop on their tour of the Americas was Argentina although they were not as well received there as in the previous countries. News arriving that the Civil War was shifting in favour of the fascist side meant that fewer and fewer footballing institutions and bodies were willing to show support for the Basque national team and its cause.

As a result, the squad spent three months in Argentina without playing any of its five scheduled games against the country's biggest clubs. It returned to Mexico, via Chile and (again) Cuba – the few countries that still welcomed them.

Once on Mexican soil, they played nine matches, and registered to play in the *Copa Oxo* (Oxo Cup) – a tournament held just before the start of the domestic league championship and which the Basques ended up winning. The situation in Spain, where the fascist troops were now heading towards inevitable victory, prompted the Basque team players to stay in Mexico as exiles. Just before this, the clubs making up the Mexican league – then known as the *Liga Mayor* – had decided to invite the Euzkadi team to take part in their championship.

The Basque footballers accepted the invitation, and their team joined the Mexican championship under the name *Club Deportivo Euzkadi*. The decision to register the Basques as a Mexican club was based on the fear that any aiding of the Basque national team could mean FIFA – now with the pro-Franco Spanish footballing federation as a member – applying punitive measures against the Mexican championship and footballing federation.

Euzkadi started taking part in the *Liga Mayor* in the 1938–1939 season being the strong favourite to win the league. This was because of the excellent results the national team had had in the *Copa Oxo* and the many friendly games it had previously played in Mexico.

In view of the victory by Franco's forces in Spain and the club's lack of financial support, CD Euzkadi decided to disband after that championship, sharing out the money it had available among its players. A long dark period of dictatorship began, ostracising a Basque national team that would take decades to go back on the pitch to play for its country. In the meantime, however, the Euzkadi team could boast, as it still can, of being the only national team that has been within an inch of winning a domestic league championship.

Bibliography

BOOKS

Archambault, Fabien, Beaud, Stéphane, and Gasparini, William (eds., 2016). *Le football des nations* (Paris: Publications de la Sorbonne)

Boniface, Pascal (2002). *La terre est ronde comme un ballon. Géopolitique du football* (Paris: Seuil)

Boniface, Pascal (2010). *Football & mondialisation* (Paris: Armand Colin)

Brohm, Jean-Marie (1992). *Sociologie politique du sport* (PU Nancy)

Brohm, Jean-Marie, and Perelman, Marc (2006). *Le football, une peste émotionelle: la barbarie des stades* (Paris: Gallimard)

Bromberger, Christian (2004). *Football, la bagatelle la plus sérieuse du monde* (Paris: Pocket)

Correia, Mickaël (2023). *A People's History of Football* (London: Pluto Press)

Curletto, Mario Alessandro (2018). *Fútbol y poder en la urss de Stalin* (Madrid: Altamarea Ediciones)

De Waele, Jean-Michel, and Husting, Alexandre (eds., 2008). *Football et identités* (Brussels: Éditions de l'Université de Bruxelles)

Dietschy, Paul (2010). *Histoire du football* (Paris: Éditions Perrin)

Dietschy, Paul, and Kemo-Keimbou, David-Claude (2010). *L'Afrique et la planète football* (Paris: Éditions epa)

Fernández Ubiría, Miguel (2020). *Fútbol y anarquismo* (Madrid: Catarata)

Foer, Franklin (2004). *How Soccer Explains the World: An Unlikely Theory of Globalization* (New York: Harper)

Foot, John (2007). *Calcio. A History of Italian Football* (London: Harper Perennial)

Frydenberg, Julio (2011). *Historia social del fútbol* (Buenos Aires: Siglo xxi)

García Candau, Julián (2007). *El deporte en la Guerra Civil* (Barcelona: Espasa)

Galeano, Eduardo (2018). *Football in Sun and Shadow* (London: Penguin Classics)

Ghemmour, Chérif (2013). *Terrain miné. Quand la politique s'immisce dans le football* (Paris: Hugo et Cie)

Goldblatt, David (2007). *The Ball is Round. A Global History of Football* (London: Penguin Books)

Gómez, Daniel (2007). *La patria del gol. Fútbol y política en el Estado español* (Irún: Alberdania)

Kuhn, Gabriel (2011). *Soccer vs. the State. Tackling Football and Radical Politics* (Oakland: PM Press)

Kuper, Simon (1996). *Football Against the Enemy* (London: Phoenix)

Kuper, Simon (2012). *Ajax, the Dutch, the War: The Strange Tale of Soccer During Europe's Darkest Hour* (New York: Nation Books)

Lara, Miguel Ángel (2019). *El poder y el balón. Episodios futbolísticos que hicieron historia.* (Seville: Editorial Samarcanda)

McGuirk, Brian (2009). *Celtic fc. The Ireland Connection* (Edinburgh: Black & White Publishing)

Montague, James (2008). *When Friday Comes. Football in the War Zone* (Edinburgh: Mainstream Publishing)

Osúa, Jordi (2019). *Vázquez Montalbán. Fútbol y política* (Barcelona: Editorial Base)

Padilla, Toni (2017). *Atlas de una pasión esférica* (Barcelona: Geoplaneta)

Peinado, Quique (2013). *Futbolistas de izquierdas* (Alcalá de Henares: Léeme Libros)

Pérès, Jean-François (2010). *Dico fou du foot africain* (Monaco: Éditions du Rocher)

Porta, Frederic, and Tomàs, Manuel (2015). *Barça inédito* (Barcelona: Editorial Córner)

Porta, Frederic, and Tomàs, Manuel (2017). *Barça insólito* (Barcelona: Editorial Córner)

Segurola, Santiago (ed., 1999). *Fútbol y pasiones políticas* (Barcelona: Temas de Debate)

Serrado, Ricardo (2009). *O jogo de Salazar. A política e o futebol no Estado Novo* (Alfragide: Casa das Letras)

Simon, Gabrielle (ed., 2014). *Sport et nationalité* (Paris: LexisNexis)

Sonntag, Albrecht (2008). *Les identités du football européen* (Grenoble: Presses Universitaires de Grenoble)

Suárez, Orfeo (2015). *Los cuerpos del poder. Deporte, política y cultura* (Barcelona: Editorial Córner)

Usall, Ramon (2011). *Futbol per la llibertat,* (Lleida: Pagès Editors)

Vassort, Patrick (2005). *Football et politique. Sociologie historique d'une domination* (Paris: L'Harmattan)

Vázquez Montalbán, Manuel (2005). *Fútbol. Una religión en busca de un Dios* (Barcelona: Debate)

Vázquez Montalbán, Manuel (2018). *Barça, cultura i esport* (Barcelona: Editorial Base)

Villalobos, Cristóbal (2020). *Fútbol y fascismo* (Madrid: Altamarea Ediciones)

Viñas, Carles (2005). *El mundo ultra* (Madrid: Temas de Hoy)

Viñas, Carles (2022). *Football in the Land of the Soviets* (London: Pluto Press)

Wilson, Jonathan (2006). *Behind the curtain. Travels in Eastern European football* (London: Orion)

SPORTS NEWSPAPERS

As
Marca
L'Équipe
L'Esportiu de Catalunya
Mundo Deportivo
Sport

OTHER PERIODICALS

11 Freunde
Desports
Four Four Two
France Football
L'Équipe Magazine
Líbero
Le Miroir des Sports
Le Monde Diplomatique
Les Cahiers du Football
Manière de Voir
Onze Mondial
Panenka
Sàpiens
So Foot
When Saturday Comes

WEBSITES

From among the multitude of websites consulted that include historical information on football, a special mention should be given to that of the Rec.Sport.Soccer Statistics Foundation (www.rsssf.com/) which provides detailed statistics from all of the football competitions in the world throughout history.

Crests

BRITAIN AND IRELAND

- Current Manchester City FC crest
- Tottenham Hotspur FC crest from 1921 to 1951
- Liverpool FC crest from 1968 to 1987
- Current crest of Forest Green Rovers FC
- There was no crest for British Ladies FC. This image shows part of a depiction of the British Ladies' first match from the cover of the weekly British newspaper *The Graphic* (30 March 1895)
- Current Celtic FC crest
- Crest of Rathcoole's Stella Maris Secondary School – the Catholic educational centre to which Star of the Sea was associated

FRANCE AND ITALY

- Current Red Star FC crest
- Current SC Bastia crest
- Juventus FC crest from 1976 to 1983
- Current Torino FC crest
- AS Roma crest from 1990 to 2013
- Inter Milan crest, then called Società Sportiva Ambrosiana, during the 1928–1929 season, with the *fascio litorio* clearly visible

IBERIAN PENINSULAR

- Current Associação Académica de Coimbra crest
- Club Atlético Aviación de Madrid's crest from 1941 to 1943
- Madrid FC crest from 1931 to 1939
- Rayo Vallecano crest from 1974 to 1995
- FC Barcelona crest in the 1940s – the early years of the Franco dictatorship – after the club was forced to incorporate the Spanish flag in the crest, as well as Hispanicise its name
- Current CE Júpiter crest

- There was no crest for the Spanish Girl's Club. This photo shows some members of the two Spanish Girls teams before their first match in 1914

CENTRAL EUROPE AND SCANDINAVIA

- Berliner FC Dynamo crest in the 1980s
- Current 1. FC Union Berlin crest
- Crest worn by SC Tasmania Berlin in the 1965–1966 season when it played in the West German football's top division
- Current FC St Pauli crest
- Current shield of Polonia Warszawa
- Ajax crest from 1928 to 1990
- Historic Hakoah Vienna crest
- Current Christiania SC crest

THE BALKANS

- Current GNK Dinamo Zagreb crest
- HNK Hajduk Split crest from 1960 to 1970
- FK Sloboda Tuzla crest in the 1970s – during Yugoslavian communism
- Current FK Velež Mostar crest
- Current Olympiacós Piraeus crest

EASTERN EUROPE AND THE CAUCASUS

- FC Olt Scornicești crest in the 1980s
- FC Dynamo Kiev crest between 1996 and 2010, with the colours of the Ukrainian flag clearly visible on the emblem
- FC Shakhtar Donetsk crest between 1960 and 1989, with the name of the team and the city in Russian and with a reference to its mining associations clearly visible
- Current FC Karpaty Lviv crest
- Since the FC Stroitel Pripyat crest is unavailable, we have included the coat of arms for the Pripyat *atomgrad* – a town created in 1970 to house staff at the Chernobyl nuclear plant and which was deserted after the 1986 disaster
- Crest of the October Revolution Club, predecessor of the current Lokomotiv Moscow, from 1922 to 1930

- Crest worn by FC Akhmat Grozny when crowned Russian Cup champions in 2004
- Current Qarabağ FK crest

MIDDLE EAST AND CENTRAL ASIA

- Current crest of Erbil SC
- Current Al-Wehdat FC crest headed by an outline of the Al Aqsa Mosque in Jerusalem
- Current crest of Shaheen Asmayee SC

AFRICA

- Racing Universitaire d'Alger's crest from 1927 to 1962
- Atlético Tetuán's crest in 1951
- JS Massira's current crest inspired by the city of Laayoune's coat of arms
- Current Hafia FC crest
- As no crest was available for the Passive Resisters SC, we have instead included the symbol for peace, created in 1958 by the British graphic designer Gerald Holtom. Despite this being produced after Gandhi's clubs were created, it faithfully portrays the philosophy behind them.

THE AMERICAS

- Current New York Ramblers crest
- Crest of FC Corinthians Paulista between 1979 and 2000
- Current CD Cobresal crest
- Colo-Colo's current crest
- Current Mushuc Runa CD crest
- CD Euzkadi crest during the 1938–1939 season, the only one of its existence

The Pluto Press Newsletter

Hello friend of Pluto!

Want to stay on top of the best radical books
we publish?

Then sign up to be the first to hear about our
new books, as well as special events,
podcasts and videos.

You'll also get 50% off your first order with us
when you sign up.

Come and join us!

Go to bit.ly/PlutoNewsletter

Thanks to our Patreon subscriber:

Ciaran Kane

Who has shown generosity and comradeship in support of our publishing.

Check out the other perks you get by subscribing to our Patreon – visit patreon.com/plutopress. Subscriptions start from £3 a month.